Evidence-Based Strategies for Effective Classroom Management

DAVID M. HULAC
AMY M. BRIESCH

THE GUILFORD PRESS
New York   London

Copyright © 2017 The Guilford Press
A Division of Guilford Publications, Inc.
370 Seventh Avenue, Suite 1200, New York, NY 10001
www.guilford.com

Printed in Canada

This book is printed on acid-free paper.

Last digit is print number: 9   8   7   6   5   4   3   2   1

Library of Congress Cataloging-in-Publication Data

Names: Hulac, David M. | Briesch, Amy M.
Title: Evidence-based strategies for effective classroom management / David
    M. Hulac, Amy M. Briesch.
Description: New York : The Guilford Press, 2017. | Series: The guilford
    practical intervention in the schools series | Includes bibliographical
    references and index.
Identifiers: LCCN 2017024154 | ISBN 9781462531752 (paperback)
Subjects: LCSH: Classroom management. | Classroom management—Psychological
    aspects. | Educational psychology. | BISAC: PSYCHOLOGY / Psychotherapy /
    Child & Adolescent. | EDUCATION / Classroom Management. | SOCIAL SCIENCE /
    Social Work. | EDUCATION / Special Education / General.
Classification: LCC LB3013 .H82 2017 | DDC 371.102/4—dc23
LC record available at *https://lccn.loc.gov/2017024154*

To the kids who've taught me what questions to ask,
and to my wife, Mary, the source of my best ideas
—D. M. H.

To my husband, Chris,
whose daily classroom adventures
have both made for many great stories
and sparked an abundance of research ideas
—A. M. B.

About the Authors

David M. Hulac, PhD, NCSP, is Assistant Professor of School Psychology at the University of Northern Colorado. He is President of the independent organization Trainers of School Psychologists and served as Program Chair for Division 16 (School Psychology) at the 2016 American Psychological Association (APA) conference. Dr. Hulac is a recipient of the Belbas–Larson Award for Excellence in Teaching from the University of South Dakota. He has multiple publications in the area of response to intervention for behavior and academics and is coauthor of *Behavioral Interventions in Schools: A Response-to-Intervention Guidebook*.

Amy M. Briesch, PhD, is Associate Professor in the Department of Applied Psychology at Northeastern University. Her primary research interests include the role of student involvement in intervention design and implementation, and the development of feasible and psychometrically sound measures for the assessment of student behavior in multi-tiered systems of support. Dr. Briesch is Associate Editor of the *Journal of School Psychology* and a recipient of the Lightner Witmer Award for early-career scholarship in school psychology from Division 16 of the APA. She has authored over 50 peer-reviewed journal articles, books, and book chapters.

Contents

PART II. PROMOTION AND PREVENTION STRATEGIES

PART III. STRATEGIES FOR ADDRESSING CLASSWIDE
BEHAVIORAL CONCERNS

PART I

OVERVIEW AND FOUNDATIONS OF CLASSROOM MANAGEMENT

CHAPTER 1

Why Classroom Management Matters

We are going to be bold and put it out there: being able to effectively manage a classroom is *the* most essential aspect of teaching. Classroom management should be the first class taught to all teachers and should be the first consideration anytime that someone is teaching a new class. Certainly having a thorough understanding of the subject matter and being able to make difficult topics easy to understand are critical to effective teaching; however, if the classroom is not under control, no teaching can occur and no curriculum can be taught. Students will probably learn—but chances are they won't learn the lessons we intended for them to learn. Rather than learning reading, social skills, history, or science, they will learn how to survive in chaos.

If you are reading this book, chances are that classroom management concerns you. Some of you may be experienced teachers who are looking for ways to increase student engagement and decrease disruption and aggression. Others may be just learning how to teach and find the prospect of working with large groups of students daunting. Still others may be administrators or school-based consultants who see teachers struggling with student behavior in the classroom and want to find a way to help. No matter what your background or current situation, you have arrived at this place because you are looking for some answers to a challenge that extends beyond individual classrooms, schools, states, and even countries.

Classroom management is not just an individual struggle, but is arguably the top concern in education today (Melnick & Meister, 2008). There is no question that student behavior in schools presents a major challenge. Within a survey of early childhood and elementary schoolteachers, more than 90% of respondents reported that they had dealt with problem behaviors that interfered with classroom instruction (e.g., disruptive behavior, defiant behavior) within the past year (Reinke, Stormont, Herman, Puri, & Goel, 2011). These behavior problems are not all minor in nature either. According to a report from the National Center on Educational Statistics, one in every 14 students in public school in the United States in 2009 was suspended from school at least once and one in every 476 students was expelled (Planty et al., 2009). Epidemics have been declared based on much more conservative estimates of prevalence.

To fight an epidemic, it is necessary to have a sufficient number of well-trained professionals who can put into place effective strategies to reduce the number of existing cases and prevent further spread of the problem. A quick Google search for the phrase "classroom management," however, swiftly brings nearly 30 million results before you can bat an eye. If you begin to scroll through the pages upon pages of results, you will find that just about everyone seems to be writing about classroom management. There are articles written by national teaching organizations (e.g., the National Education Association and the National Council on Teacher Quality), national periodicals (e.g., *Education Week*), and institutions of higher education (e.g., New York University, Vanderbilt University). You can also find numerous "tips," "secrets," and "strategies" on websites with promising names like Education Oasis and Teacher Toolkit, and popular social networking sites such as Pinterest and Edmodo. The sheer amount of information at your fingertips can become overwhelming. Where do you start? Who do you trust? How do you know that any of these self-proclaimed "quick fixes" will have any effect on the problems you are having?

Despite the abundance of information that we have available to us in the Information Age, practicing teachers still report that classroom management is the number one problem that they struggle with (New Teacher Project, 2013). Unfortunately, this constant struggle, combined with a seeming lack of solutions, can be a main contributor to teacher burnout (Aloe, Amo, & Shanahan, 2014; O'Neill & Stephenson, 2011). In fact, many teachers have even reported leaving the field due to frustrations with student behavior problems (U.S. Department of Education, National Center for Education Statistics, 2000–2001). Although we can never know the individual circumstances of these teachers, it is possible that this unfortunate end to their stories might have been avoided had these teachers been armed with effective strategies for better managing their classrooms.

WHAT IS CLASSROOM MANAGEMENT?

Before we go any further, it is important to make sure that we are all talking about the same thing when we use the phrase "classroom management." Classroom management refers to practices that a teacher follows to ensure that (1) students behave in ways that are not disruptive to the learning of others and (2) teachers are able to focus on academically relevant material. Some criticize behavioral management techniques by claiming that the changes in student behavior do not generalize to other environments. We agree. The purpose of classroom management is not to teach life lessons; rather, classroom management allows life lessons to be taught.

Academic instruction is effective only when instruction occurs without interruption and students can practice new skills without distraction. A teacher can individualize instruction when other students are on task and quiet, social skills improve because social skills instruction can take place without incident, and fewer problematic social skills are modeled. Student mental health also improves because students are bullied less and social–emotional learning such as self-relaxation and impulse control training can take place more effectively. As displayed in Figure 1.1, classroom management is the bedrock on which learning occurs. Classroom management isn't the teaching, but without it, students won't learn what we want them to learn. Our goal in this book is to provide you with strategies that will help to minimize the amount of time teachers spend transitioning from one activity to another, addressing problem behavior, and engaging in other noninstructional activities that detract from classroom learning.

Effective classroom management is also the foundation of a multi-tiered system of support (MTSS). MTSS refers to the coordinated system of instruction, assessment, and intervention that allows schools to meet the needs of a variety of students (Lane, Menzies, Ennis, & Bezdek, 2013). An MTSS typically consists of three levels of service delivery, wherein the intensity of both assessment and intervention increases as one moves from one level to the next. Whereas Tier 1 focuses on providing universal supports to all students in a school, Tier 2 and Tier 3 direct increasingly focused and intensive supports at those students at risk for or demonstrating academic or behavioral problems. When student performance is judged to be nonresponsive to the supports provided at one level, the decision is made to move the student to the next tier of service delivery. One of the fundamental assumptions in judging nonresponse, however, is that the student has received high-quality, evidence-based instruction. This is where classroom management comes in. On the academic side, the effectiveness of classroom instruction will likely diminish without classroom management, meaning that many students without learning problems will begin to look like they have learning problems. In addition, on the behavioral side, a poorly managed classroom in which behavioral expectations are unclear will increase the likelihood of students displaying poor social skills, exhibiting behavioral problems, and struggling with mental health problems.

Although having a well-managed classroom may be important in the immediate place and time, you may wonder just how much of a difference it will really make in the long run. The simple answer is that well-managed classrooms can make a huge difference and

FIGURE 1.1. Classroom management is the foundation upon which quality learning and development occur.

these differences may be long lasting. Oliver, Wehby, and Reschly (2011) conducted a meta-analysis of those studies in which teachers implemented universal classroom management practices in typical public school settings (e.g., general/special education). Across 12 studies, the authors found that classroom management practices had a large and significant effect ($d = 0.80$) on student behavior. (If you are not sure what an effect size refers to, imagine that you were able to increase somebody's IQ from 100 to 112. That is what an effect of 0.8 looks like. In social science research, this effect is considered large.) Positive classroom management has also been shown to be significantly related to lower levels of bullying behavior (Ttofi & Farrington, 2012) and higher levels of school connectedness (McNeely, Nonnemaker, & Blum, 2002). Furthermore, it has the potential to not only reduce existing problem behavior but also to prevent the development of new problems and disorders (Hester et al., 2004; Myers, Simonsen, & Sugai, 2011).

To provide one specific example of the potential power of classroom management, let us take a moment to describe a longitudinal study conducted with a large number of students in inner-city Baltimore (Dolan et al., 1993; Kellam, Rebok, Ialongo, & Mayer, 1994; Kellam et al., 2014). The researchers randomly assigned students to different first-grade classrooms, and then ensured that each classroom had a similar number of students who had displayed problem behaviors in kindergarten. Half of these classrooms were then randomly assigned to receive an evidence-based classwide behavioral intervention called the Good Behavior Game (GBG; see Chapter 6 for a complete description of this intervention) and the other half served as control classrooms. By the end of the spring semester of first grade, teachers reported significant decreases in aggressive behavior for those children receiving the GBG intervention. The most notable effects were found, however, for those students who began the year with the highest levels of aggressive behavior (Dolan et al., 1993). The students who displayed the most aggression in kindergarten were then tracked into sixth grade. Those aggressive kindergarten boys who had received the GBG were twice as likely to display aggressive behaviors in sixth grade than the nonaggressive students. However, those boys with high initial levels of aggression who did not receive the intervention were 25 times more likely to be aggressive in sixth grade than nonaggressive students (Kellam et al., 1994). Kellam and colleagues (2014) also followed up with those students when they were 19–21 years of age. Again, they found that those students who received the GBG in first and second grade were less likely to display sexual violence, be diagnosed with antisocial personality disorders, and have suffered from drug abuse (Kellam et al., 2014). This research shows that not only do teachers make a difference each and every day but that they make a difference that lasts.

WHAT IS *EVIDENCE-BASED* CLASSROOM MANAGEMENT?

Believe it or not, there are lots of things that we do in schools to try and improve student behavior that the research tells us are ineffective. Counseling, for example, is effective in treating disorders such as depression and anxiety; however, its effect is negligible on classroom behavior and student performance (Baskin, Slaten, Sorenson, Glover-Russell & Merson, 2010; Prout & Prout, 1998; Stage & Quiroz, 1997). Many individuals have argued that adopting school uniforms decreases problem behaviors and improves student learning; however, analysis of data from the National Education Longitudinal Study found that uniforms appear to have little effect on student behavior (Brunsma & Rockquemore, 1998). Even most disciplinary practices, such as suspensions, are frequently accompanied by high degrees of recidivism, arrest rates, and anger directed toward school staff members (Blankenship & Bender, 2007; Skiba & Nesting, 2001).

Although many strategies can fall under the umbrella of classroom management, the specific focus of this book is on *evidence-based practices*—that is, we have deliberately chosen to present you with only those strategies that we see as evidence based. Evidence-based practice means that an educator uses knowledge and research-based interventions to inform his or her practice (PACER Center, 2011). The Every Student Succeeds Act (2015) requires that schools utilize practices that have a research base behind them. There are, however, many different ways in which the term "evidence based" has been defined and interpreted. The Council for Exceptional Children (2014), for example, outlines that studies must have been conducted using either group comparison or single-subject experimental designs. The U.S. Department of Education, Institute of Education Services (2003), on the other hand, has noted that strong evidence comes from two or more randomized controlled trials conducted in typical school settings. Within this book, we take a less conservative approach, considering evidence-based practices to be those interventions and strategies that have been shown to be effective across multiple controlled research studies. Although these studies may have been conducted using either group comparison or single-case designs, the majority of research we review has come from the single-case literature.

With all the talk about evidence-based practice nowadays, some readers may find themselves asking "What's the big deal?" The reason why evidence-based practice is so important is because it gives us some confidence that what we choose to try will actually work. Even when some interventions are used frequently in practice, there is no guarantee that these interventions will have positive results—and they may perhaps even be harmful in some cases. Although evidence-based practices are not guaranteed to work in every situation, there is a much higher likelihood given prior successes.

There is also an important distinction that should be made between what has been termed "effective classroom management" and "evidence-based classroom management." Much of what has been written about classroom management is based on observational studies that were conducted in the 1970s of effective teachers. The goal of this line of research was to identify teachers who were believed to be effective and then observe them in the classroom in order to better understand the practices in which they engaged. In the seminal study published in 1970, Jacob Kounin looked at the practices of teachers who were believed to be effective classroom managers as well as the practices of those teachers who were believed to be ineffective. What he found was that both groups of teachers used similar practices to address problem behaviors when they arose. There was, however, one main difference between the two groups that Kounin identified. Rather than waiting until problems arose, those teachers with well-managed classrooms used preventative strategies that made problem behaviors less likely and on-task behaviors more likely to occur. In particular, Kounin (1970) focused on the way in which an effective teacher would move through a lesson: ensuring the active participation of students, managing smooth transitions, and remaining aware of what was going on in all corners of the classroom at all times. These findings were further supported by later researchers utilizing observational approaches to understanding those teacher behaviors most associated with student performance (e.g., Emmer, Evertson, & Anderson, 1980; Sanford & Evertson, 1981).

Although studies such as the one by Kounin (1970) certainly contributed to the dialogue around classroom management practices, it is important to highlight the correlational nature of this work—that is, although use of proactive strategies was related to higher levels of both teacher and student performance, it is impossible to say whether one actually caused the other. In the 1980s, however, researchers began to conduct the first experimental studies focused on classroom management. Emmer and colleagues, for example, found that those teachers who received specific training in classroom management strategies had higher levels of appropriate student behavior in their classrooms than those teachers in a control condition (Emmer, 1984). Since this time, numerous experimental studies have been conducted in order to better delineate both what effective classroom management should look like and how necessary strategies should be taught.

Although the research base is quite dense, findings from the experimental literature fortunately suggest that the recipe for effective classroom management is both understood and straightforward. Interestingly, three major reviews of the experimental and quasi-experimental research on effective classroom management practices (Epstein, Atkins, Cullinan, Kutash, & Weaver, 2008; Oliver et al., 2011; Simonsen, Fairbanks, Briesch, Myers, & Sugai, 2008) have all come to similar conclusions. As highlighted by Greenberg, Putman, and Walsh (2014), there are the "Big Five" classroom management strategies that have emerged from over 60 years of research in this area. First, positively stated expectations must be made clear by establishing, teaching, and practicing a small set of classroom rules. Second, predictable routines for navigating different settings and situations within the school day must be developed and taught. Third, teachers should use positive and specific praise to reinforce students for appropriate behavior. Fourth, inappropriate behavior should be responded to consistently with an appropriate level of consequence. Fifth, student engagement should be kept high by facilitating opportunities for active engagement and ensuring that the instructional content is interesting and meaningful. Most importantly, all of these practices are things that must be planned before students enter the classroom. Without deliberate, systematic lesson planning and preparation, classrooms may be chaotic where no learning can occur.

So if we know what works, we should assume that everybody is doing this, right? Unfortunately, what we know is that most teacher education programs are not equipping their graduates with the classroom management tools that they need. The National Council on Teacher Quality (Greenberg et al., 2014) published a report that investigated whether teacher education programs were training teachers in classroom management. They made three key findings:

1. Most teacher education programs are not deliberately teaching the science of classroom management in class and clinical settings.
2. Most programs function under the belief that "instructional virtuosity" will render the need for classroom management moot because all students will be enthralled with the flawlessly executed lesson that they will be unable to act out.
3. Teachers are encouraged to come up with a *philosophy* for classroom management based upon their own beliefs about child development.

The findings of this report raise a number of serious concerns. Imagine going to a physician complaining of a chronic heart problem. Rather than following a standard procedure that is based upon years of science, the doctor has instead been trained to come up with his or her own philosophy for solving heart problems based upon his or her own beliefs about how a heart works. Or, imagine if the physician merely believed that following a healthy diet and regular exercise would remove the need for any treatment. A practice that would be intolerable in medicine unfortunately continues to be standard practice in education, which boasts a substantial research-to-practice gap (Burns & Ysseldyke, 2008; Carnine, 1997; Cook & Odom, 2013).

Just as we would not want a doctor to enter surgery without the right instruments, we do not want teachers entering classrooms without the proper management tools. However, when it comes to student behavior, over 40% of teachers participating in the Schools and Staffing Survey (Epstein et al., 2008) indicated that they felt "not at all prepared" or "only somewhat prepared" to handle behavioral issues in the classroom. It should therefore come as no surprise that teachers find the job stressful, or even sometimes decide to leave the field. Intervention is sorely needed in order to change this trajectory. We do not fool ourselves into thinking that this book is the only answer, but we do hope that it will serve as a critical important tool in an educator's toolbox.

WHAT IS TO COME

Now that we have explained what we mean by evidence-based classroom management—and hopefully convinced you of just how important it is—you are probably eager to hear more about the concrete strategies that are available to you. Before we jump to this, however, we want to say a few words about what our goals for this book are and what you can expect as a reader.

This book seeks to avoid long and theoretical discussions about classroom theory, but to instead focus on tangible strategies that can immediately be put into place. We aim to equip beginning teachers with concrete strategies that have been proven effective through rigorous research. In addition, we see the information presented within this book as being valuable to experienced teachers and educators who may be looking to ensure that their practices are up-to-date, research based, and most importantly, effective. In the chapters to come, we present you with those classwide strategies that have shown the greatest promise in promoting and supporting appropriate student behavior. All of these strategies have been repeatedly subjected to empirical testing and therefore can be classified as evidence based. Although prior research suggests that these strategies are likely to be successful in your setting, there are a few important caveats to keep in mind as we move forward into the book.

First, behavior is not something that is ever totally fixed. One of the most important things to keep in mind about classroom management practices is that they never *eliminate* problems. There are very few things that we as educators do that work perfectly. Human beings are extraordinarily complex, and when large groups of complex beings come together in places like schools, unexpected things may happen. When teachers implement evidence-based classroom management procedures with fidelity, there is a good likelihood that problems will be *reduced*. Although we would like to see a situation go from complete chaos to calm in 5 seconds, it is important to keep realistic goals in mind and to celebrate each small victory. After all, if we can reduce the number of acting-out behaviors from 10 per day to four per day, we have made a huge improvement.

Second, nothing lasts forever. As you will read in this book, having clear expectations that are taught and consistently reinforced reduces problem behaviors. Sometimes, however, these problem behaviors start to return after time has passed. For example, there may be times when our practices work for a month and then unexpectedly just stop working. When something like this happens, we first need to rejoice in the fact that we had a better month. After that, we either need to perform a series of reminders (booster sessions), or we may need to try something else entirely (new intervention). Imagine, for example, a middle school in which the students received extensive opportunities to learn and practice specific social skills at the start of the school year; however, come November, they have stopped using good eye contact and seem to be unable to accept "No" as an answer. In such a case, the team may either reteach the expectations, or they may change the way expectations are reinforced.

Third, this book is not specifically meant to address the needs of students with serious behavioral difficulties. Those students on the autism spectrum, or those who display impulsive behaviors, tend to perform much better in classrooms that are well managed; however, the strategies discussed herein are designed to address the needs of the general population. Although we recommend working with a school-based mental health consultant to support the needs of these students, the behavior plans that you implement will be more effective when procedures are clear, expectations are taught and reinforced consistently, and problematic behaviors are addressed fluently and immediately (Witt, VanDerHeyden, & Gilbertson, 2004). This book may therefore be considered a critical base to prevent many more serious problem behaviors.

The book is divided into several broad sections. In the remainder of the first section, Chapter 2 provides you with the theoretical underpinnings for the book and a brief overview of the principles of applied behavior analysis. We believe that understanding these principles is essential to the effective implementation of the strategies that are described in subsequent chapters. The second section, "Promotion and Prevention Strategies," describes the basic interventions that all teachers should use to prevent classroom behavior problems and to reinforce desired behaviors in an effective manner. Within the third section ("Strategies for Addressing Classwide Behavioral Concerns"), we outline additional, more structured interventions that can be used if the strategies described in Chapters 3 and 4 are insufficient. Chapter 5 introduces classwide token economies, Chapter 6 addresses group contingencies, and Chapter 7 provides methods for helping students manage their own behavior. The final section outlines strategies that teachers can use to evaluate classroom behavior (Chapter 8), to determine whether the interventions are being implemented correctly (Chapter 9), and to individualize interventions for those students who need more structure or feedback than others in the class (Chapter 10).

Finally, it is important to mention that many of these chapters include coach cards. These coach cards break the interventions down into steps and offer checklists that may be helpful in planning as well as during implementation. These checklists can be used by teachers to make sure they don't "miss something" when putting a new procedure into practice. In addition, these coach cards can be used by coaches who are interested in helping a teacher with a new practice and providing integrity checks. We encourage you to make copies and use them within your own classroom or for your own practice.

CONCLUSIONS

We know that teaching children is a high calling. The fields of psychology and education know a tremendous amount about learning and behavior, though our practices in schools tend to fall behind our knowledge base. This book seeks to close that gap by providing teachers with the best science to date on managing classroom behaviors. We want to provide you with the best tools and information so you can provide your students with the best supports possible. Before we can equip you with specific tools, however, we do believe that a basic understanding of behavioral principles is necessary to successful implementation. We therefore spend Chapter 2 providing the reader with much of the theoretical basis for the rest of the text.

Understanding Behavioral Theories Relevant to Supporting a Well-Managed Classroom

As educators, there are some things that we have control over and others that we simply do not. Come the beginning of the school year, most of us do not get to select the students who will join our classrooms. Rather, we are provided with a roster and then cross our fingers that this group of students will get along well—both with one another and ourselves. We also have no control over biological factors within each student, such as one's DNA, brain functioning, or nervous system functioning. Students are born with different levels of ability and operate at different levels of functioning. We can certainly put in place strategies and accommodations to improve student learning and functioning in the classroom, but there is no way that we can directly change a child's neural structures through surgery! Furthermore, we do not get to select the parents and families that we work with, or the structure of the homes that these children come from. We might wish, for example, that all students would have someone watching over them at home to make sure that homework is completed correctly and the student is in bed at a reasonable hour; however, we know that this is not always going to happen. What is true is that more than half of public school students in the United States live in poverty (Suitts, Barba, & Dunn, 2015), and many of our students come from food-insecure households in which homework completion is a relatively insignificant problem. National statistics also tell us that many students are victims of abuse and neglect, with as many as 12 out of every 1,000 children estimated to be victims of maltreatment (U.S. Department of Health and Human Services, Administration on Children, Youth, and Families, 2007). These are problems that are inarguably very concerning, but largely outside of our control as educators.

We also cannot directly control children's behavior in the classroom. Yes, you read that last sentence correctly. As educators, we have no control over the choices that a child makes in a particular moment. We are not puppet masters with strings that can control the motor and vocal behaviors of students. Rather, each child is free to make his or her own individual choices. Although we may like to believe that we can control behavior, the truth is that it is impossible.

In presenting you with these realities, we do not mean to paint a bleak picture. The truth is that although teachers cannot directly control students' behavior, they have an incredibly important role to play in promoting student outcomes. In order to gain a better understanding of the major influences on student academic achievement, John Hattie (2008) reviewed over 50,000 studies that had been conducted with over 80 million students. Hattie classified the factors that influence achievement into six overarching categories: student, teacher, parent, principal, schools, and peers. The factors that predicted the largest amount of variance in student performance were student factors such as intelligence and personality, which accounted for almost half of the variance. However, the second largest predictor of student performance was teacher variables. In fact, teacher variables had as much of an influence on student achievement as parent, home, school, and principal variables combined!

So if we can't control students' behaviors, how is it that teachers have such a large influence on student achievement? This chapter provides an overview of behavioral science. As the name implies, behavioral science is concerned with understanding why humans (and animals) behave in the ways that they do. A chief assumption of behavioral science is that although we cannot directly control others' behaviors, we can control the environments in which those behaviors occur. Where our control lies as behavior change agents is in how we proactively structure the environment (e.g., physical layout of the classroom, our expectations and rules) as well as how we respond to students' behaviors (both appropriate and inappropriate). These sources of control are the focus of this book over the next several chapters.

TEACHER ATTRIBUTION THEORY

Before we begin to talk about what teachers can *do*, we first wish to stop and talk a bit about what teachers *think*. This is because the way that we respond to behavior is based upon our beliefs as to why a student is exhibiting a particular behavior. We all know that siblings will frequently get involved in fights in which one of them hits the other. The fight is rarely about whether the actual blow took place. Instead, it devolves into a "You did it on purpose!" versus "No, I didn't, it was an accident!" What is important to note here is that the child who was on the receiving end of the blow will usually be much angrier when he or she believes that the other sibling meant to do it—that is, if he or she believes that the strike was under the control of the offending sibling. This refers to a psychological concept known as attribution theory. Attribution theory deals with how we use information to come up with an explanation for why someone acted a certain way or why something occurred (e.g., what caused a student to behave in a particular way).

Weiner (1993) described three dimensions of attribution (see Table 2.1):

1. Locus of control: Is the behavior due to internal or external causes?
2. Controllability: Are the causes under someone's control?
3. Stability: Are the causes fixed or do they change?

Typically, if a person believes the causes of a behavior are internal, controllable, and stable, those causes are seen as being dispositional, whereas causes that are external, uncontrollable, and unstable are considered situational. Understanding the attributions that an individual makes is important because these attributions often influence the degree to which the individual believes he or she can effect change (i.e., self-efficacy). For example, if a teacher believes that the causes of a student's behavior are both stable and uncontrollable, that teacher is much less likely to intervene (Mavropoulou & Padeliadu, 2002). Attributions can also more generally influence what strategies we select to address a problem. For example, Soodak and Podell (1994) found that teachers were more likely to suggest parental involvement as a strategy when they believed a student's problems were attributable to home factors and more likely to suggest classroom intervention when they believed a student's problems were attributable to school factors.

Research has found that many teachers tend to view student problem behaviors as dispositional (Wiley, Tankersley, & Simms, 2012). This suggests that teachers believe that

TABLE 2.1. Understanding the Dimensions of Attribution Theory

	Situation	
	Student failing an exam	Student getting sent to the office
Locus of control		
Internal	"He just doesn't have the smarts."	"He's just a bad seed."
External	"The test was probably just too hard."	"Some of the teachers are just too hard on him."
Controllability		
Controllable	"He just didn't study hard enough."	"He just didn't think before he acted."
Uncontrollable	"He's just unlucky."	"He's just not in control of his own actions."
Stability		
Stable	"He's just not good at math."	"Trouble just always finds him."
Unstable	"Maybe he was just having a bad day."	"Maybe something happened before school."

student problem behaviors are due to stable factors that are unique to the child and within the child's control. In fact, in a survey of teachers conducted by Stage et al. (2008), 65% of teachers attributed the students' problem behaviors to their thoughts or feelings, whereas only 25% attributed them to classroom variables. Furthermore, a majority of teachers (57%) indicated that the most helpful intervention would be individual counseling, whereas only 14% indicated a more structured and detailed classroom management plan would be useful (Stage et al., 2008).

It is common for teachers to attribute student behaviors to a child's home environment. Across several studies, teachers have been provided with a vignette describing a student who struggled behaviorally in the classroom. When asked to identify the most likely causes of these problems, the two most frequently endorsed explanations have been either internal factors or home factors (Mavropoulou & Padeliadu, 2002; Soodak & Podell, 1994). Across these studies, teachers attributed student misbehavior to various home variables, including parental attitudes, poor modeling, and the parents' level of education.

Much less research has been conducted on the attributions that students make for their own behavior or the behavior of their peers. In a study by Cothran, Kulinna, and Garrahy (2009), secondary school students were asked about their beliefs regarding the causes of student misbehavior within a physical education class. Among the more common explanations provided by students were that students misbehaved because they were uninterested in the subject matter or were trying to get attention and thereby achieve a higher social status. These findings suggested that students perceived misbehavior as under the individual's control. In contrast, however, studies by Guttmann (1982) and Sargeant (2012) suggested that student misbehavior may instead be explained by relational variables. Problems in the teacher–student relationship were noted across both studies, including the student being misunderstood and the teacher simply not liking the student.

One of the few studies to directly compare the attributions of teachers and students was conducted by Guttmann (1982). Results of this study highlighted several important differences in the nature of the attributions made regarding student misbehavior. Whereas students were more likely to see problem behavior as the result of classmates' behavior or being punished too much by the teacher, teachers were more likely to identify the student's psychological problems or need for attention as possible causes. Together, these findings present an interesting conflict—that is, it seems that both students and teachers attribute problematic behaviors to factors outside of themselves. This may not be surprising given the frequency with which we are bound to hear comments such as "He just needs to put in more effort" or "That teacher just has it out for me!" over the course of a school day. However, adopting such an external attribution serves to create two emotions that are counterproductive to effective classroom management: anger and helplessness.

When you see a student displaying inappropriate behavior, what attributions do you make about the reason for the behavior? Do you assume that the student is deliberately causing problems because it is in his or her nature? That the behavior was instigated by one of his or her classmates? That the misbehavior stems from unmet needs as a child? That the behavior is the result of a skill deficit? The attributions that we make to explain problem behavior provide insight into our theoretical beliefs about human behavior and why we act the way that we do. You may not necessarily have thought about yourself as ascribing to a particular theory of human behavior; however, your answer to the question above may say something about which theory your beliefs align with. For example, a psychodynamic perspective views behavior as being determined by the unconscious mind and the experiences that we had in childhood. Cognitive psychologists, on the other hand, believe that behavior can be explained by understanding what is going on in the human mind (e.g., how we process, store, and use information).

Within this book, however, we take a decidedly behavioral approach. Behaviorism views individual behavior as being determined by factors in the environment. Have you ever noticed that students behave differently in different settings? We have all worked with the student who can't sit still during a reading lesson, but is incredibly focused during physical education class. Other students behave well in art, but not in mathematics. In fact, very few students behave the same in all environments. If we approach student misbehavior from a behavioral perspective, we are interested in understanding how the events in one's environment affect behavior—and how we can best harness this knowledge to support student functioning.

We spend the rest of this chapter outlining a number of key theories and principles that are essential for understanding behavioral science. We hope that this chapter will therefore lay the conceptual foundation for understanding the interventions that we discuss in this book.

FOUNDATIONS OF BEHAVIORAL SCIENCE

A long time ago in a school district far, far away, David was working with a middle school teacher who did not know what to do about a student who repeatedly called his classmates racially offensive names. Each time this boy—we will call him Joe—called his classmate a name, the other students would yell at Joe and tell him to stop. This created a hectic classroom scenario, in which none of the students were able to complete work, and the teacher was completely frustrated. In order to try and curb the behavior, the teacher had tried many things. She asked Joe to stop. She asked him to please stop. She yelled at Joe to stop. She moved his seat to the front of the room. She sent him to the principal's office. She offered Joe a reward if he stopped. After each intervention or attempt to control the behavior, Joe continued calling others racist names. No matter what she seemed to try, the behavior persisted. The teacher knew that Joe had been diagnosed with attention-deficit/hyperactivity disorder (ADHD) and oppositional defiant disorder (ODD), and began to wonder whether her own efforts to curb the behavior were simply wasted. This scenario may sound hopeless, but fortunately (especially for the teacher!) there is a satisfactory ending to the story. Before we get there, however, we want to highlight a few critical principles that may explain this student's behavior (see Table 2.2 for a summary of these six principles).

TABLE 2.2. Principles of Behavior

Principle	What is it called?	In other words . . .	Classroom example
Principle 1: We are more likely to engage in behaviors that generate pleasurable consequences.	Law of effect	*I'll eat my broccoli for Skittles, but won't eat my Skittles for broccoli.*	A student is more likely to complete his or her assignment quickly if it means he or she can go to recess early, than if it results in being assigned more work.
Principle 2: We can promote behavior through reinforcement.	Reinforcement	*I'll do anything for Skittles!*	A student who desires attention will be more likely to follow directions if doing so results in teacher praise.
Principle 3: We can reduce or eliminate behavior through extinction.	Extinction	*If you stop giving me Skittles, I'll stop doing what you ask.*	That same attention-seeking student will stop following directions if it no longer results in teacher praise.
Principle 3a. We can reduce or eliminate behavior through punishment.	Punishment	*If you give me lemons, I won't do something anymore.*	A student who does not want to stay after school will stop calling out in class if it results in detention.
Principle 4: We tend to engage in those behaviors that bring the greatest reinforcement.	Matching law	*Lots of Skittles! Right now? Little effort? Yes, please!*	If a student who desires attention can get it immediately from peers by making jokes as opposed to having to wait until recess if he or she sits in class quietly, he or she is more likely to make jokes.
Principle 5: What we find rewarding once may not always be so.	Motivating operations	*My wants are always changing!*	
Principle 5a: When we have had too much of something, it is no longer reinforcing.	Satiation	*I'm tired of Skittles! I want M&M's!*	A student who receives constant praise for everything that he or she does may come to no longer desire it.
Principle 5b: When we have too little of something, it is more reinforcing.	Deprivation	*I haven't had Skittles for a while. I want them now!*	A student who has not received any attention from the teacher may find the smallest compliment highly reinforcing.
Principle 6: We look for cues to tell us whether reinforcement is likely.	Discriminative stimulus (*Look, reinforcement is available!*)	*I can see that you bought more Skittles and I'm ready to work!*	A typically reserved student might begin to act out after seeing a classmate act out and get attention from the teacher as a result.

PRINCIPLE 1: We Are More Likely to Engage in Behaviors That Generate Pleasurable Consequences (or, I'll eat my broccoli for Skittles, but won't eat my Skittles for broccoli).

In 1898, Edward Thorndike first described the law of effect, which now serves as the basis for the science of behaviorism. A student of animal learning, he was interested in how cats behaved when placed in a puzzle box. Thorndike would place a cat inside the box and lay a piece of fish outside. The cat could open the box (and access the fish!) by pressing down on a lever; however, the cat obviously did not know this. Thorndike was interested in seeing what strategies cats would use to try and get out of the box and how long it would ultimately take for them to escape. The cats would often make several unsuccessful attempts to get out before unintentionally pressing the lever—and opening the door. What Thorndike found was that after pressing the lever and releasing the door, the cats became faster and faster at getting out during subsequent trials. These puzzle box experiments ultimately led him to propose the law of effect.

The law of effect states that a behavior that is followed by a pleasurable occurrence is more likely to occur in that situation, whereas a behavior that is followed by an unpleasurable occurrence is less likely to occur in a similar situation. In other words, we will keep engaging in a behavior if something good comes of it and stop doing it if it results in something bad. When the cats found that pressing the lever released the door (and got them fed!), they were more likely to press the lever the next time. Other strategies that did not result in the opening of the door, however, were less likely to be used again. This law was profound for its time because it focused not on the internal psychical structures of the individual (remember Sigmund Freud's id, ego, and superego?), but instead looked at the relationship between behaviors and events in the environment in which those behaviors occurred. In other words, Thorndike suggested that most behavior is situational.

The idea that behavior is largely situational probably does not shock most of us today. Indeed, if an adult were to strip off all of his or her clothes and sing Kiss's "Rock and Roll All Night" (Stanley & Simmons, 1975) at the top of his or her lungs, this behavior would be responded to very differently depending on the context. If performed downtown on a Friday night, this behavior would likely be followed by an arrest, which would (hopefully!) reduce the likelihood that the behavior occurred again in the future. On the other hand, there would likely be no response at all if the individual was home alone in the shower, such that the behavior would be much more likely to repeat in the future! Same behavior but different contexts, and thereby very different outcomes.

The other part of the law of effect that is worth noting has to do with the vague definition of something pleasurable versus unpleasurable. We may think of something that is pleasurable as being universally so; however, this is in fact not true. The first reality is that what is pleasurable for one person is not necessarily pleasurable for another person. For example, David does not like chocolate, whereas Amy absolutely loves it. Therefore, offering David a box of chocolates to assist with an accreditation report is likely to be seen as much less motivating than it would be to Amy. The second reality is that our own perception of pleasurability may vary across time, or we might find something pleasurable in one context but not in another. For example, having friends and family sing "Happy Birthday" in the comfort of one's own home may be enjoyable, whereas having it sung by a rowdy group of restaurant waiters when surrounded by strangers can feel more awkward than comforting.

PRINCIPLE 2: We Can Promote Behavior through Reinforcement (or, *I'll do anything for Skittles!*).

Roughly 60 years after Thorndike (1898) introduced the law of effect, B. F. Skinner (1966) expanded upon this idea by introducing the principle of reinforcement. You may remember hearing about the Skinner box in Introduction to Psychology. Similar to Thorndike's experiments, Skinner placed a hungry rat in a box that contained a lever. When the lever was pressed, food pellets would be dispensed into the box. Although it sometimes took a while for the rats to initially discover the lever, eventually they would go straight to the lever when placed in the box. The rats continued to press the lever because they had learned that doing so would result in a desired consequence.

Skinner suggested that anything that strengthens the likelihood of a behavior occurring in the future should be considered reinforcement. Thus, *people* are not reinforced, *behavior* is reinforced. In general, most behaviors are reinforced by something in the environment—some sort of an outside action. We suspect that this outside action is serving to reinforce a particular behavior if (and only if!) the behavior continues to occur when it is followed by that outside action.

Types of Reinforcement

Skinner (1966) also distinguished between two types of reinforcement: positive and negative. Because we often think of positive as being associated with something good and negative as being associated with something bad, the definitions of positive and negative reinforcement are a bit counterintuitive. Here, the positive and negative refer instead to whether something is given or taken away. Positive reinforcement refers to something that an individual *receives* that leads to an increase in the behavior occurring in the future. This may look similar to a reward (e.g., receiving a gold star or a prize), but does not necessarily look so in every situation. For example, being yelled at by a teacher could be a form of positive reinforcement if the problem behavior continues occurring after the student receives this attention from the teacher. Negative reinforcement refers to something aversive that is *taken away from or avoided* that leads to an increase in the behavior occurring in the future. Perhaps the most common example of negative reinforcement is the familiar nagging buzzer that sounds as soon as you start up your car's ignition. The annoying buzzing noise goes away as soon as you fasten your seat belt, which (for the majority of us) increases the likelihood and swiftness with which we fasten our seat belt the next time that we get in the car.

Let's consider some examples:

- Your colleague has a jar of candy in his or her office. When you walk into the office, you take some candy from the jar, and so you walk into the office more frequently. The candy reinforces your entering the office.
- When you log into Facebook, you get a notification that somebody has commented on one of your posts. As a result, you check your posts more frequently. The comments from friends reinforce your Facebook-checking behavior.
- A student is given a difficult assignment that she does not want to complete. The student knows that if she swears at the teacher, she will be sent to the principal's office and will get to chat with the principal's secretary instead of doing her work. The student therefore continues to swear. Getting to hang out in the principal's office reinforces the swearing behavior.

Notice that all of these examples involve an increase in behavior. Even the last example (which is intended to decrease a problem behavior!) actually functions to increase the problem behavior. Sending the student to the principal's office was reinforcing because the student was able to avoid having to do a difficult assignment. Additional examples of both positive and negative reinforcement are provided in Table 2.3.

Schedules of Reinforcement

As Skinner (1966) continued his study of animal behavior, he discovered something interesting by accident. His supply of food pellets was drawing thin and he didn't have enough time to make the new pellets that were needed. He decided to try and extend his remaining supply of food by providing the rat with food once every minute instead of once every time

TABLE 2.3. Types of Reinforcement

Positive reinforcement (gaining/accessing)	Negative reinforcement (losing/escaping)
Attention	
• Getting attention from adults	• Avoiding attention from adults
• Getting attention from peers	• Avoiding attention from peers
Activities	
• Getting to do a preferred activity	• Avoiding a boring activity (e.g., doing difficult math assignments)
Objects	
• Getting to play with a particular toy, book, or use an instrument	• Avoiding a frightening animal such as a dog, snake, or spider

that it pressed the lever. What he found was that the rat's lever-pressing behavior actually became stronger when reinforcement was presented intermittently. Through subsequent trials, Skinner developed the concept of schedules of reinforcement.

If you think about what is going on in a classroom, there are multiple behaviors that a child can choose to engage in. As described in the first chapter, a child can yell in class, throw spit wads, work on assignments, or stare out of the window. In a classroom setting, each of these behaviors is reinforced on a different reinforcement schedule. Some behaviors may be reinforced continuously, meaning something in the environment occurs every single time the student performs a behavior. Other behaviors are reinforced periodically on an intermittent reinforcement schedule. We provide a few concrete examples of what these reinforcement schedules look like next, highlighting the strengths and limitations of each approach (see Table 2.4).

Continuous Reinforcement Schedules

Within a continuous reinforcement schedule behavior is reinforced each and every time that it occurs. Imagine, for example, what would happen if you had a job making paper airplanes. Each time you finished a paper airplane, a person gave you one quarter. What would you likely do? You would likely continue making paper airplanes and start saving up for a night out on the town! But what would happen if you suddenly stopped getting quarters? You might continue to make one or two more airplanes, but chances are that you would stop once it became clear that the funds had dried up. Continuous reinforcement systems can be incredibly useful when you are looking to establish a new behavior because the learner comes to quickly realize that engaging in the desired behavior will reliably lead to something good. At the same time, however, these types of systems are both time and resource intensive and may create a situation in which a student's behavior is entirely dependent on receiving a reward.

TABLE 2.4. Schedules of Reinforcement

Fixed	Variable
	Continuous
Not applicable	Not applicable
	Interval
Fixed period of time	Random period of time
• After working for 5 minutes	• After working for between 3 and 7 minutes
• After playing appropriately for 10 minutes	• After playing appropriately for 8–12 minutes
	Ratio
Fixed number of responses	Random number of responses
• After completing 10 problems	• After completing 8–10 problems
• After raising hand three times	• After raising hand two to four times

Intermittent Reinforcement Systems

The alternative to providing continuous reinforcement of behavior is providing reinforcement intermittently. Returning to the example above, rather than paying you after each airplane is completed, someone might choose to instead pay you for working a certain period of time or after completing a certain number of airplanes. Intermittent reinforcement systems can further be classified into either interval or ratio systems.

INTERVAL REINFORCEMENT SYSTEMS

Within an interval reinforcement system, behavior is reinforced after a certain period of time (i.e., interval). This period of time may be constant (i.e., fixed) or it may vary across time (i.e., variable). Fixed interval systems are probably the most familiar to us, as this is the system often used by employers. Typically, people either get paid a set amount for each hour worked (i.e., hourly wage) or one larger sum in exchange for many hours worked (i.e., salaried income). Applied to our paper airplane example, we might get paid $10 an hour for making paper airplanes. As a worker on the origami assembly line, a fixed interval reinforcement system is desirable because we know that we will reliably get paid for each hour worked. The potential disadvantage for the employer, however, is that this system does not necessarily encourage high levels of productivity—that is, because an individual gets paid the same amount regardless of whether he or she makes three airplanes or 30, there may not be sufficient external motivation to produce. In a random interval system, on the other hand, we would not necessary know how long we would need to work before we got paid. Sometimes we might get paid $10 after a half hour of work and other times we may need to work for 90 minutes to earn the same amount. Such a system often results in a steady rate of behavior over a long period of time; however, behavior occurs at a modest rate. This is because the reinforcement that the individual receives is independent of the behavioral response rate.

RATIO REINFORCEMENT SYSTEMS

Within a ratio reinforcement system, behavior is reinforced based on the number of times it occurs. As with interval systems, the number of necessary occurrences may be constant (i.e., fixed) or it may vary across time (i.e., variable). Within a fixed ratio system, you might get paid $5 every time you made 20 paper airplanes. In this case, most of us would work very quickly to finish the 20 paper airplanes so we could get paid. A ratio reinforcement system therefore typically results in fast responding; however, producing in terms of quantity may come at the cost of quality. In our daily lives, far more behaviors are reinforced according to variable ratio schedules. The most common example of a variable ratio system is a slot machine, for which the odds may be known (1 in 20 is a winner!) but for which the payoff during any particular play is uncertain. What would happen if you were making paper airplanes and you received $5 after making one airplane, and then another $5 after making seven airplanes, and another $5 after three airplanes, such that you couldn't quite predict when you might get paid next? Behaviors that are reinforced on a variable ratio schedule tend to persist and continue because the individual cannot predict when the payout will come. As such, this has been shown to be the most powerful schedule of reinforcement.

PRINCIPLE 3: We Can Reduce or Eliminate Behavior through Extinction and Punishment (or, *If you stop giving me Skittles, I'll stop doing what you ask*).

Reinforcement can be used to strengthen desired behaviors; however, B. F. Skinner (1966) also discussed ways in which to weaken or eliminate undesired behaviors (see Figure 2.1). The first is through the use of punishment. Whereas reinforcement was seen as strengthening the likelihood of a behavior occurring in the future, punishment was seen as weakening the likelihood of a behavior occurring in the future. Similar to reinforcement, punishment can be of two forms: either positive or negative (see Table 2.5). If something is received for engaging in a problem behavior and this decreases the likelihood that the problem behavior will occur again, it is called positive punishment. Common examples of positive punishment include being yelled at or getting a speeding ticket for driving too fast on the highway. Negative punishment, however, occurs when something is taken away and this decreases the likelihood of the problem behavior occurring in the future. For example, a student might have to stay inside during recess for engaging in problematic behavior or have his or her phone taken away for playing with it during class. Sending a student to time-out may also serve as a form of negative punishment if doing so removes the student from desired attention from peers.

The second strategy for weakening behavior is through the process of extinction. Extinction occurs when a behavior that was previously reinforced is no longer reinforced. Imagine, for example, that one of your students thrives on attention from peers. In order to get that attention from peers, the student begins to tell jokes during whole-class instruction. Each time that the student tells a joke, he or she reliably gets a laugh from classmates. If, however, you provide the class with explicit instructions regarding how to ignore the behav-

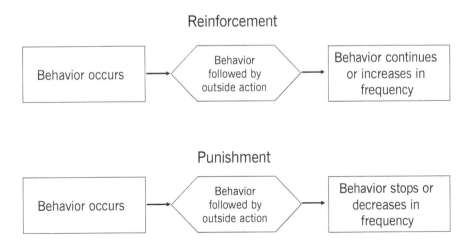

FIGURE 2.1. Distinguishing reinforcement from punishment.

TABLE 2.5. Types of Punishment

Positive punishment (gaining/accessing)	Negative punishment (losing/escaping)
Attention	
• Being reprimanded • Being given an office referral	• Being sent to time-out • Having seat moved away from friends
Activities	
• Having to serve detention	• Having to stay in from recess
Objects	
• Having to wear an ugly shirt	• Having a toy taken away

ior (e.g., turn away from the student and remain silent), the student will eventually find that his or her comedic efforts are ineffective, and will stop making jokes. Although the process sounds so simple, teachers who implement extinction procedures are often bedeviled by what is called an extinction burst. An extinction burst refers to an increase in a behavior that occurs when reinforcement stops. Because the student knows that telling jokes was so effective in gaining peer attention in the past, he or she may try harder—making jokes louder or more dramatic—in order to try and regain that lost attention. Usually, the extinction burst is short-lived and the behavior does eventually stop; however, unfortunately, the behavior can often get much worse before it begins to get better.

It is important to also keep in mind that extinction can occur with desired behaviors. For example, you might know that one of your students is likely to complete more assignments if the student knows that doing so will allow him or her to receive a salty snack. You therefore decide that every time the student turns in five assignments, he or she will receive a small snack. This fixed ratio reinforcement strategy proves very effective; however, eventually you come to realize that you can no longer afford to give out salty snacks so often. What is likely to happen if you suddenly stop doing so? Probably the same thing that would happen if you stopped receiving a paycheck: The work will stop.

PRINCIPLE 4: We Tend to Engage in Those Behaviors That Bring the Greatest Reinforcement (or, *Lots of Skittles! Right now? Little effort? Yes, please!*).

After Skinner had laid the foundation for understanding how reinforcement and punishment operate, R. J. Herrnstein (1961) began to explore the role that choice plays in determining behavior. Like Skinner's rats—and Thorndike's cats before him—Herrnstein was studying learning behavior in his laboratory with pigeons. Within an experimental chamber, he this time placed two different keys. Pressing either key would result in the release of food; however, each key was set to a different variable interval schedule of reinforcement. For example, the pigeon might receive food on average every 2 minutes if it pressed the first key but only every 5 minutes if it pressed the second key. What Herrnstein found was a strong relationship between the rate of responding (i.e., how often the pigeon pressed the key) and the relative rate of reinforcement (i.e., how often the pigeon received food for pressing one key as opposed to the other). This quantitative relationship came to be known as the matching law.

Extended to the understanding of human behavior, we know that there are often multiple behaviors that we can choose to exhibit in a given situation. However, most of us will choose to exhibit those behaviors that will result in the best outcomes. In general, we are most likely to choose those behaviors that get us the greatest amount of reinforcement, with the least amount of effort, and as quickly as possible. This is why although most of us like to think that we would choose the salad when approaching a buffet line, we all know that the broccoli and garbanzo bean containers stay full while the cheesecake goes very quickly!

There are a couple of important implications of the matching law to consider when we think about student behavior. The first is that in any situation there are likely to be competing sources of reinforcement. If your own efforts to change student behavior through reinforcement or punishment have been largely unsuccessful, it is important to consider whether the problem behavior is being reinforced by something or someone other than yourself. If a student is receiving higher rates of reinforcement for engaging in the problem behavior than exhibiting what is desired, the problem behavior will likely continue to persist. We therefore need to set up our classrooms so that earning reinforcement through problem behaviors is unlikely, whereas receiving reinforcement through desirable behavior is more likely. Of the multiple behaviors that are possible, we want to make the undesirable behavior difficult and the desirable behaviors easy. The second thing to keep in mind is that the conditions that are reinforcing a behavior may vary over time and across settings. Because there are always multiple things going on in a classroom, it can sometimes be difficult to understand the multiple competing contingencies at play. For example, a student may find teacher attention reinforcing when his or her peers are busy, but may find teacher attention embarrassing if peers are with him or her. Assuming that the value of a particular form of reinforcement is a constant for an individual would therefore be problematic.

PRINCIPLE 5: What We Find Rewarding Once May Not Always Be So (or, *I'm tired of Skittles! I want M&M's!*).

One of the interesting things to note is that the value of a particular type of reinforcement or punishment is not necessarily a constant over time. Rather, a reinforcer may have a very strong influence on our behavior in one situation and a much more weak influence in another. Imagine attending a reception where you have just eaten cake. If someone were to bring back the leftover cake and place it in the break room, you would not be especially motivated to get up and get a piece because your sweet tooth had already been satisfied. However, had you decided to skip the reception and found yourself in need of a sugar boost to make it to the end of the day, you would likely be much more motivated to venture down the hallway to grab a slice. In this example, cake became less desirable when it was preceded by another event (i.e., attending the reception). An event that changes the value of the reinforcer is called a *motivating operation.*

To draw another example using student behavior, imagine if you will that a middle school student has just returned to third period after spending all of first and second periods sitting alone quietly in the principal's office. The student is typically fairly attentive, but today cannot seem to sit facing forward and is constantly turning to talk with classmates. Despite prompts to pay attention, the student continues to talk at inappropriate times throughout the entire period. Under typical circumstances, the student is not someone whom you would consider a chatterbox—this inappropriate talking is therefore seen an unusual behavior for him or her. However, in this particular situation, there was an event that made the attention from the student's peers more powerful—namely, the fact that he or she had been deprived of any attention during first and second periods. This situation is depicted in Figure 2.2. In this example, being deprived of attention in the office was the motivating operation that made talking to classmates more desirable.

In the first example, the fact that you were already satiated by cake meant that the opportunity to eat more cake was not reinforcing. In the second example, the fact that the student was deprived of attention at the start of the day meant that attention from peers became even more reinforcing. Together, these examples illustrate the two most common types of motivating operations: satiation and deprivation. We are less likely to engage in a behavior if we have already been in frequent contact with the reinforcer and more likely to engage in a behavior if we have not received that form of reinforcement in quite some time. The implications of this for the classroom are as such. If a previously effective reinforcer appears to lose its value, this may possibly be explained by satiation. When possible, one might switch out reinforcement to another form (e.g., providing the student with free time instead of stickers); however, alternatively, it may be necessary to limit access to the reinforcer until it regains its former value.

PRINCIPLE 6: We Look for Cues to Tell Us Whether Reinforcement Is Likely (or, *I can see that you bought more Skittles and I'm ready to work!*).

The last important concept to understand when looking at an individual's behavior is the idea of a discriminative stimulus. A discriminative stimulus is something that signals to an

FIGURE 2.2. Example of a motivating operation.

individual that reinforcement is available. When I am driving home from work and come to an intersection with a stoplight, I stop. I stop even though I want to get home and driving through the stoplight might get me home a bit sooner. In this case, the red traffic light signals to me that it is not a good idea to cross the street because it is unsafe or I may get a traffic ticket. In this case, the red light signals that reinforcement is not available, whereas a green light signals that reinforcement is available and that it is safe to drive.

As another example, think of a middle school boy who has a crush on a girl in his class. He finds her attention extremely reinforcing and is therefore routinely willing to sing in class, call her name, or talk about the clothes she is wearing so that she will say something to him. Although she has not paid attention to him all day and he is starved for her attention, he does not act out as your class begins today. Why? Because the girl is tardy and has not yet arrived. When she finally walks into the class, however, the student begins his normal routine of verbally wooing the girl. It is the act of walking into the classroom that signals to the boy that reinforcement (i.e., attention) is now available.

PUTTING IT ALL TOGETHER

Now that we have laid out the basic behavioral principles upon which the strategies presented in this book will build, let us return to the case of the middle school student we presented earlier in order to provide further illustration. To refresh your memory, the middle school teacher was frustrated (to put it mildly) with one of her students, who continually called other students racially offensive names. Although his teacher had tried several strategies to curb this behavior (e.g., sending to the office, administering rewards), the most typical response was for both the teacher and the other students to yell at him to stop.

We next reexamine the principles that we have described throughout this chapter with regard to the student's use of offensive language.

The Law of Effect

The law of effect essentially says that we will keep engaging in a behavior if something good comes of it and stop doing it if it results in something bad. Each time that Joe called his classmates offensive names, they would yell at him to stop. The fact that Joe continued to engage in the behavior—despite seat changes and reprimands and trips to the principal's office—suggests that he took great pleasure in the attention that he was getting from his teacher and classmates. Although most of us would not find having others yelling at us pleasurable, we must keep in mind that what is pleasurable for one person is not necessarily pleasurable for another.

Reinforcement

As we noted above, each time that Joe made negative comments, he received peer and teacher attention. The fact that the problem behavior continued to persist when followed by negative attention suggests that attention was reinforcing the behavior. Because the reinforcement was something that Joe received (i.e., attention), this suggests an example of positive reinforcement. When we stop to think about the schedule of reinforcement, we realize that Joe was being reinforced on a continuous schedule—every time he insulted a classmate, the rest of the class told him to stop. This meant that the behavior was being strongly reinforced. However, this also meant that the behavior may have had low resistance to extinction. In other words, if the class had simply ignored the behavior, it may have gone away.

Punishment

When we think about the word "punishment," we often think about some penalty that is imposed for doing something wrong. When Joe's teacher yelled at him, moved his seat to the front of the room, and sent him to the principal's office, she was attempting to punish him for his inappropriate behavior—that is, she thought that applying these consequences would stop the behavior from occurring in the future. Unfortunately, however, what we sometimes expect to be negative consequences don't end up being quite as aversive as we hoped. In Joe's case, the fact that the behavior persisted—rather than abating—after these consequences were applied suggests that none effectively served as forms of punishment.

The Matching Law

The matching law suggests that although there are multiple behaviors that we may engage in, we tend to choose those behaviors that result in the greatest level of reinforcement. At one point, Joe's teacher moved away from relying solely on punitive strategies and offered Joe a reward if he stopped making inappropriate remarks. She was well-intentioned and hoped that perhaps Joe would be so motivated to earn extra recess time that he would clean up his verbal act. The fact that the reinforcement strategy did not work, however, suggests that the recess time reward was not powerful enough. This is likely because Joe was receiving higher rates of reinforcement for engaging in the problem behavior than he was for speaking kindly to his peers—that is, whereas he could only receive extra recess time once a day, he was receiving attention from peers every time that he made an inappropriate remark.

Motivating Operations

A motivating operation is an event that changes the value of a reinforcer. In this case, the fact that Joe was calling his classmates inappropriate names day in and day out suggests that there was not a motivating operation at work. However, if Joe's day was structured so that he was able to access a lot of peer attention at the start of the day—thereby satiating the need for attention—he may be less likely to call his classmates names in order to obtain attention as the day went on.

Developing an Intervention

Given what we now know about Joe's problem behavior, designing an appropriate intervention plan becomes a much more straightforward task. At the foundation of this plan, our goal should be to ensure two things: (1) that Joe does not continue to receive attention for calling his classmates inappropriate names and (2) that the reinforcement Joe receives for using kind words in the classroom is sufficiently powerful to maintain the behavior. David therefore worked with the teacher to implement a program known as a group ignore. Through this process, the other students in the class were rewarded for ignoring Joe's inappropriate behavior. Every time Joe yelled a racially inappropriate name, the teacher would look at the rest of the class. If they said nothing, they earned a point that could be exchanged for 15 seconds of free time at the end of the class. After eight shouts with no response, Joe stopped calling out. In addition, procedures were put into place to reinforce him for using kind words in the classroom. Given that Joe seemed to find peer attention reinforcing (albeit the negative kind!), his classmates were taught to provide Joe with positive attention each time that he used appropriate language or otherwise interacted appropriately with them. In addition, a contingency was put into place whereby Joe could earn 5 minutes of free time each hour to chat with a friend if he said at least five kind things to his classmates and had no instances of inappropriate language.

CONCLUSIONS

Much as it would be difficult to understand a chemistry lesson if you did not have a handle on the necessary terminology (e.g., "compounds," "electrons," "elements"), fully understanding the interventions described in this book would be challenging without a basic understanding of behavioral principles. Our goal in this chapter was therefore to provide the reader with much of the theoretical basis for the rest of this text. Some people have objections to a behavioral approach to managing classes. These concerns are addressed in Appendix 2.1 at the end of this chapter. As we move to discuss specific intervention techniques in future chapters, we return to these basic principles to provide a rationale for why it is important to carry out procedures in a certain way. Chapter 3 addresses methods for both promoting positive behaviors and making sure that problem behaviors are not unintentionally rewarded. Chapters 4–7 focus on different strategies for utilizing the principles of reinforcement to reward the behaviors we want to see and to extinguish problematic behaviors.

APPENDIX 2.1. FREQUENTLY ASKED QUESTIONS

Q: Are you suggesting that we treat our kids like laboratory animals?

A: Not at all. Even though many of these theories were tested and developed using animal models, an entire field of study called applied behavior analysis has been created that applies these theories to humans. Humans are certainly much more complex than animals, but these same principles apply.

Q: Are you saying that we need to give students something every time they do what they are supposed to do?

A: No, not at all. In this chapter, we are not making recommendations. Instead, we are making observations about the ways that behaviors increase and decrease.

Q: Don't behavioral techniques kill a student's intrinsic motivation?

A: This is a question that we frequently get. We have both worked with a number of teachers who believed that rewards kill students' intrinsic motivation or their willingness to do something just because they think it is important. There are a few things to consider:

1. For a student to be intrinsically motivated to do something, he or she must already be able to do it, and do it well. Most of the behaviors that we teach in school are things that students have not mastered and have no intrinsic motivation for. For most of these situations, extrinsic motivators are needed if the students do not find the skills motivating. Once a behavior is under stimulus control, or we know how to motivate it, intrinsic motivation may be facilitated by fading the intervention using self-monitoring techniques (see Chapter 7) and by the student's mastery of the skills.
2. If students are given rewards for a behavior that they already find intrinsically motivating, they may or may not lose intrinsic motivation. However, using reductive strategies such as overt punishment to control a student may actually serve to decrease intrinsic motivation.

Q: Don't students already know how to behave when they come to school?

A: Human beings learn to adapt to a variety of environments. Some students come from environments that are similar to school, and some do not. Students know how to behave in the environments in which they have experience.

Q: Won't students have learned proper behavior from their previous teachers?

A: This does not always happen. Different teachers have differing amounts of expertise in classroom management. However, one should never assume that students know how to behave in *your* classroom.

Q: Isn't this just another education fad?

A: We are all used to seeing educational "fads" come and go. Most of the time, the fads are based on weak evidence (e.g., learning styles, whole-language reading instruction) or there are inadequate supports put into place to allow those ideas to take shape. Classroom management practices have some of the strongest theoretical and empirical support, but are frequently not implemented with integrity. Chapter 9 of this book addresses the issue of intervention integrity. Classroom management practices require practice and feedback.

PART II

PROMOTION AND PREVENTION STRATEGIES

CHAPTER 3

Structuring the Classroom for Success
Preventing Problems before They Happen

> What distinguishes our intellect from animals' is not that we can go against
> our environment—most of us can't, not in the long run—but rather that we can
> purposefully alter our environment to shape our behavior in ways we choose.
> —FREEDMAN (2012)

Have you ever observed that your behavior changes in different situations? For example, most people are far more likely to exercise if the air temperature is 70 degrees than if it is 0 or 105 degrees. We are more likely to check our Facebook page if we've been receiving notifications frequently than when we have not. We tend to eat healthier food when we are at home where there are apples on the counter than when we are traveling and it is easiest to pick up snacks at a convenience store. We talk louder at parties with a lot of background noise than we do when we are sitting in a church, synagogue, or mosque. We are more likely to get work done if the setting is quiet and has minimal distractions than if someone is playing a video game in the same room. Walmart even recently changed the way it laid out the items in its stores because it found that consumers tend to buy more when shelves are higher and more items are stacked in the middle of the aisles!

Although there are certainly always exceptions, our behavior is somewhat predictable. Given a specific situation, adults are more likely to engage in a particular response. The same is true for kids. Have you ever noticed how high schoolers behave differently in gym and art class than they do in English? How an entire class performs well for their classroom teacher but displays abhorrent behavior for a substitute? The point is that environments matter and have a profound effect on behavior long before a student even thinks about acting up. Teachers who recognize that environments affect behavior are more likely to look for environmental solutions to classwide behavior problems that are preventative. This chapter addresses the preventative methods that teachers may employ to foster environments that minimize disruption and maximize learning. In other words, we focus on those things that teachers can do proactively in order to make problem behaviors less likely to occur.

WHY ARE PREVENTATIVE STRATEGIES IMPORTANT?

Prevention is about getting in early to stop something before it occurs. Although most of the time there is widespread consensus as to the importance of preventing something undesirable (e.g., bullying, crime, violence), this is not necessarily always so. For example, currently in the United States there is disagreement regarding whether vaccines are necessary in order to stay healthy and prevent disease, or whether they make children more susceptible to illness by weakening the immune system. This same type of debate extends to preventative classroom management practices. Although some teachers believe that preventative classroom management strategies are necessary in order to prevent problem behavior, we have heard many other teachers express concern that classrooms that are too highly structured will prevent kids from being able to think critically. In other words, they fear that these students will not receive sufficient opportunities to make mistakes, learn from natural consequences, and figure out how to navigate social hierarchies. By the time these students grow up, these teachers worry that students will not be able to function independently as adults. We want to address this concern by acknowledging two realities.

The first reality is that many students come to school with some type of disadvantage. In 2013, roughly 20% of school-age children in the United States were living in poverty (Kena et al., 2015). Children living in poverty have a higher likelihood of risk factors including lead exposure, limited access to mental and physical health care, and increased exposure to substance abuse. These home factors may make it more difficult to attend to instruction when students enter the classroom. Furthermore, the National Survey of Children's Exposure to Violence found that one in 10 youth in the United States had personally experienced maltreatment and more than one in four youth had witnessed victimization at home or in their communities (Finkelhor, Turner, Ormrod, & Hamby, 2009). Students who have experienced violence may come to school with some degree of anxiety or may alternatively imitate the aggression that they have witnessed elsewhere. For many of these students who have experienced disorder or uncertainty outside of school, a highly structured classroom setting is the best way to keep them safe and to remove distractions from learning.

The second reality is that if a classroom is poorly structured, *all* students are likely to miss out on learning opportunities because instructional time is lost to managing behavior problems. As a result, instructional periods are likely to be much less efficient. For example, even a student who is generally very attentive and engaged in classroom lessons may find him- or herself having to use mental energy to ignore distractions in a classroom characterized by high levels of disruptive behavior. Because energy has to be directed toward purposefully ignoring distractions, the student ultimately has fewer immediate cognitive resources to allot to mastering complicated academic material. On the other hand, if a classroom is well structured and disruptions are minimized, it is easier not only to teach the intended curriculum but also to teach independent living skills such as social and emotional regulation.

WHAT ARE EVIDENCE-BASED PREVENTATIVE STRATEGIES?

Throughout the remainder of this chapter, we present evidence-based strategies for managing student behavior that are proactive in nature. Many of the decisions regarding preventative strategy usage can be made before the first student even enters the classroom. In fact, research has shown that those teachers who are most effective spend a great deal of time teaching and planning for the management of student behaviors at the start of the year (Everston & Emmer, 1982). Although the specific execution of each of these strategies may differ depending on the age of the student, the underlying principles do not. Broadly speaking, preventing classroom problems requires addressing three areas:

1. Creating physical structures in the classroom that reduce the likelihood of behavior problems.
2. Teaching students expected behaviors.
3. Engaging in effective teaching behaviors that elicit desired behaviors.

Creating Physical Structures

One of the first things that most classroom management textbooks talk about is how structuring the classroom setting is key to promoting appropriate behavior and maximizing learning. This is likely because changing seating arrangements is an easy and inexpensive method for managing student behavior. Like much of the classroom management literature, early studies examining classroom layout were largely correlational (e.g., Kritchevsky & Prescott, 1969; Zifferblatt, 1972)—that is, researchers entered different classrooms and tried to account for the behavioral differences observed by highlighting variations with regard to the physical space. Although the authors of these studies made recommendations with regard to classroom layout (e.g., limit number of desks in a cluster), the correlational nature of these investigations meant that definitive conclusions regarding the effect of classroom configuration could not be made.

Beginning in the late 1970s, however, researchers began to conduct experimental studies in order to better understand the influence of seating arrangement on student behavior. Wannarka and Ruhl (2008) conducted a review of those empirical studies in which desk arrangement was directly manipulated. Several of the identified studies examined the differential effect of arranging desks in rows versus clusters or circles on off-task behavior (see Table 3.1). Results suggested that structuring desks in rows resulted in lower levels of off-task behavior during independent seatwork than other configurations (e.g., clusters, circles). These results held across elementary (e.g., Hastings & Schweiso, 1995) and secondary (e.g., Axelrod, Hall, & Tams, 1979) settings, but were found to be most pronounced when exam-

TABLE 3.1. Studies Examining the Effects of Classroom Configuration

Study	Setting	Comparison	Design	Outcome
Axelrod, Hall, & Tams (1979), Study 1	Second-grade classroom during independent seatwork	Desks in rows versus clusters	BCBC design within one classroom	Higher levels of on-task behavior in rows
Axelrod et al. (1979), Study 2	Seventh-grade life sciences class	Desks in rows versus clusters	BCB design within one classroom	Greater number of talk-outs in clusters
Bennett & Blundell (1983)	Fourth-grade inclusive classrooms during independent seatwork	Desks in rows versus groups	BCB design across two classrooms	Higher levels of work production in rows
Hastings & Schweiso (1995)	9- to 11-year-old students during independent seatwork	Desks in rows versus groups	BCB design across two classrooms	Higher levels of on-task behavior in rows
Wheldall & Lam (1987)	Two classrooms of 12- to 15-year-old students in a special school for behaviorally troublesome students	Desks in rows versus clusters	ABAB across three classrooms	Higher levels of on-task behavior in rows

ining the behavior of students with behavior problems (Wheldall, Morris, Vaughan, & Ng, 1981).

Teaching Students Expected Behaviors

We know that there is wide variation from one school to the next with regard to philosophies of learning and the ways of doing business. There are some schools that eschew traditional teacher-led instruction and instead encourage students to initiate their own learning opportunities. At the same time, other schools are characterized by a high level of structure, order, and discipline. However, the one thing that all schools have in common is that there are agreed-upon expectations for student behavior. Such expectations are necessary given that a large number of students have to manage the limited resources of space, materials, and teacher attention in any one given classroom. Therefore, once the physical environment has been structured, classroom management next involves identifying the behaviors that students need to exhibit—or should avoid exhibiting—in order to maximize learning in the classroom. These behaviors that we wish to see students exhibit (or suppress!) are not necessarily ones that students need in order to be successful later in life. As adults, we rarely need to get hall passes, line up for lunch, or sit on a specific square on a carpet. Yet, these may be behaviors that are necessary for students to move safely through a school or to be able to meaningfully participate in a group activity. One way of classifying these behaviors is as either being instructionally relevant or instructionally irrelevant.

All of the following student behaviors are ones that we generally wish to increase and could be considered instructionally relevant: answering teacher questions, individually completing a worksheet, mixing chemicals together in a laboratory, playing an instructional game, helping another student with classwork, and collaborating on a group project. We could probably brainstorm a list of 100 behaviors that are of potential relevance in school settings; however, identifying all possibilities is probably of limited utility for two reasons. First, we know that there are probably very few behaviors that each and every teacher finds to be instructionally relevant. For example, one classroom teacher may require students to stay seated and facing forward throughout instruction, whereas another teacher may encourage students to get out of their seats to release energy intermittently. Neither is necessarily right or wrong; they are simply two different ways of structuring the classroom that result in different interpretations of "instructionally relevant" behavior. Second, we know that what is relevant in one setting is not necessarily relevant in another. For example, bouncing a ball off of the floor may be instructionally relevant in physical education, but would likely be looked upon with discouragement during literacy instruction. It is therefore important to consider context when determining instructional relevance.

We would like to think that students spend the majority of their school days engaged in instructionally relevant behaviors; however, we know in reality that this is not necessarily true. Instructionally irrelevant behaviors are those that do not directly pertain to instruction. Most of the time when we think of instructionally irrelevant behaviors we think of problem behaviors that teachers aim to decrease: talking or getting out of a seat without permission, playing with a smartphone, fighting, calling other students names, engaging in horseplay, writing graffiti on walls, cheating . . . the list goes on. However, not all instructionally irrelevant behaviors are necessarily considered problem behaviors. In any classroom, there are times when students may be doing tasks that do not directly relate to math or reading or science but are necessary to ensure that everybody is prepared to learn and that instruction moves forward. Examples include putting materials away, getting snow gear on and off, lining up, sharpening pencils, turning in assignments, and finding another activity when classwork is finished. These transitional activities are critical to classroom success because they allow students to stay safe while being in the right place with the right tools. Although the nature of these instructionally irrelevant and transitional behaviors is certainly very different, too much of either can be problematic. After all, the more either of these types of behaviors occurs, students spend less time participating in—and benefiting from—the class curriculum. Maximizing learning time requires that a teacher establish and teach rules, expectations, and routines to make sure that the classroom functions smoothly.

Establishing Rules and Expectations

One way to help ensure that students engage in higher rates of instructionally relevant behaviors is to establish clear rules and expectations for student behavior. We have yet to see a classroom management book that does not recommend having clear expectations for student behavior, and there are very few classrooms in which rules are not in place. In fact, when you think back to your own elementary school experience, you can probably picture the list of boldly written reminders not to eat, cheat, or fight hung on the wall! The terms "rules" and "expectations" are often used interchangeably to refer to guidelines for student behavior; however, these concepts can be differentiated by their scope, both in terms of how they are framed and where they apply.

Merriam-Webster (2017) defines an expectation as "a belief that something will happen or is likely to happen," whereas a rule is defined as "a statement that tells you what is or is not allowed in a particular game, situation, etc." Expectations are therefore broader in scope, in that they are generally stated and apply across settings. The expectation that students be kind to one other, for example, is a general expectation for how we would like students to behave that is not typically limited to the lunchroom or the hallways. Rules, on the other hand, tend to be narrower in scope. Rules describe specific behaviors that we would like to see students demonstrate and that apply to specific settings. Just as the rules in a game of Go Fish are not the same as those in Capture the Flag, the rules for student behavior on the playground are not necessarily the same as those in the classroom.

Within the positive behavioral interventions and supports (PBIS) literature, recommendations have been made for establishing both rules and expectations. In general, both rules and expectations should be realistic, age appropriate, and understandable for the students. This means setting ambitious but not unrealistic expectations and wording these rules or expectations in a way that makes sense to the target population. Rules and expectations should also be positively stated, describing what students should do rather than what they should not. Finally, both lists of rules and expectations should be limited in number so that it is easy for students to remember them. Although there are no clear research-based criteria for how many rules are too many, one recommendation that has been made is that classes should have approximately four to six rules (Gable, Hester, Rock, & Hughes, 2009; see Coach Card 3.1).[*]

CLARIFYING CHANGING EXPECTATIONS

One of the challenges with rules is that they are often context specific and vary depending on the time of day. It has therefore been suggested that a visual signal may be useful for students to understand when different expectations are in place (Skinner & Skinner, 2007). One strategy for clarifying expectations involves the use of a color wheel system (Skinner, Scala, Dendas, & Lentz, 2007). Within this system, a different set of expectations is developed to correspond with the colors red, yellow, and green. Typically, red is the most restrictive in terms of expectations for student behavior and reflects what students should be doing when the teacher is giving directions. For example, students may be expected to sit quietly in their seats with their eyes on the teacher. Green, on the other hand, is the least restrictive in terms of expectations and reflects what students should be doing during free-time activities. For example, students should keep their hands and feet to themselves, respect others, and use inside voices. Yellow lies between red and green and reflects expectations during

---

[*] All coach cards appear at the ends of chapters.

typical instructional periods (e.g., independent seatwork, lecture). During these times, students are expected to sit quietly in their seats with their eyes on their work and raise their hands if they have a question or need to leave their seats. In one study utilizing the Color Wheel intervention within an urban fourth-grade classroom, a fourth segment was added in order to signify expectations during cooperative learning activities (Blondin, Skinner, Parkhurst, Wood, & Snyder, 2012). Specifically, during these times students were expected to use quiet voices, talk only when it was about assigned work, ask three students a question before asking the teacher, keep their hands and feet to themselves, and follow directions.

Once the expectations have been operationalized, a tricolored wheel (i.e., equal parts green, yellow, and red) is constructed and placed at the front of the classroom. The teacher then explains that appropriate behavior looks different depending on what is going on in the classroom. The three sets of expectations are explicitly taught to the students and practiced using role plays (Skinner et al., 2007). Each day, the teacher reviews the three sets of expectations with the class and then cues the students each time that the color wheel is turned. In one variation, a stoplight was used rather than a color wheel to signal changes in expectations (Choate, Skinner, Fearrington, Kohler, & Skolits, 2007). Both improvements in on-task behavior and decreases in disruptive (e.g., out of seat, inappropriate vocalizations) behavior have been observed in empirical studies of the Color Wheel intervention within elementary classrooms (see Table 3.2).

TABLE 3.2. Empirical Studies Examining the Color Wheel Intervention

Study	Setting	Intervention	Design	Outcome
Blondin, Skinner, Parkhurst, Wood, & Snyder (2012)	Fourth-grade general education classroom	Color Wheel	ABAB design across seven students	Large increases in on-task behavior
Choate, Skinner, Fearrington, Kohler, & Skolits (2007)	First-grade general education classroom	Color Wheel	AB design within one classroom	Large decreases in out-of-seat behavior
Fudge et al. (2008)	Second-grade general education classroom	Color Wheel	BCBC design within one classroom	Large increases in on-task behavior
Kirk et al. (2010), Study 1	Third-grade general education classroom	Color Wheel + IGC	ABCDC design within one classroom	Fewer inappropriate vocalizations during Color Wheel + IGC than IGC alone
Kirk et al. (2010), Study 2	First-grade general education classroom	Color Wheel + SCM	BCDC design within one classroom	Fewer callouts during Color Wheel + SCM than SCM alone

Note. IGC, interdependent group contingency; SCM, standard classroom management procedure.

SAMPLE RULES AND EXPECTATIONS

Because rules and expectations provide a clear set of boundaries that serve as cues for students and teachers alike, they should be both observable and enforceable. When David began teaching, he found that he would accuse his students of breaking rules that he had never established. If two students were talking to each other, he would tell them that they were violating the classroom rules even though he had never told them ahead of time that talking was not allowed. Rightfully, the students complained. Eventually, it was the act of sitting down to establish rules for the class that crystalized what his expectations actually were. Although rules can be established for a wide range of contexts and situations, our goal here is to provide you with a few diverse examples of situations in which proactively establishing rules in advance may pay off in dividends (see Box 3.1 for additional examples).

• *What type of space should students give each other?* One of the most consistent problems that teachers have is students who violate each other's space. For example, in a residential treatment setting, it is important to establish boundaries because there are frequently problems with horseplay and physical interactions that border on bullying. In this setting, students may not be allowed to touch each other while they are in school unless it is a handshake or a fist bump. More commonly, however, students simply struggle with understanding the concept of a personal bubble. Within preschool settings, for example, children may be taught to put a Hula-Hoop around their waists in order to understand how much space their classmates may need. Because guidelines for how much space students need will differ depending on the age and cultural context of the students and the

---

BOX 3.1. Questions That May Be Used to Establish Proactive Rules/Expectations

- How loud can students talk?
- How should students line up?
- What materials should students come to class with?
- What should students do to show they are paying attention?
- What should students do when they finish their assignments early?
- What should students do when they need help?
- What should students do when they need to use the restroom or drinking fountain?
- When can students leave their seats?
- When can students work with classmates?
- Where can students move in the classroom?

target setting, these expectations should be explicitly taught to students from the beginning.

• *What movement is allowed?* The amount of movement that is tolerated in the classroom will inevitably vary based on the activity. During individual work time, students may need to stay seated in order to complete their assignments and avoid disturbing other students. During a science lab, on the other hand, it may be perfectly acceptable to get up and walk around the room. The rules regarding what type of movement is permissible and when should be clearly outlined for students in order to avoid any confusion. When establishing these rules, however, it is beneficial to keep in mind the importance of movement in promoting students' emotional, cognitive, and academic health. Regular activity is needed in order to maintain glucose and oxygen levels to the brain, which help to promote focus and attention (Reilly, Buskist, & Gross, 2012). One study found that incorporating just one brief 10-minute physical activity break into the daily classroom schedule led to improvements in students' on-task behavior (Mahar et al., 2006).

• *What should students be doing during teacher-directed instruction?* Research has found that rates of disruptive or inappropriate classroom behavior tend to be much higher during whole-class instruction (e.g., Greenwood, Horton, & Utley, 2002; Hollo & Hirn, 2015). This may be explained by the fact that students tend to have fewer opportunities to respond and actively engage in instruction. Establishing expectations for what students should be doing during teacher-directed instruction clarifies what it means to be engaged when one is not necessarily actively working on an assigned task. One popular expectation for student behavior during classroom instruction involves the use of the acronym SLANT: Sit up, Lean forward, Ask questions, Nod your head, and Track the speaker. Research has shown that teaching students to observe and monitor their SLANT behaviors may help to improve overall levels of on-task behavior (e.g., Amato-Zech, Hoff, & Doepke, 2006; Briesch, Hemphill, & Daniels, 2013).

• *How should students respond to classmates' misbehavior?* When working in general education classrooms, we come to expect that there will be some students who will exhibit impulsive behaviors, some who will act out when things are not going their way, and still others who will display the inevitable behavioral meltdown. Unfortunately, however, students who act out are often reinforced by the behavior of their classmates. A student who makes inappropriate jokes in order to gain peer attention may get the laugh from his or her neighbors that he or she was hoping for. Or a student who begins to cry during recess when he or she isn't able to play with a toy that he or she wants may be given that item by an empathetic peer. It can therefore be beneficial to teach students strategies for responding up front. For example, one facility had a procedure called "awareness," whereby students had to turn their heads away from a student who was acting out and be silent. When problems are anticipated, proactively teaching students concrete strategies helps to avoid further escalation of problems.

EMPIRICAL RESEARCH ON RULES AND EXPECTATIONS

The National Council on Teacher Quality (NCTQ) describes the explicit teaching of rules and expectations as a strategy with "strong aggregated research support." Researchers have even suggested that ensuring students have a clear understanding of the rules and expectations can do more for school safety than security cameras, security guards, and higher levels of supervision (Mayer & Leone, 1999). It is important to note, however, that there is no research to show that clear rules and expectations, by themselves, have a significant impact on student behavior (Gable et al., 2009). Across two studies conducted in elementary school classrooms, teacher-created rules that were only introduced to the class but not reinforced were shown to have no effect on problem behaviors (Greenwood, Hops, Delquadri, & Guild, 1974; Madsen, Becker, & Thomas, 1968). However, when students received feedback and reinforcement for demonstrating expected behaviors, significant improvements in classroom behavior were observed. We talk more about the reinforcement of student behavior in Chapter 4.

Establishing Routines

In addition to rules and expectations, it is also important to establish routines. Whereas rules describe what students should and should not do, routines describe specific step-by-step responses that students should exhibit during daily classroom activities in order to ensure that materials, furniture, and bodies are in the right place for the activity. One of the things we know about teachers who are identified as most effective is that they spend most of their time during the beginning of the year establishing routines and teaching procedures (Bohn, Roehrig, & Pressley, 2004; Rubie-Davies, 2007).

There are many different routines that we may establish. Although some routines are likely applicable to any classroom (e.g., using the bathroom), others may be idiosyncratic to a particular classroom context (e.g., cleaning the class pet's cage). Furthermore, we may establish some routines from the outset of the school year, whereas others may arise during the middle of the school year (we present a case example to illustrate how the need for new routines may be identified in Box 3.2). The best way to begin to think about which routines should be taught in your classroom is to write down the different transitions that occur throughout the day. For example, there are specific steps that students must follow when they first enter the classroom that are distinct from those that they must follow when getting ready to go home at the end of the day. In Table 3.3, we have provided several examples of both academic and nonacademic routines to help get you started in thinking about which routines you may wish to target.

When developing a routine, there are several things that a teacher needs to consider. First, how long should the routine take? If the routine involves transitioning from one activity to another, a 2-minute time frame may be appropriate. If a routine involves clearing the classroom in case of a serious disruption, however, 20 seconds may be a more appropriate time limit. Second, what is the end goal of the routine—that is, once the routine is completed, what should the classroom look like? Communicating clear expectations for what it

BOX 3.2. Illustration of Establishing Routines

I (David) was once working with a sixth-grade class that typically sat at two-person tables. For group activities, however, all students needed to sit in chairs in a circle in the middle of the room. The first time that the students were asked to move their desks and chairs, there were several problems. Some students dragged the tables across the tile floor, which made a horrible noise. In order to get the best seat, several other students ran with their chairs, narrowly missing hitting or running into their classmates. The students also placed a number of tables directly in front of the classroom door, creating a fire hazard. When the chairs were finally moved to the center of the room, they formed an oval, which meant that some students sitting at the far ends would have difficulty participating in the conversation. To top it all off, the transition took 5 minutes, which was much longer than the 2-minute target that I had in mind. After bringing these concerns to the students, the class created the following checklist for what transitioning to group activities should look like:

1. The classroom should have all desks placed to the side of the room while still ensuring easy access to the door.
2. All chairs should be carried by one person. All tables should be carried by two persons.
3. Students will walk at all times.
4. All of the chairs should be placed in a circle.
5. The transition will take no longer than 90 seconds.

The class then practiced this transition five times until they met all of the criteria. Of course, teaching the routine took nearly an entire class period; however, the next time that the class met, the transition took only 90 seconds and they were able to begin the group activity immediately.

TABLE 3.3. Examples of Academic and Nonacademic Classroom Routines

Academic routines	Nonacademic routines
• Asking questions	• Entering the classroom
• Finishing an assignment early	• Using the bathroom/water fountain
• Getting/putting away materials	• Evacuating the room in case of emergency
• Making up missed work	• Lining up
• Turning in assignments	• Preparing for bus departure
• Getting help	• Cleaning up at the end of the school day
• Note taking	• Sharpening a pencil
• Discussing work in groups	• Blowing one's nose
• Completing the "starter" assignment	• Taking off and putting on snow gear

means to have put all of your materials away, for example, will avoid some students having cleared their desktops, whereas others have created tidy piles of books and papers. Third, what level of scaffolding is needed for students to successfully carry out the routine? More or fewer teacher-delivered prompts may be necessary depending on the students' age, as well as their familiarity with the routine. Consideration of each of these factors will assist in developing the most effective routine procedures for a given situation.

Teaching Rules and Routines

Once rules and routines have been established, they must then be explicitly taught to students. Whether you are teaching rules or routines, arithmetic or writing, the same principles of effective instruction apply—that is, teaching a new skill involves a four-step process of telling, showing, doing, and generalizing (see Coach Card 3.2). The first two steps represent indirect training, in which the students passively listen and learn. The second two steps represent direct training, in which the students take a more active role in practicing and rehearsing the skill. To illustrate these steps, imagine that you have never been on skis before and the instructor's task is to teach you to get down the bunny slope successfully. Initially, the teacher explains what the skill involves and why it is important (i.e., tell). A novice skier might be told to form a "wedge" with his or her skis in order to control his or her speed down the hill. Forming a V with one's skis helps to create resistance and thereby slows you down. Next, the teacher demonstrates for the student how to perform the skill (i.e., show). The ski instructor might put on his or her skis and model the wedge technique while the student watches. Providing examples of both good and bad (e.g., legs too far apart, leaning too far back, looking down at the ground) form will help the student to better understand what creating a wedge should look like. Third, the student is provided with multiple opportunities to perform the skill (i.e., do) and receives feedback from the teacher in order to improve performance. This means that the novice skier actually puts on his or her boots and skis and tries to slow him- or herself down using the wedge method. If the instructor sees ways in which the novice could improve, he or she provides the skier with concrete suggestions. Finally, the student receives different opportunities to apply the skill in order to build fluency (i.e., generalize). This might first entail additional practice opportunities (e.g., repeatedly going up and down the bunny slope); however, eventually the novice should apply the skill in different contexts (e.g., on a different or more challenging hill) in order to promote skill generalization.

When teaching rules and routines, there are a few things to keep in mind. First, never assume that a student knows what a routine or an expectation is. To understand the degree to which teachers' expectations vary, all that you need to do is to walk down the hallway during after-school dismissal. The student may have been taught an expectation or routine previously; however, it may not look exactly like the one you wish to establish. Second, never assume that simply telling a student how something should be done will result in behavior change. No matter how many instructional videos you watch on YouTube, you are unlikely to be able to do the Napoleon Dynamite dance until you actually practice. Just like us, children don't learn by listening—they learn by doing. Third, never assume that practicing a routine once is sufficient. We know that with most things repeated practice is necessary in order to build fluency with a skill. Fourth, never assume that feedback is unnecessary. When we practice a skill in the absence of feedback, we risk practicing that skill incorrectly. Students need to receive performance feedback in order to ensure they fully understand what is expected. Finally, never assume that your routines will be perfect the first time. We may spend time developing a routine, teach it to our students, and then realize that we have forgotten an important step. Or, particular steps may become less necessary over time. Routines must be viewed flexibly and subject to modifications as needed.

Engaging in Effective Teaching Behaviors

In an educational utopia, we might simply teach students what we expect them to do, click our heels three times, and they would magically follow every rule and routine that we had laid out before them. In reality, we know that additional effort is needed in order to ensure that classrooms continue to run smoothly. In this final section, we highlight those small strategies that teachers can implement on a daily basis in order to elicit desired behavior from their students. These strategies fall into several broad categories: effectively communicating instructions, increasing opportunities to respond, and actively supervising the classroom.

Effectively Communicating Instructions

There are many times in a given day when teachers need to give directions. Directions refer to those expectations communicated by teachers that are unique to that particular activity or period of time. Directions can be used to describe the behaviors necessary to complete an assignment, or to communicate to students how to move from one place to another. If a teacher does not give clear directions, however, a student may not know what the expectations are. Many beginning teachers struggle when giving directions and make one of several common mistakes. First, they may fail to get the students' attention before giving a direction so that it falls on deaf ears. In such a situation, students do not even have the opportunity to hear the direction in the first place. Second, some teachers give directions as requests (e.g., "Would you mind moving to another desk, please?"). Although such requests come across as very polite, they also communicate to the student that the direction is optional (when, in fact, it may not be). Third, teachers may give long directions (e.g., "Take out your science books, turn to page 56, read the first full paragraph on that page, and then write down a few key points from your reading"), causing students to lose track of what they are supposed to do. Fourth, teachers may ask students to do things that are not behaviorally measurable. Asking a student to "Improve your attitude," "Try harder," or "Pay attention" involves changing some internal state that we cannot observe. As a result, it can be difficult to judge whether the student actually achieved what was being asked of him or her. Fifth, teachers may create a power struggle by standing immediately over a student and waiting for him or her to comply. This may increase a student's anxiety level as well as the likelihood that the student may shut down or respond in a manner that is aggressive or attention seeking. For some students with challenging behaviors, this may actually reinforce the noncompliant behavior by providing teacher attention. Finally, teachers may forget to check to make sure that the student actually followed the direction. By failing to follow up, and thereby communicating the importance of following instructions to the student, the student may learn that directions are only suggestions and not worth following. The empirically supported strategies, which are described below, address these problems that teachers frequently encounter when communicating with students.

MAKING PRECISION REQUESTS

A precision request is one that includes the student's name as well as a description of the required behavior, is delivered using a polite tone, and builds in wait time for the student to comply. When delivering a precision request, it is important to use the child's name to make sure he or she knows to whom you are speaking. For many children (although this may vary based on the child's cultural background), use of direct eye contact can help to ensure that the student is paying attention. Care should also be taken to make the request in as few words as possible using language that clearly states what you would like the student to do. For example, "Please bring that book to me" communicates a much clearer request than "Can I have that book?" After the initial request has been made using the word "please," you should then do something else (i.e., not staring intensely at the student!) for approximately 5 seconds before checking to make sure the student has followed the directive. The 5-second delay is particularly important given empirical evidence that compliance may be thwarted if an insufficient wait time is employed (Forehand, Gardner, & Roberts, 1978). If the student follows the direction, he or she should receive some form of praise. If not, the direction is given again—this time incorporating the word "need" (e.g., "You need to bring that book to me"). Again, if the student responds to the second request, praise is delivered; however, failure to follow the directive may be followed by some form of reprimand (see Coach Card 3.3).

Although precision requests can effectively be used to solicit desired behavior from most students, they may prove particularly beneficial with those students demonstrating problem behaviors (see Table 3.4). For example, research has shown that the use of precision requests may substantially increase student compliance (De Martini-Scully, Bray, & Kehle, 2000; Neef, Shafer, Egel, Cataldo, & Parrish, 1983). De Martini-Scully and colleagues (2000) found a substantial reduction in noncompliance when teachers used precision commands, which even maintained after the teacher stopped using the technique. Musser, Bray, Kehle, and Jenson (2001) also found that precision techniques increased compliance with students who had been identified with serious emotional difficulties.

MAKING HIGH-PROBABILITY REQUESTS

As we shared with you in Chapter 2, both of us have different perspectives on chocolate. Given that Amy finds chocolate to be very enjoyable, she would be highly likely to say yes if asked to eat some. This is what we call a high-probability request. Asking David to do so,

TABLE 3.4. Empirical Studies Examining Effective Communication of Requests

Study	Setting	Intervention	Design	Outcome
Ardoin, Martens, & Wolfe (1999)	Second-grade students in general education	High-probability requests	Multi-element design	Notable increase in compliance for two-thirds of students
De Martini-Scully, Bray, & Kehle (2000)	Second-grade students in general education	Precision requests + token economy with response cost	ABAB and multiple baseline across two students	Notable decreases in disruptive behavior
Killu, Sainato, Davis, Ospelt, & Paul (1998)	Preschool students with developmental delays	High-probability requests	Multiple baseline across three students	Substantial increases in compliance
Mackay, McLaughlin, Weber, & Derby (2001)	12-year-old female with intellectual disability	Precision requests	ABAB design across three settings	Substantial decreases in noncompliance
Musser, Bray, Kehle, & Jenson (2001)	8- to 10-year-old students in a special education classroom for students with emotional/ behavioral disorders	Precision requests + mystery motivator with response cost	Multiple baseline across three students	Substantial decreases in disruptive behavior
Wehby & Hollahan (2000)	13-year-old student in general education	Compared low- versus high-probability requests	BCBCBDC design	Substantial decrease in latency to compliance

however, would be followed by some resistance. Because David dislikes chocolate, asking him to eat some would be considered a low-probability request. Sometimes we can increase the chances of a student following a low-probability request (e.g., "Please write a paragraph about your day") by making a high-probability request first (e.g., "Please pick up your pencil"). Once a student starts to do something, we then hope that the principle of behavioral momentum will kick in. Behavioral momentum refers to the idea that once we start doing something, it is difficult to stop. Filing our taxes is a difficult task to start, but once we do it, it becomes easier. The same is true for exercise, doing chores, and grading student work. In much the same way, we hope that once a student has complied with one request, he or she will continue to comply with subsequent requests.

Teachers can improve student compliance without students even knowing it by using a combination of high-probability requests and behavioral momentum. The process is fairly straightforward. Begin by asking students to do something they have no problem doing (e.g., "Give me a high five"). Then, ask them to do something they may be less likely to do (e.g.,

"Now tell me what happened on the playground"). Oliver and Skinner (2002) wrote about a substitute teacher who used the "Hokey Pokey" when working with her students (e.g., "Put your right hand in, put your right hand out") before asking them to do other things. The song had the advantage of lots of high-probability tasks as well as a rapid sequence of requests. High-probability tasks may also be interspersed within low-probability tasks in order to improve student compliance (Axelrod & Zank, 2012). Lee (2005) conducted a meta-analysis of 28 studies examining the use of high-probability requests and found the intervention to be effective in promoting compliance in preschool through high school-age students (see Table 3.4 for information regarding specific studies).

Increasing Opportunities to Respond

David spent some time working at a school that was attached to a residential treatment facility. During the 2 weeks of winter break, he and his coworkers worked in the students' living units and were responsible for organizing activities to keep the girls entertained. Most of the activities were not very popular (e.g., movies, games, discussions, sports); however, one activity was consistently associated with high levels of enjoyment and exemplar behavior. It was the Bingo group. No matter what group of students participated in Bingo, the event went well. Why was that? One of the great things about Bingo is that it is high paced. Because a new number is called out every 30 seconds, there isn't enough time for students to tune out or get into any trouble. If they want to have a chance of winning the round, students have to sit quietly, listen carefully, and remain vigilant as the numbers are announced. Providing students with lots of opportunities to participate ultimately served to reduce the number of behavior problems exhibited.

Teachers can also use this proactive strategy by increasing the number of opportunities students have to respond during classroom instruction. Opportunities to respond (OTRs) refer simply to the number of times a student has the opportunity to provide an answer. Classroom teachers most typically ask students to raise their hands, and then call on individuals to provide correct answers. This approach has been used for decades; however, it frequently oversamples the most enthusiastic and confident students while leaving out those students who are struggling with the material. As a result, teachers may be given false optimism about the entire class's understanding of material. In order to promote the participation of all students in the classroom, two alternatives to individual hand raising have been supported within the research literature: choral responding and response cards.

Rather than having students respond individually when questions are posed, use of both choral responding and response cards entails having the entire class provide an answer simultaneously. One of the other key elements across both strategies is ensuring a sufficient instructional pace, which allows students less time to act out and increases the amount of time that students are on task (Carnine, 1976; West & Sloan, 1986). The difference between the two strategies, however, simply lies in how those answers are provided. With choral responding, all students respond verbally in unison to a teacher-posed question. Although some successful examples of choral responding can be found in both self-contained special education (e.g., Sindelar, Bursuck, & Halle, 1986) and general education (e.g., Haydon et al.,

2010) settings, the number of studies that have examined behavioral outcomes is relatively small. Furthermore, the challenge with choral responding is that it can be difficult to monitor individual responses, particularly the voices of those students who are less confident.

The use of response cards involves providing students with whiteboards or other slates so that they may write down answers and hold them up in the air. Responding may be facilitated by cell phones or laptops using websites like *polleverywhere.com* (for anonymous responding) or *socrative.com* (which allows teachers to track individual responses). Students can also respond to their partners or the person sitting next to them. Over the past 30 years, the majority of studies have examined the use of response cards in order to improve academic performance (e.g., Cavanaugh, Heward, & Donelson, 1996; Maheady, Michielli-Pendl, Mallette, & Harper, 2002; Narayan, Heward, Gardner, Courson, & Omness, 1990); however, positive effects have been seen for classroom engagement and disruptive behavior as well. Successful examples of the use of response cards within general education settings have been found in both elementary (e.g., Lambert, Cartledge, Heward, & Lo, 2006; Wood, Mabry, Kretlow, Lo, & Galloway, 2009) and secondary (e.g., Cavanaugh et al., 1996; George, 2010) settings (see Table 3.5).

TABLE 3.5. Empirical Studies Examining Opportunities to Respond

Study	Setting	Strategy	Design	Outcome
Armendariz & Umbreit (1999)	Bilingual third-grade general education classroom during math lecture	Response cards	ABA design within one classroom	Decrease in disruptive behavior
Haydon et al. (2010)	Second-grade general education classrooms during teacher-directed whole-class instruction	Choral responding; mixed (individual and choral) responding	Alternating treatments design across six students	Disruptive and off-task behavior lowest during mixed-responding condition
Lambert, Cartledge, Heward, & Lo (2006)	Fourth-grade general education classrooms during math instruction	Response cards	ABAB design across four students	Decrease in disruptive behavior
Sutherland, Alder, & Gunter (2003)	8- to 12-year-old students in a self-contained classroom for students with emotional/behavioral disorders	Teachers receive daily feedback regarding opportunities to respond	ABAB design within one classroom	Decrease in disruptive behavior; increase in on-task behavior
Wood, Mabry, Kretlow, Lo, & Galloway (2009)	Kindergarten classroom during circle time	Response cards	ABAB design across four students	Decrease in off-task behavior

The relative effectiveness of a response card intervention was further demonstrated in a study by Godfrey, Grisham-Brown, Schuster, and Hemmeter (2003). These authors used an alternating treatments design that directly compared the effectiveness of individual hand raising, choral responding, and response cards. Each intervention condition was implemented classwide during the morning calendar activity in a preschool classroom (e.g., "What is the month?" "What is the day today?"); however, data were collected only for four target students who struggled with attention. Whereas the number of inappropriate behaviors exhibited during the calendar activity was roughly similar during the hand-raising (range = 8–14) and choral-responding (range = 6–17) conditions, much lower rates of inappropriate behavior were observed when using response cards (range = 2–6). The greatest improvements in on-task behavior were also noted within the response card condition.

Actively Supervising the Classroom

I (David) have a confession to share with the readers. Sometimes, I got into a little bit of trouble in school. Not a lot of trouble, but I could be disruptive—especially with friends nearby. My favorite teachers were those who stayed in the front of the room, and would never come by and "bother" me while I was "working" (*read*: having a serious conversation about after-school plans). However, when the teacher was standing near me, I was much less likely to act out, make paper airplanes, or play Dungeons & Dragons. Teacher presence had a significant influence on my behavior.

Ironically, when I was a beginning teacher, it took me a while to learn this lesson. I sat at my desk in the front of the classroom and rarely got up. My students could be fairly confident about where I would be at any one time. This meant that some students got away with sneaky behaviors such as writing notes, stealing other students' stuff, and making comments under their breath. Rather than trying to head off problem behavior before it occurred, I waited until I saw a transgression to publicly confront the student. On occasion, the student would stop the behavior, but other times the confrontation led to arguing, threatening, or simply ignoring. What I didn't realize was that these problems might have been prevented from occurring in the first place had I simply gotten up from my desk, moved around the room, and used active supervision.

Active supervision consists of two important components (see Coach Card 3.4). First, the teacher needs to move around the classroom, scan the environment, and frequent those parts of the classroom where behavior problems frequently occur. The less predictable the teacher's location, the less likely that students will be to engage in problem behaviors. Second, the teacher should have frequent interactions with students to make sure that they know the teacher is around. These interactions can range from greeting students with a friendly tap on the shoulder to providing praise (De Pry & Sugai, 2002). Through these actions, teachers are able to communicate "with-it-ness" to their students, or the sense that they are aware of what is going on in the classroom at all times (Kounin, 1970).

Within the literature, active supervision has been successfully used with elementary (De Pry & Sugai, 2002; Colvin, Sugai, Good, & Lee, 1997), middle (Schuldheisz & Mars,

2001), and even high school students (Johnson-Gros, Lyons, & Griffin, 2008). As displayed in Table 3.6, active supervision is a vital component for managing a variety of schoolwide behavior problems. Use of active supervision in classrooms, hallways, and playgrounds has been shown to reduce problem behaviors ranging from playground accidents to tardies. Use of active supervision can also help teachers to provide higher rates of behavioral feedback, such as praise and reprimands. We talk more about using praise and reprimands effectively in the classroom setting in Chapter 4.

CONCLUSIONS

Preventing behavior problems before they occur is critical to effective classroom management, whether it be at the preschool or high school level. Before the first student steps in the classroom in the fall, we can already work to head off problem behavior by carefully considering physical layout and structure. Next, explicitly teaching classroom rules and routines helps students to understand what behavior is expected and provides fewer triggers for problem behaviors. Behavioral expectations can also be made clear through the use of pre-

TABLE 3.6. Empirical Studies Examining Active Supervision

Study	Setting	Strategy	Design	Outcome
Colvin, Sugai, Good, & Lee (1997)	Elementary students during before-school transition	Active supervision versus typical supervision	Multiple baseline across settings	Decrease in problem behaviors across each setting when active supervision implemented
Heck, Collins, & Peterson (2001)	Students in grades K–3 on playground	Active supervision with social skills instruction versus typical supervision	Multiple baseline across grades	Reduction in the misuse of playground equipment
Johnson-Gros, Lyons, & Griffin (2008)	High school hallway	Active supervision versus typical supervision	Multiple baseline AB across class periods	Reduction in office discipline referrals for tardies
Kartub, Taylor-Greene, March, & Horner (2000)	Middle school hallway	Precorrection and social skills training + active supervision versus typical supervision	AB design across three grade levels	Reduction in noise levels across all grades
Lewis, Colvin, & Sugai (2000)	Elementary school playground	Active supervision and precorrection during typical supervision	AB design across recess periods	Decreased problem behavior

cision commands and high-probability requests, which are structured to avoid ambiguity in interpretation. Teachers can also work to curb disruptive behavior by making sure that students remain actively engaged in instruction. Increasing the number of opportunities that students have to respond through techniques, such as choral responding or response cards, minimizes the likelihood of problem behavior. Finally, active supervision signals to students that the teacher is aware of everything that is going on in the classroom. This ultimately makes the problem behavior more costly by increasing the likelihood that the teacher will find out. Now that we have talked about what to do *before* problem behavior occurs, it is time to answer the question "What should I do *after* a behavior has already occurred?"

COACH CARD 3.1.
Establishing Rules and Expectations

1. Ensure rules and expectations are:

   ☐ Age appropriate.

   ☐ Easily understood by students.

   ☐ Enforceable.

   ☐ Limited in number (e.g., four to six).

   ☐ Observable.

   ☐ Positively worded.

   ☐ Realistic.

2. When possible, use visual signals to clarify when different expectations are in place.

COACH CARD 3.2.
Teaching Rules and Routines

Teaching any new skill should involve a four-step process of:

☐ *Telling* the students what the rule or routine is.

  • Explain what following the rule looks like.

  • Explain the specific steps needed to follow a routine.

☐ *Showing* the students what following the rule or routine looks like.

  • Provide both examples and nonexamples.

☐ Having the students *do* what you have taught them.

  • Ask the students to practice the rule or routine.

  • Provide performance feedback.

☐ Having the students *generalize* the skill.

  • Have the students rehearse the rule or routine in different contexts.

COACH CARD 3.3. Delivering Effective Precision Requests

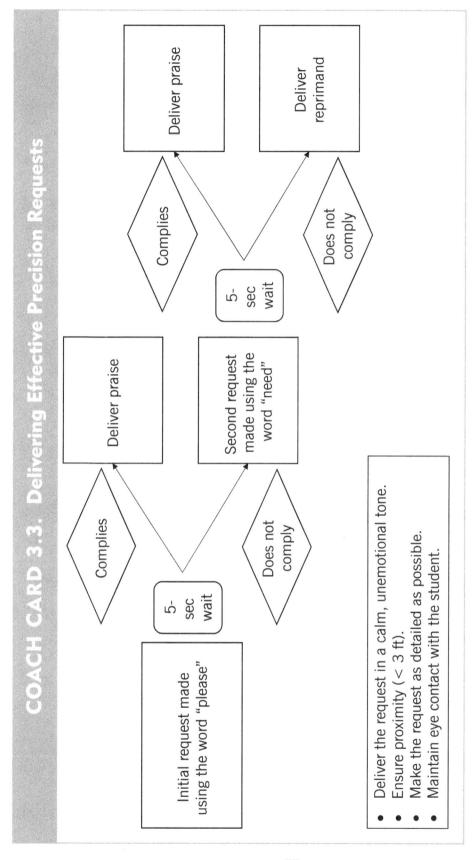

- Deliver the request in a calm, unemotional tone.
- Ensure proximity (< 3 ft).
- Make the request as detailed as possible.
- Maintain eye contact with the student.

COACH CARD 3.4. Active Supervision

Actively supervising a classroom involves:

☐ Frequently interacting with students.

☐ Moving around the classroom.

☐ Providing feedback for both appropriate and inappropriate behavior.

☐ Scanning the environment to look for problem behavior.

☐ Spending more time in those parts of the classroom in which behavior problems frequently occur.

CHAPTER 4

Providing Students
with Behavioral Feedback

As humans, we are well accustomed to both delivering and receiving feedback. We receive feedback regarding how well we are performing our jobs when we meet with our boss at the end of the year. We provide other motorists with feedback concerning how well they are driving when we decide to honk our car horn. We receive feedback from our children as to how much they enjoyed our cooking when they leave most of the food on their plate uneaten. Feedback is important in our daily lives because it helps us to know whether our efforts were correct and accurate, or whether they were wrong and off base. Feedback is particularly important in the classroom, however, because it provides an opportunity to overcome a discrepancy between the expectations that we as adults have for students, and the behaviors that they are displaying (Hattie & Timperley, 2007). In fact, feedback has been identified as one of the most powerful instructional practices known to education (Hattie & Timperley, 2007).

Although we know that feedback is incredibly important, it is the type of feedback that we give a student that can dramatically affect the power the feedback has on student learning and behavior. Consider the example of a small child first learning to talk, who has heard his or her parents speak with perfect grammar, syntax, and elocution, but still commits grammatical mishaps. If the child says, "I is going to the park," and the parent simply says, "That's not how you say it," the child's speech is unlikely to improve. Simply telling a child that he or she is wrong or right provides little help in closing the discrepancy gap between your expectations and the child's behavior. By merely telling the child that he or she has done something wrong, you have communicated implicitly two things: (1) you are not doing what I expect you to do and (2) I want you to change your behavior. Instead, the best feedback answers the following questions for a child: (1) What are the goals?; (2) What kind of progress am I making toward those goals?; and (3) What do I need to do to better meet those goals? (Hattie & Timperley, 2007). In the example above, the parent has not communicated what appropriate syntax is, has not alerted the child to the exact error that he or she made, and has not provided a way for the child to fix the error. Thus, the best feedback ensures that the child understands what he or she has done incorrectly and what needs to be done to correct it. Even when corrected, the child will likely make the same error again. It is only after receiving clear and consistent feedback over repeated trials, however, that the behavior will hopefully improve. If we did not receive this type of feedback as toddlers, our collective grammar would be even worse than most English teachers lament that it is today!

Within the previous chapter, we discussed the importance of explicitly teaching students behavioral expectations. However, just as toddlers need feedback regarding verb conjugation even after they have heard perfectly constructed sentences, students in school settings often require behavioral feedback even if they have been taught what to do. In other words, Chapter 3 dealt with what to do before a behavior even occurs, whereas the current chapter answers the question of what to do after a behavior occurs. Note that in making this distinction we did not qualify the word "behavior" with "desirable" or "problematic." Students need feedback on all behaviors—whether those behaviors are the ones that you want to see or the ones you really hope not to. The type of feedback that we provide, however, can either help to support appropriate behavior or it can have unintended results. Our aim in this chapter is to provide guidance regarding how feedback can be used for good, as well as to make clear how the wrong kind of feedback can create more problems than it solves. We begin by looking more closely at the structure of feedback.

ANATOMY OF FEEDBACK

Feedback is part of a contingency. Think of a contingency as an "if–then" statement. If something happens, then something else will happen. Consider the following contingency: If Beatrice's desk is clean at the end of the day, Beatrice will receive a homework pass from the teacher. The contingency has multiple components:

1. The behavior of interest: A desk is clean.
2. The person responsible for the behavior: Beatrice.
3. When the behavior is supposed to happen: At the end of the school day.
4. When the behavior will be evaluated: At the end of the school day.
5. Who will receive the reward or punishment: Beatrice.
6. What reward or punishment Beatrice will receive: A homework pass.
7. Who will give that reward or punishment to Beatrice: The teacher.

When we think of contingencies in this way, we realize that they can be quite flexibly constructed. Consider what would happen if we were to change some aspects of this contingency. Let's change each component one at a time and think about the effect the change might have on a classroom. One easy modification might involve changing the person who is responsible for the behavior and who will receive the reward:

If Monica's desk is clean at the end of the day, Monica will receive a homework pass from the teacher.

However, what if we just changed the person who was responsible for the behavior but not the one receiving the reward?

If Monica's desk is clean at the end of the day, Beatrice will receive a homework pass from the teacher.

At first blush, this seems unfair and somewhat capricious. But imagine working with a child who enjoys peer attention. One way to do this is to allow the child to give away a reward to another student. This may even be a method for sharing gratitude. (Note: When using such an approach, it is usually wise not to inform the other students of this contingency beforehand, in case the behavior is not performed. After all, if we were to inform Beatrice that a homework pass was coming to her if Monica performed a particular behavior, Beatrice may be angry that Monica's desk is not cleared.)

Although contingencies may be quite flexibly constructed, a few key questions must be answered in order to ensure that the contingency will be effective. In addition to determining who will administer the contingency and to whom the contingency and reward/punishment will apply, it is necessary to consider what behavior is expected, when the behavior should occur, when the behavior will be evaluated, and what the student will receive.

What Behavior Is Expected?

We can provide a student with positive feedback for a variety of behaviors including keeping desks clean, turning work in accurately and on time, raising hands, walking down the hallway, getting ready for class at the start of the day, or standing in line without fighting. Conversely, it may sometimes be necessary to provide negative feedback when a student turns work in late, calls out during instruction, runs in the hallway, comes to class unprepared, or gets in fights in the lunch line. Before selecting a target behavior, however, it is important to ensure that it is one that is within the student's behavioral repertoire. Behavioral repertoire refers to the behaviors that a child is capable of doing. The following behaviors are within both of our behavioral repertoires: typing, speaking in English, and reading most educational and psychology textbooks that are written in English. In contrast, the following behaviors are not in either of our repertoires: flying like Superman, speaking Mandarin Chinese, and dunking a basketball. If somebody were to offer either of us $10 million to fly ourselves to China, trash-talk Yao Ming during a game of one-on-one basketball, and slam-dunk a ball, we would certainly be motivated to do so but would find it impossible because we are incapable of actually performing any of those behaviors. There are, of course, also some slightly more realistic, classroom-based examples that illustrate the concept of a behavioral repertoire. Whereas some students may be unable to sit in a chair for more than 25 minutes, others could theoretically stay seated all day long. There are also some students who may not know how to line up or how they should get help if they are struggling during independent work time, whereas other students perform these behaviors quite naturally. The first question we must ask ourselves when a student is not performing a required behavior is whether that student actually has that behavior within his or her repertoire. If not, as educators we may need to teach a child a behavior so that it can be added to his or her repertoire.

As we explained in Chapter 3, however, it is important that both expected and prohibited behaviors are clear so that both the student and the teacher can agree on what appropriate and inappropriate behaviors are. In other words, if a clean desk is expected, the student and teacher should have a shared sense of what a clean desk looks like. If the definition is not made explicit and both individuals are instead left to come up with their own definitions of what a clean desk looks like, problems are likely to arise. Whereas the classroom teacher might expect all papers to be filed away in folders and writing implements to be stored in a pencil case, an organizationally challenged student might consider a "clean desk" to be one in which all items that were formerly on top of the desk are quickly stuffed inside! It is critical that this discrepancy gets resolved so that the student clearly understands the expectations for receiving positive feedback and is not frustrated if negative feedback is received.

When Must the Behavior Occur?

The time of the behavior is also important. Some behaviors have to occur immediately (such as following a direction), whereas other behaviors can occur at a later period of time (such as completing an assignment). In this context, however, we typically think of periods of the day when certain behaviors are expected. For example, we may expect that students raise their hands frequently during carpet time or during a classwide discussion, but rarely during a test. The time period when the behavior occurs is therefore important to define.

When Will the Behavior Be Evaluated?

In the desk-cleaning example above, when the behavior must occur happens to be the same time that the behavior is evaluated (i.e., at the end of the day). However, sometimes the time that the behavior must occur will be different from when the child will receive feedback on the behavior. Following a direction, turning in an assignment, or raising a hand is a discrete behavior that occurs once and can therefore be reinforced immediately. Other behaviors may be more difficult to reinforce because they need to occur for a long period of time (e.g., working on an assignment, staying quiet while a teacher is talking). There are several ways that ongoing behaviors may be reinforced. If you think back to Chapter 2, you may recall that behavior can be reinforced according to four different types of schedules. The most predictable are the fixed interval and fixed ratio. According to these schedules, behavior is either reinforced after a fixed amount of time (e.g., every 5 minutes) or a fixed number of responses (e.g., after every other correct answer). Fixed schedules of reinforcement are rather easy and straightforward to employ, but also tend to be the least effective in terms of promoting behavioral change. This is because students may quickly learn exactly how long or frequently they have to perform a behavior in order to receive reinforcement . . . and then stop performing it once they receive what they were after. Variable schedules of reinforcement, on the other hand, reinforce behavior after a variable amount of time (e.g., every 3–7 minutes) or number of responses (e.g., after every third to fifth correct answer). Variable schedules of reinforcement tend to be more effective in producing behavioral change because learners cannot reliably predict when reinforcement will occur. For example, variable interval reinforcement schedules have been shown to be effective in changing student behavior (Hulac, Benson, Nesmith, & Shervey, 2016) because the child does not know when feedback will come. To implement a variable reinforcement schedule, teachers often have timers that buzz at random intervals to remind themselves to praise the students who are staying on task or listening quietly during story hour.

What Does the Child Receive?

The final question to answer concerns what reinforcement or punishment the child will receive. There are many different ways to respond to student behavior. We can smile, scream, lecture, encourage, reward . . . the list goes on. Generally, we assume that students will find the same things to be rewarding or aversive as we do ourselves (e.g., appreciating a compliment while avoiding criticism). As explained in Chapter 2, however, what serves as a reinforcer for one child may very well serve as a punisher for another child. The only way to know whether something is serving as a reinforcer or a punisher is to watch what happens with the behavior over time. If the behavior continues or gets stronger, this indicates that the student found the adult response to be one that was desirable. If the behavior weakens or stops, this indicates that the adult response was punishing.

Feedback is something that can serve as either reinforcement or punishment. Over the course of the next few chapters, we discuss strategies for providing students with more tangible forms of feedback (e.g., stickers, privileges); however, within this chapter we first focus on the administration of verbal feedback to students in the classroom. Verbal feedback can be provided via three central routes: negative feedback (e.g., reprimands), positive feedback (e.g., praise), and planned ignoring. We describe each, as well as the research available to support them, next.

NEGATIVE VERBAL FEEDBACK

Negative verbal feedback is what we deliver in hopes of discouraging someone from exhibiting a particular behavior again. If you are scolded for arriving late to work or lectured for not submitting your grades on time, the expectation is that you will find being talked to aversive enough that you will work extra hard to ensure it does not happen again. When we are dealing with problem behavior in the classroom, one of the more familiar forms of negative verbal feedback unfortunately is yelling. In eighth grade, David had a wonderful social studies teacher who had the capacity to generate excellent work from the most difficult students. Because she was funny, charismatic, and passionate, her students loved her. One day, however, the class had a substitute teacher. This substitute teacher walked into class and saw two students sitting on a counter before the bell rang. With vehement anger in her voice, she yelled, "GET OFF OF THAT COUNTER RIGHT NOW!!!" The whole class heard her yell and responded not by sitting in their seats or quieting down, but by laughing. The next 20 minutes of class were humiliating for this teacher, who was tormented by the class until she eventually called down to the vice principal's office. The problem behavior stopped once the administrator walked into the classroom, but the class had clearly lost all respect for the substitute (see Box 4.1).

What went wrong? Well, the substitute teacher made several mistakes that you might choose to point out (e.g., not making her expectations clear, not taking the time to build relationships); however, the decision to yell at the students is what we want to focus on here. There are times when yelling makes student behaviors *seem* better. If students are being loud or disruptive but stop when the teacher yells, from the teacher's perspective, the yelling worked (i.e., the negative reinforcement trap; Maag, 2001). When you think about the situation a bit more, however, it is not surprising that the misbehavior stopped. After all,

---

BOX 4.1. Addressing Serious Problem Behaviors

Many teachers want to know what they should do when a serious infraction occurs. For example, what needs to happen if a student verbally abuses another student, makes a threat, blatantly insults the teacher, or gets into a fistfight? The goals in these situations are to keep other students safe and return the classroom to its normal functioning. Unfortunately, there is little research that has experimentally examined different approaches used to manage behavioral outbursts. However, there are a few things that we can do to make things better.

1. **Stay calm.** Teachers who use very loud voices or start screaming exacerbate these types of situations.
2. **Determine the threat level.**
   a. If other students are in imminent danger of being hurt, use a classroom-clearing routine to make sure the students are safe. At the same time, seek out extra adult help to manage the situation.
   b. If the classroom is disrupted by the behavior, an office discipline referral may be needed immediately.
   c. If the classroom is not disrupted, it may be useful to say something like "I am going to address this, but I need to take care of something first." This way, the lesson may continue, and when there is a natural break, it may be more appropriate to either call the office or to talk to the student individually.
3. **Determine if an individual behavior plan may be necessary.** For this, we suggest consulting with a school psychologist or other professional with training in behavior management.
4. **Determine a reentry plan.** Once the student has left a classroom, a conversation between the teacher and the student needs to occur. A restorative consequence that allows the student to make amends for the transgression should be put into place.
5. As always, review classroom management systems to identify methods to prevent the behavior from occurring again.

the students were probably scared. When any of us are scared, our instinctive reaction is often to freeze. If the fear is sufficient, students sometimes learn not to engage in a behavior again just to avoid being yelled at. This is an example of positive punishment (see Chapter 2). Unfortunately, being scared changes the way we learn. Learning new, difficult, or abstract concepts is difficult when we are feeling overly fearful. The cognitive resources that should be spent learning are instead spent trying to avoid getting into trouble.

It is also critical to keep in mind that many students have had traumatic experiences that were precipitated by yelling. When students experience frequent traumatic events, they develop habitual responses that may include violence, yelling, extreme anxiety, or dissociation. For some students, these responses become "hardwired" and automatic. Thus, for some students, yelling may actually trigger a traumatic response. Sometimes, these responses will be violent and loud, and at other times the responses will be subdued, as students may dissociate when faced with a trigger for trauma. Either way, however, the student is less likely to benefit from a learning environment.

Yet another problem is that not everyone finds yelling to be punishing. There are other students in the classroom for whom yelling actually serves to trigger more problem behavior. Going back to the example of the eighth-grade substitute teacher, for many of the students in that class, they saw the teacher yell at the top of her lungs and realized she was "out of bullets"—that she had no other tools to manage their behavior. This served as a signal to the students that they could act out and not get in trouble, or could act out, make the teacher angry, and receive peer attention for being "hilarious." Some of those students enjoyed seeing the teacher lose her temper and found the "show" enjoyable. Chaos reigned.

Thus, as an everyday method of classroom management, yelling runs the risk of creating learning problems, promoting other behavior problems, and even triggering traumatic reactions in some students who have been exposed to trauma. There are, however, some situations in which yelling may be necessary. Obviously, we support yelling in those rare situations in which a child is at immediate risk of being harmed. When used infrequently by adults who have demonstrated care for their students, yelling may stop fights or prevent students from doing something dangerous such as running into a street. In these circumstances, having a child freeze momentarily can prevent further action (e.g., stopping them from running into the street or stopping a fight). By and large, however, yelling should be avoided.

Delivering Effective Reprimands

Although we would generally recommend against yelling, there are other more productive ways to discourage behavior. Reprimands are a common form of behavior intervention and are used after a student displays a behavior that is a violation of classroom rules or norms. Some research has suggested that for students who display average levels of problem behavior, reprimands may serve to increase on-task behaviors, increase compliance to directions, and reduce problematic behaviors (Redd, Morris, & Martin, 1975). Over the years, a number of studies have manipulated different aspects of how reprimands are delivered in order to determine what is most effective (see Table 4.1). These studies found that reprimands

TABLE 4.1. Studies Examining the Use of Reprimands

Study	Sample	Intervention	Design	Results
Abramowitz, O'Leary, & Futtersak (1988)	Students in grades 2–3 in a special education program for students with hyperactivity	Compared use of short and long reprimands	Alternating treatments design	No significant differences in off-task behavior between short and long reprimands
O'Leary, Kaufman, Kass, & Drabman (1970)	Students in grades 2–3 referred for disruptive behavior	Compared use of soft and loud reprimands	BCBC across six students	Lower rates of disruptive behavior when using soft reprimands
Rosén, O'Leary, Joyce, Conway, & Pfiffner (1984)	Students in grades 2–3 in a special education program for students with hyperactivity	Loud, public, emotional reprimands delivered for problem behavior	ABACDE within one classroom	Decrease in on-task behavior when public reprimands used
Van Houten, Nau, McKenzie-Keating, Sameoto, & Colavecchia (1982)	9- to 12-year-old boys referred for behavioral problems	Compared verbal reprimands delivered in firm tone and close proximity to the student with verbal reprimands paired with eye contact and physical touch	ABAB across two students with alternating treatments within intervention phase	Decrease in disruptive behavior when both types of reprimands introduced; however, lower rates of disruptive behavior with use of verbal plus nonverbal reprimands

were most effective when (1) brief (Abramowitz, O'Leary, & Futtersak, 1988); (2) delivered immediately using a calm, firm, and unemotional tone (Rosén, O'Leary, Joyce, Conway, & Pfiffner, 1984); and (3) paired with eye contact and provided in close proximity to the student (Van Houten, Nau, MacKenzie-Keating, Sameoto, & Colavecchia, 1982). Thus, reprimands should be delivered succinctly, individually, and quietly, and should include specific feedback about what a student should be doing instead (see Coach Card 4.1). An example of an effectively delivered reprimand would be placing a hand on the back of the student's chair when he or she is talking to the student behind him or her and quietly stating, "You need to turn around in your seat and face the front of the classroom now." The message is clear and to the point—it is unambiguous as to (1) what the student is doing wrong and (2) what the student needs to do to correct the problem.

When administering a reprimand, there are a few things to consider. The first is that a public reprimand can work against a teacher in two ways. Many students are embarrassed when a teacher tells them that they are doing something wrong. This embarrassment may cause a student to become anxious, which means he or she is not focusing on his or her class-work. In other cases, students may enjoy the reprimand and use it as an opportunity to draw attention to themselves. On these occasions, the student may actually start acting out more when reprimands are given instead of less. Furthermore, those students who demonstrate aggressive behaviors may have negative reactions to teacher reprimands and may therefore be more likely to respond aggressively (Van Acker, Grant, & Henry, 1996). In light of these potential reactions, it is often more effective to provide reprimands quietly and individually than publicly in front of other students.

The second thing to consider is that vague reprimands may backfire. Telling a student to "Stop that!" often engenders the response, "Stop what?" In some cases, the student is saying, "Of the many things I was doing wrong, which one did you see?" More often, however, the student is probably simply unsure what infraction he or she is breaking. Reprimands therefore need to be specific if they are to actually change behavior. Only when the teacher is specific can a student know which behavior he or she is supposed to change. Furthermore, telling a student what *not* to do still leaves many options for ways to act out. A reprimand should therefore include a redirection whereby students are told or reminded what the specific expectation is.

Finally, it is important to keep in mind that time spent delivering a reprimand is time that students are not receiving academic instruction or supervision. If a reprimand takes 2 minutes to deliver, those are 2 minutes during which the student is receiving a high level of teacher attention but no academically relevant instruction. In addition, because the teacher's attention is focused on one particular student, this may be allowing other students to act out while the teacher is not paying attention. Therefore, reprimands should be delivered quickly before returning to instruction.

POSITIVE VERBAL FEEDBACK

Whereas reprimands may be used to discourage inappropriate behavior, one of the simplest and potentially most effective forms of feedback that has received a great deal of attention over the past decade is praise. Despite variations in the literature, definitions of praise generally involve directing positive attention (either verbal or nonverbal) toward a behavior being demonstrated by an individual (Jenkins, Floress, & Reinke, 2015; see Box 4.2). The fact that praise is delivered in response to specific student behaviors differentiates it from teacher warmth more generally (Brophy, 1981). Beginning in the 1960s, a number of studies were conducted within the behavior analytic world to explore the effect of teacher praise on student behavior. Studies documented changes in a range of school-based behaviors including academic performance (Hughes, 1973; Witmer, Bornstein, & Dunham, 1971), social behavior (Becker, Madsen, Arnold, & Thomas, 1967; Madsen et al., 1968), and study behavior (Hall, Lund, & Jackson, 1968).

Praise has many advantages—the most important being that it is inexpensive and easy to deliver. It is therefore surprising that low levels of teacher praise have generally been identified in actual classroom settings. One of the first studies to examine teachers' rates of

---

**BOX 4.2. Case Example:
Using Praise to Promote Appropriate Behavior**

We worked with a ninth-grade student who frequently came to school angry. If the teacher asked him what was wrong, he would snap back "NOTHING!!!" and display clear body language that he wanted to be left alone. When teachers redirected and reprimanded him, he argued back and would sometimes mutter threats under his breath. One teacher chose to try something different. In the morning, when the student entered her class, she simply said to him, "Good morning, I'm glad you're here," and then she walked away. Later in class she said to him, "I read your essay and appreciated the insight you had about the main character of the book," and then again walked away. Each day, she made an effort to recognize something that she could praise him for. She knew the praise had to be authentic and given privately—after all, this student was an expert on adults who were insincere. The student's behavior did not take a dramatic turn, but slowly she noticed the student remaining on-task more, and he occasionally smiled.

---

naturally occurring praise and criticism was conducted by White in 1975. Using an observational system called the Teacher Approval and Disapproval Observation Record (TAD), White examined teacher behavior across 104 classrooms from first through twelfth grade. She found that there were relatively low rates of teacher approval across classrooms, with levels of approval dropping off sharply at the higher grade levels (e.g., 1.3 approval statements per minute in third grade vs. 1 approval statement per 5–10 minutes in the higher grades) as levels of disapproval increased. Since this time, many studies have been conducted in order to examine teachers' rates of praise not only in the United States (Fry, 1983; Heller & White, 1975; Nafpaktitis, Mayer, & Butterworth, 1985) but in Australia (Russell & Lin, 1977), Britain (Merrett & Wheldall, 1987; Wheldall, Houghton, & Merrett, 1989), Hong Kong (Winter, 1990), and New Zealand (Thomas, Presland, Grant, & Glynn, 1978) as well. Across time and studies, general trends have been found in terms of increasing rates of teacher approval; however, overall, teachers tend to respond more frequently with disapproval than approval when it comes to addressing social behavior (Beaman & Wheldall, 2000).

How to Provide Praise

Before we move forward, it is important to keep in mind that when we talk about praise, we are referring to a very specific type of praise that has been supported in the literature—that is, just saying something nice to someone is not necessarily going to cut it. Imagine that you are working at your desk and someone comes up to you and says, "You're really a great person." Although you may appreciate the compliment, it's really difficult to know what spurred the positive feedback. Did the person like your work? Was he or she impressed by your outfit? Or was there something about your demeanor that caused the person to pause and say something? When praise is general like this, there is no way of knowing what behavior should be continued. In contrast, imagine that a person came up to you and said, "While you were working with that student in that really difficult situation this morning, I was so impressed with how calm you stayed." This type of praise is specific and you can therefore do much more with the information provided. In this particular case, if you wanted to continue to receive accolades from that person, you would know to focus on remaining calm during the next stressful situation that arose.

Now, let's extend the example to working with students. Saying "Great job!" to a student is nice to hear, but it does not communicate any behavioral information. It would be far more effective to say to the child, "Right now, I expect all students to be on task, and I notice that you are working on the assignment" or "When Michael was just yelling, you did a really nice job ignoring him by reading your book." Both of these statements include elements that are vital to the provision of effective feedback. First, the feedback is *specific*, in that it provides information regarding exactly what the student was doing correctly (see Table 4.2 for examples of specific vs. general praise). Second, the feedback is *contingent,* in that it is delivered only following the behavior that the teacher hopes to increase. Although most researchers have empirically emphasized the importance of these two elements (e.g., Chalk & Bizo, 2004; Jenkins et al., 2015), Brophy (1981) also noted that praise has to be sincere and believable. Saying to a student, "Great work, you managed to get one whole math addition problem finished in that last hour" will function as a reprimand and a put-down. Similarly, if a student has been acting out and then receives praise from a teacher for doing something well, the student may not believe it. Finally, as emphasized by Partin, Robertson, Maggin, Oliver, and Wehby (2009), it is important that the student's skill level be taken into consideration when providing praise—that is, those students at a lower level of performance may require praise for less significant or what are often considered prerequisite behaviors

TABLE 4.2. Examples of General versus Specific Praise

General praise	Behavior-specific praise
"Nice job!"	"Marcus, nice job taking the time to sound out that word!"
"I'm so proud of you!"	"Karina, I know it can be hard to introduce yourself to someone new. I'm so proud of you for sitting next to a new friend today!"
"Thanks for doing that!"	"Susan, thanks for pushing in your chair quietly!"
"Way to go!"	"Jameson, I'm so impressed that you were able to finish all of your math problems before recess. Way to go!"
"Well done!"	"Sophie, I really liked the way that you sat down right away and got out your materials. Well done!"

(e.g., simply getting out materials as opposed to actually starting to work), whereas providing praise for more substantive behaviors may be more effective for those students with well-developed behavioral repertoires (see Coach Card 4.2).

Just as studies conducted in natural classroom environments have found that teachers tend to acknowledge appropriate behavior less frequently than inappropriate behavior, recent work has similarly indicated that teachers tend to use general praise more frequently than behavior-specific praise. In examining rates of praise across kindergarten to third-grade classrooms, Reinke, Herman, and Stormont (2013) found that teachers used general praise roughly three times more frequently (25.8 times per hour) than specific praise (7.8 times per hour). Research conducted across four kindergarten classrooms produced similar results, with general praise being noted nearly 40 times per hour as opposed to specific praise, which was utilized less than 10 times per hour (Floress & Jenkins, 2015).

Despite low rates of actual usage, there are important advantages of teacher-delivered behavior-specific praise. For one, when delivered publicly, explicit praise statements not only reinforce what one particular student has been doing well but also remind his or her classmates of the behavioral expectations (Stormont & Reinke, 2008). Additionally, there is a growing body of evidence suggesting that use of behavior-specific praise can significantly improve the behavior of a wide range of students. We review some of this research base next.

Empirical Examples

Over the past four decades, researchers have examined the effects of behavior-specific praise across a range of student ages and contexts (see Table 4.3). For example, within a preschool setting, teachers were trained to deliver behavior-specific praise during problematic classroom transitions (e.g., "I am so proud of the way you put all the cars in the bin"; Fullerton, Conroy, & Correa, 2009). Higher rates of teacher-delivered praise during the intervention phase were associated with higher levels of compliance across four students. Similarly positive findings have been evidenced at the elementary level, with higher rates of behavior-specific praise shown to reduce disruptive behaviors (Becker et al., 1967) as well as increase work completion (Reinke, Lewis-Palmer, & Martin, 2007). Furthermore, praise has even been shown to have an effect on students who are not personally receiving the praise. For example, increased amounts of teacher attention to one second-grade student led to an increase in attending behavior for a second student seated at an adjacent desk (Broden, Bruce, Mitchell, Carter, & Hall, 1970)!

Research has also demonstrated that behavior-specific praise may be effective for students with emotional/behavioral disorders (EBDs). In a study involving fifth-grade students in a self-contained classroom for students with EBDs, for example, increases in teacher-delivered behavior-specific praise were associated with improvements in students' on-task behavior during social skills instruction (Sutherland, Wehby, & Copeland, 2000). Specifically, on-task behavior increased from less than 50% of intervals during baseline to more than 80% during intervention phases. Allday and colleagues (2012) sought to answer a slightly

TABLE 4.3. Studies Examining the Use of Praise

Study	Sample	Intervention	Design	Results
Blaze, Olmi, Mercer, Dufrene, & Tingstrom (2014)	High school students in general education	Compared quiet versus public praise	ABCAC design across four classrooms	Both forms of praise resulted in significant improvements in engaged and disruptive behavior; no significant differences between conditions
Cihak, Kirk, & Boon (2009)	19 third-grade students in general education	Tootling	ABAB within one classroom	Decrease in disruptive behavior with introduction of tootling intervention
Fullerton, Conroy, & Correa (2009)	Preschool children in university-based early childhood centers	Use of specific praise	Multiple baseline across four students	Increase in both engagement and compliance with instructions with use of specific praise
Grieger, Kaufman, & Grieger (1976)	Kindergarten students	Peer reporting	ABAB design (averaged across two classes)	Modest improvements in cooperative play; more notable effects for aggressive acts
Jones, Young, & Friman (2000)	13-year-old students in a residential program for delinquent adolescents	Positive peer reporting	Multiple baseline across three students	Increase in number of cooperative statements made with introduction of positive peer-reporting intervention
Lambert, Tingstrom, Sterling, Dufrene, & Lynne (2015)	36 fourth- and fifth-grade students in general education	Tootling	ABAB across two classrooms	Notable reductions in disruptive behavior and improvements in appropriate behavior
Sutherland, Wehby, & Copeland (2000)	Nine fifth-grade students with emotional/behavioral disorders in a self-contained classroom	Behavior-specific praise	ABAB within one classroom	Increased on-task behavior when praise introduced

different question, which was whether delivering behavior-specific praise to all students in the classroom would result in behavioral improvements on the part of those students at risk for behavioral disorders specifically. Across four elementary classrooms (i.e., grades K, 1, 2, and 6), teachers were instructed regarding the difference between general and behavior-specific praise and provided with feedback regarding their use of behavior-specific praise. All four students demonstrated higher levels of on-task behavior, even though three of the four target students received less teacher praise themselves.

When examining the literature on praise, however, it is important to note that these studies tend to involve elementary and early middle school classes. The effectiveness of praise for secondary students is less understood. For example, high school students who display symptoms of anxiety and depression may respond better to praise than do students who are disruptive (Lane, Wehby, Robertson, & Rogers, 2007). We suspect that increasing the amount of praise may prevent some negative behaviors from occurring by removing an antecedent for power struggles; however, some high school students may be less affected by adults than by peers in these settings (Hawkins & Heflin, 2011). Furthermore, whereas studies at the elementary level have generally focused on publicly delivered praise, those conducted with secondary students have more typically incorporated the use of quiet, private praise. This may be true in light of findings that secondary-level students report preferring no praise or silent praise to public praise (Elwell & Tiberio, 1994).

Peer-Delivered Praise

Although most research has focused on teachers' use of praise in the classroom, it is important to note that teachers do not have to be the only purveyors of praise. In fact, one of the difficulties with relying exclusively on teachers to provide students with behavioral feedback is that they may not observe or be aware of positive behaviors as they are occurring, particularly those that are prosocial in nature (Skinner, Neddenriep, Robinson, Ervin, & Jones, 2002)—that is, a teacher who is already working to balance the complexities of delivering engaging instruction while managing student misbehavior may have limited cognitive resources left over to provide positive feedback to the students who are doing what is expected of them. An additional concern is that many students may not find teacher praise to be reinforcing—in other words, they may not care what the teacher thinks about them. However, they may still find peer attention reinforcing. One alternative approach is therefore to shift responsibility for behavioral monitoring and reinforcement to the students themselves.

One of the earliest studies to utilize students as positive informants was conducted by Grieger, Kaufman, and Grieger (1976). Following a period of free play, kindergarten students were asked to identify one peer who had done something nice for them and these identified students were provided with a sticker. This simple intervention resulted in both improvements in cooperative play and decreases in observed aggression on the playground. Several studies conducted in the 1990s used a similar "positive peer-reporting" approach in order to improve peer perceptions of individual students. These studies found significant improvements in positive social interactions (e.g., Bowers, McGinnis, Ervin, & Friman,

1999; Ervin, Miller, & Friman, 1996), as well as cooperative statements (Jones, Young, & Friman, 2000).

Whereas positive peer reporting focuses on improving peers' perceptions of particular students, tootling is a classwide intervention strategy whereby students identify and acknowledge any and all of their peers who are demonstrating prosocial behaviors (Skinner, Cashwell, & Skinner, 2000). Each time that a student observes a peer helping someone else during the day, he or she is encouraged to write down the act on an index card, which is given to the classroom teacher. At the end of the day, the teacher counts up all of the tootles and can either read them aloud or keep them private so as to avoid embarrassment. If the class meets their goal for the number of tootles earned, the class receives a prize. In this way, tootling is essentially the opposite of tattling, wherein students tell the teacher when their peers have engaged in inappropriate behaviors. Tootling has been shown to result in significant reductions in classroom disruptions (Cihak, Kirk, & Boone, 2009; Lambert, Tingstrom, Sterling, Dufrene, & Lynne, 2015) and increases in academic engagement (McHugh, Tingstrom, Radley, Barry, & Walker, 2016).

Strategies for Increasing Rates of Praise

Given the demonstrated benefits of behavior-specific praise, paired with the fact that low rates of teacher praise have been generally noted in classrooms, a growing body of research has focused on the evaluation of intervention strategies for changing teacher behavior. One of the more common approaches used across studies has involved providing teachers with (1) explicit instruction in the appropriate delivery of praise and (2) verbal feedback regarding the frequency of praise delivery (e.g., Hawkins & Heflin, 2011; Sutherland et al., 2000). One of the feasibility concerns with this coaching approach, however, is that it necessitates the presence of an external observer in order to determine the frequency of praise delivery. Another option for increasing teacher-delivered praise is to use self-monitoring. As described more fully in Chapter 7, self-monitoring involves having an individual observe and record his or her own behavior. For example, in a study by Kalis, Vannest, and Parker (2007), a high school special education teacher was first provided with examples of what behavior-specific praise should look like and then asked to keep track of the number of behavior-specific praise statements she made using a handheld counter. Following each lesson, a consultant and teacher met to review the data on praise frequency and compared it with a predetermined goal.

Across two studies (Myers et al., 2011; Thompson, Marchant, Anderson, Prater, & Gibb, 2012), a multi-tiered approach was used to provide teachers with the appropriate level of consultative support in order to promote use of behavior-specific praise. At the universal level, all teachers were provided with instruction regarding the delivery of praise (e.g., why it is important, what it should look like, how often it should be delivered) within the context of a brief inservice training. Those teachers who were deemed unresponsive to the universal intervention (as determined by either personal report or external observations) were then selected to receive a targeted intervention. The targeted intervention was designed to be more feasible in that it did not require the daily involvement of an external consultant.

In a study by Thompson and colleagues (2012), for example, targeted intervention involved video self-monitoring, in which teachers videotaped themselves delivering a lesson and then counted the number of behavior-specific praise statements made while reviewing the footage. At the tertiary level, however, more intensive supports were provided across both studies for those teachers who continued to demonstrate low rates of praise. For example, consultants in the study by Myers and colleagues (2011) provided teachers with daily performance feedback following each observation session. Teachers in the study by Thompson and colleagues (2012) were also provided with a tactile prompting device, which would help to remind them to provide praise. Results of both studies confirmed the need to differentiate supports provided to teachers in order to promote the effective use of praise.

COMPARING POSITIVE AND NEGATIVE FEEDBACK

Over the years, few studies have sought to directly compare the effects of positive and negative teacher feedback on student behavior. Acker and O'Leary (1987) instructed a classroom teacher to provide feedback in one of four ways: (1) only reprimands for off-task behavior, (2) only praise for on-task behavior, (3) reprimands for off-task behavior and praise for on-task behavior, or (4) neither reprimands nor praise. High levels of on-task behavior were noted when students were reprimanded for exhibiting off-task behavior; however, the addition of praise for on-task behavior was not found to be incrementally effective. The researchers, however, suggested that the lack of effect for the delivery of praise may have been attributable to a ceiling effect. The same year, Abramowitz, O'Leary, and Rosén (1987) examined the effects of different types of teacher feedback on student behavior in a remedial summer school program. Following a baseline condition in which the teacher provided students with no feedback, experimental conditions were implemented in which the teacher either provided students with (1) encouraging feedback, (2) a reprimand when they were observed to be off task, or (3) no feedback at all. Significantly lower levels of off-task behavior were noted during the reprimand condition than during the no-feedback or encouraging-feedback conditions. Work completion, however, was noted to be significantly higher during the encouraging-feedback condition than when students received no feedback at all. These results appear to suggest that although positive effects have been noted for the use of both praise and reprimands, these strategies may be used most effectively in combination with one another.

PLANNED IGNORING

An action bias refers to the desire that many of us have as human beings to act when something goes wrong. If a drink has spilled, we need to clean it up. If somebody is injured, we need to provide first aid. Sometimes, however, it really is most appropriate to do nothing. The first circumstance in which it is most appropriate *not* to respond is when a child makes a mistake and begins correcting it immediately on his or her own. When that happens, the child has demonstrated learning and no reinforcement or correction is needed. Similarly, if a child does something wrong accidently, and it causes no harm, there may be no need to respond.

The second circumstance that calls for ignoring occurs when extinction is appropriate. Sometimes, inappropriate student behavior is actually reinforced by a teacher responding. Many of us have worked with students who love talking to us. When we respond by politely asking the student to stop talking, he or she lures us into an argument—which inadvertently reinforces his or her talking! After all, it is not uncommon for teachers to reinforce students' blurting out by reprimanding them. Under these types of circumstances, doing nothing may be the best choice.

Finally, there are periods of time when giving a reprimand may be disruptive to the flow of the class. By reprimanding one student, we may actually stop paying attention to other students whose behavior may become problematic. If a behavior is not serious, the classroom instruction should go on. Of course, doing nothing is not always the best choice. In these circumstances, providing some kind of feedback is recommended.

To address many of these situations, a planned ignoring intervention can be put into place (see Coach Card 4.3). Planned ignoring essentially means not responding to a particular behavior. It uses the principles of extinction: essentially, a behavior that is no longer reinforced will stop. By not responding, the teacher continues to teach and conduct the lesson as if nothing had occurred. A case example describing the use of planned ignoring is provided in Box 4.3, which illustrates both the difficulty and the effectiveness of doing nothing. The effectiveness of planned ignoring has typically been investigated in combination with praise. Across two studies designed to improve the classroom engagement of elementary

BOX 4.3. Case Example: Planned Ignoring

We once worked with a middle school teacher who had a student who really enjoyed drawing the teacher into an argument. When the teacher would say, "Write 150 words and spell them correctly," the student would say, "Can I just write the word 'I' 150 times?" When the teacher would ask all of the students to push their chairs in, the same student would wait until everybody else pushed their chair in, look at the teacher, and try to get the teacher to say specifically, "Hudson, please push your chair in." The teacher described this situation as annoying, but only disruptive if she began reprimanding the student. When that happened, the student would argue back, and a long argument would often result that would disrupt the class. However, the student's behavior was not a danger to others.

To address the problem, the teacher ultimately chose to ignore the student's behavior. She set a personal goal for herself. Every time the student said something out loud that she judged as an effort to get her to react, she ignored the student and kept a running tally of the number of times she ignored the problem behavior. If she successfully ignored the student 150 times, she would reward herself with a latte from her local coffee shop. Alas, the story has a bittersweet end—after ignoring the behavior 15 times, the student stopped calling out to try and make her respond, and the teacher never got the chance to reach her goal of 150 ignores!

school students (Hall et al., 1968; Yawkey, 1971), the classroom teacher was instructed to provide students with praise for exhibiting on-task behaviors while ignoring inappropriate behaviors. This strategy resulted in significant improvements in on-task behavior across both studies and eight students.

The use of planned ignoring in isolation, however, may have less promising results. Madsen and colleagues (1968), for example, found that the use of planned ignoring alone had little effect on inappropriate student behavior. However, as other studies have suggested, the pairing of ignoring inappropriate behavior and praising appropriate behavior was highly successful in improving student behavior. These results suggest that ignoring should rarely be implemented as a stand-alone procedure, but should be paired with positive reinforcement of an alternative behavior. In other words, if a 10-year-old boy raises his hand, he should receive teacher attention. If he uses other strategies to gain attention, these inappropriate strategies should be ignored. This process, whereby a student receives a reward (i.e., attention) for doing what is desired and the problem behavior is ignored, is also called *differential reinforcement of an alternative behavior* (DRA).

One thing to keep in mind when using planned ignoring is that things often will get worse before they get better. Think about what might happen to the 10-year-old who likes getting teacher attention, and does so by blurting out answers during a classwide discussion. If the teacher suddenly stops responding, the student is likely to blurt out even more. After all, if something has worked in the past, then maybe more of it would work better. This extinction burst, which we discussed in Chapter 2, may cause the teacher to respond to the student in an effort to control the behavior. Unfortunately, when attention is intermittently provided for behaviors that should be ignored, the behavior is likely to become resistant to future extinction efforts. Thus, it is important to make sure that you are willing to cope with an extinction burst if you want to include an ignoring intervention.

NONCONTINGENT ATTENTION

Recall our discussion from Chapter 2 about motivating operations—if a person has been deprived of something, he or she is more likely to do something to get it. For example, if a child has been deprived of attention (such as through a planned ignoring intervention), he or she may be more likely to do something disruptive in order to get attention back. One way to more appropriately provide students with the attention they desire may therefore be through the use of noncontingent attention. When attention is given noncontingently, a teacher will reinforce students' behavior by providing attention frequently through the school day. For example, some teachers greet their students at the door when they come into the classroom. Other teachers simply engage students who are working on an assignment or who are in the middle of a transition. From a behavioral perspective, students who receive frequent attention have less of a need to "misbehave" in order to get it.

Of course, teachers may not be the only ones to provide attention. In a positive peer-reporting intervention, Morrison and Jones (2007) found that noncontingent attention was effective at reducing acting-out behaviors. They speculated that the "dose" of attention reduced the need of some students to act out for the purpose of getting attention. A primary advantage of noncontingent attention is the ease with which the intervention may be implemented (Vollmer, Iawata, Zarcone, Smith, & Mazaleski, 1993). After all, attention is easy to provide and can be done on a regular basis. Simply put, noncontingent attention may be provided at any time for any reason.

CONCLUSIONS

Our look at the evidence leads us to believe that reinforcing desirable behavior is more effective for most children than waiting for a behavior problem to occur and then reacting to it. That is not to say that educators should focus only on positive behavior and simply hope and pray that problem behavior does not occur. Rather, problem behavior should be handled in a careful, deliberate, and systematic way. As we mentioned in the previous chapter, rules alone have little impact on behavior. When paired with feedback, however, rules do result in behavioral changes (Madsen et al., 1968). The type of feedback that we provide may involve praise, reprimands, or ignoring. The research seems to suggest that a beneficial procedure to follow is to reinforce those behaviors that you want to see with praise or some other kind of positive attention while also ignoring the smaller forms of inappropriate behavior that continue to occur. When coupled with use of the strategies we described in Chapter 3 (e.g., delivering effective instructions, proximity, active supervision), we can expect to find notable improvements in student behavior. However, a more systematic approach may be needed for classrooms with higher than usual levels of disruption. Under these circumstances, a classwide token economy may be useful.

COACH CARD 4.1. Delivering Effective Reprimands

In order to be most effective, reprimands should be:

☐ Brief.

☐ Delivered immediately.

☐ Delivered quietly.

☐ Delivered individually.

☐ Made using a calm, firm, unemotional tone.

☐ Paired with eye contact.

☐ Paired with specific feedback regarding what the student should be doing instead.

☐ Provided in close proximity to the student.

☐ Specific regarding what the student is doing wrong.

☐ Followed by the teacher moving away from the student while the student modifies behavior.

COACH CARD 4.2. Delivering Effective Praise

In order to deliver praise most effectively:

1. Select the best behavioral targets.

   ☐ Those behaviors that are new to the students.

   ☐ Those behaviors that students need to perform more often.

   ☐ Those behaviors that are incompatible with problem behavior.

   ☐ Students who are infrequently praised.

2. Provide praise immediately following the behavior you wish to increase.

3. Ensure the praise will **PASS** the test.

   ☐ **P**roximity: Be close enough to the student so the praise can be given in private and quietly.

   ☐ **A**ge appropriate: Praise students for things that they would expect to be praised for—not for things they would find insulting.

   ☐ **S**incere: Students know when we are lying. Be sincere about the praise you are giving.

   ☐ **S**pecific: Make sure that the student knows exactly what he or she is doing correctly.

COACH CARD 4.3.
Effective Use of Planned Ignoring

Steps involved in using planned ignoring:

☐ Identify behavior that you want to ignore.

☐ Determine if you can handle an extinction burst (if not, select a different intervention).

☐ Create a plan for managing an extinction burst.

☐ When behavior occurs, continue teaching as if nothing happened.

☐ When the appropriate behavior occurs, provide student with attention.

Alternative: When a student is displaying an attention-seeking behavior, some teachers respond with a phrase like "I can respond only to students who are raising their hand" or "I would be happy to answer your question once the room is quiet." This approach may be effective for some students, but may serve as reinforcement for others to increase their acting-out behavior.

PART III

STRATEGIES FOR ADDRESSING CLASSWIDE BEHAVIORAL CONCERNS

CHAPTER 5

Implementing Token Economies

As we saw in Chapter 4, praise can be a powerful reinforcer for many students. Research studies have shown that providing students with specific, contingent praise leads to both improvements in appropriate behavior and decreases in disruptive behavior (e.g., Blaze, Olmi, Mercer, Dufrene, & Tingstrom, 2014; Lambert et al., 2015). Praise can be an effective motivator for many students because as human beings, we want to understand those things that we are doing correctly and know that someone else appreciates those things. However, even though praise is cheap and easy to deliver, it is unlikely to be universally useful for *all* students. There may be circumstances in which praise loses its reinforcing value, or there may be students who do not find adult attention reinforcing (Case in point: One student David worked with was praised for working hard on a statewide standardized test and turned to him, saying, "Why should I care what you think of me? You're not my friend"). In these types of situations, teachers and school administrators may need additional strategies to manage student behaviors. One alternative approach, which makes positive reinforcement more concrete and tangible, is the use of a token economy system.

Within a token economy, positive verbal feedback is paired with the delivery of tokens. Tokens may come in various forms, including plastic chips, points, and tickets. These tokens serve as a type of classroom currency, which can be used to "purchase" different forms of extrinsic reinforcement. The idea of providing rewards for good behavior is nothing new. In fact, in the 15th century, Erasmus argued that teachers should replace their use of a cane to punish bad behavior with the provision of cakes and cherries for good behavior (Skinner, 1966). What is different about a token economy, however, is that students are rewarded systematically and frequently (O'Leary & Drabman, 1971). Decision rules are established ahead of time that clearly outline what students need to do to earn a token so that reinforcement is consistent and predictable.

When the use of praise has been compared with the use of a token economy, stronger effects have generally been found for the token economy system (e.g., Breyer & Allen, 1975;

Broden, Hall, Dunlap, & Clark, 1970; O'Leary, Becker, Evans, & Saudargas, 1969). The most obvious explanation for this has been that the external reinforcement is seen as more desirable—and therefore more motivating—to the students than teacher praise. One alternative explanation, however, is that the act of giving out tokens forces the teacher to more closely monitor his or her own behavior (Breyer & Allen, 1975)—that is, whereas providing verbal feedback requires the teacher to independently remember to do so amid instruction and classroom management, tokens provide a more tangible reminder of the need to recognize and reward when students are engaging in appropriate behavior.

To understand token economies, it is worth looking at the concepts of primary and secondary reinforcers. In Chapter 2, we outlined our cordial disagreement regarding the deliciousness of chocolate. Assuming that we wanted to reinforce Amy for completing an accreditation report, imagine what would happen if we gave her chocolate each time she completed writing one page. Two problems could arise. The first is that she might become tired of the chocolate (although this does seem impossible, right?) and it may lose its reinforcing value—that is, whereas chocolate might have been very motivating in the beginning, over time Amy may become satiated and less motivated to work for the sugary treat. If, however, she doesn't grow tired of the chocolate, the second problem relates to the amount of work needed to keep good, high-quality chocolate readily available. Chocolate is difficult to store and also potentially expensive, so keeping it available throughout all 500 pages of an accreditation report could prove tricky. What we need instead is to have an intermediate step between completing a page and earning the chocolate. This is where the tokens come in. Tokens can be administered at the point of performance (i.e., when the behavior actually occurs), and then exchanged for reinforcement at a later time.

The ultimate token that we use in our everyday life is money. Imagine if you went to work and, instead of providing you with money, your employer provided you with housing, food, transportation, entertainment, travel, flowers that you could send to a loved one, hygiene products, furniture, health care, dental care, shoes, clothing (formal, informal, and business attire, of course!), a computer, pictures to hang on the wall, and appliances for your house (clearly, the list could go on). Although this would enable you to get the things that you both need and want, you may not always get the things you want exactly when you want them. It is impossible to meet an individual's exact desire at every moment. Instead, money is a great substitute because it allows us the flexibility to purchase what we want when we want it. We can choose what to spend it on or whether to save it. The same advantages also extend to the classroom. Providing students with tokens that they can exchange when they want, and for what they find most motivating, can work to efficiently meet the needs of the many different students in a classroom.

In this chapter, we outline the critical components that constitute a token economy system, highlighting a number of decisions that must be made along the way regarding implementation. In addition, we describe ways in which token economy systems have been modified within the literature over the past half century. Although some of the discussion may focus on individual students, the primary focus is on developing token economy systems that are applicable to large groups of students in a classroom setting.

IMPLEMENTING A TOKEN ECONOMY SYSTEM

When it comes to implementing a token economy system, there are four essential components that must be in place. First, one must determine at what level the token economy will be implemented. Second, it is necessary to establish a set of behavioral expectations so that students understand what behaviors will be reinforced. Third, there must be a process for delivering tokens contingent on appropriate student behavior. Fourth, there must be clear guidelines for how tokens will be exchanged for backup rewards. Each of these components is discussed in further detail next (see also Coach Cards 5.1 and 5.2).

At What Level Should the Token Economy Be Implemented?

Before setting out to establish the specifics of a token economy system, it is first important to determine the level at which the system will be applied. Depending on the circumstance, a token economy may be used to support one student's behavior or an entire school. Although many examples of successful implementation of token economy interventions at the individual level can be found in the literature, there are several advantages of implementing a token economy at the classwide level (Filcheck, McNeil, Greco, & Bernard, 2004). First, using a classwide system can be more efficient for the teacher than managing multiple individual behavior plans. Rather than having to keep track of which behaviors are being targeted for whom and what each student's individual goals are, one consistent set of expectations and procedures can be used for all students in the classroom. Second, using a classwide system prevents bringing unnecessary attention to individual students. Students who are receiving an intervention may feel singled out because their behavior is being monitored more closely than that of their classmates. At the same time, classmates may feel envious of those students who are receiving an intervention because they have the opportunity to receive special rewards (Filcheck et al., 2004).

Implementation of a schoolwide token economy system offers additional benefits. For one, the expectations for student behavior are made consistent across all settings in the school and can therefore be consistently reinforced throughout the students' day. Students also receive an additional layer of behavioral support across time, as they do not need to learn new expectations as they move from one grade to the next. One of the earlier examples of a schoolwide token economy system was provided by Boegli and Wasik (1978), who implemented the intervention within a K–6 elementary school of nearly 500 students. Teachers at each grade level (e.g., K–1, 2–3) came together at the beginning of the year to generate a list of behavioral objectives that were developmentally appropriate for that particular age group. For example, completing homework was considered appropriate at the intermediate grades but not targeted for younger students. Token delivery was a shared responsibility among all adults in the building, including the principal, counselor, teachers, teaching aides, office staff, and custodians; however, tokens could be exchanged only within the students' classroom. In addition to this classroom token exchange, schoolwide auctions were also held periodically, in which students could bid on items that had been donated by parents or community members (e.g., magazines, toys, candy). Following the implementation of the intervention, the researchers observed a notable drop in classroom disruptions, improved reading and arithmetic achievement scores, and a decrease in the number of suspensions.

A schoolwide token economy system is also considered to be one of the core Tier 1 components within a schoolwide positive behavioral interventions and supports (SWPBIS) model. Within schools implementing SWPBIS, the school team first establishes a set of three to five positively worded expectations for student behavior that can apply to all settings in the school. For example, the expectation may be that all students should be safe, respectful, and responsible. Once the broad expectations are established, the team works to specify what meeting these expectations would look like in different settings in the school. For example, being responsible in the classroom may mean completing assignments, whereas being responsible in the lunchroom may mean throwing away one's trash in the proper receptacle. Both the overarching expectations and situation-specific behaviors are explicitly taught to all students at the beginning of the school year with booster sessions incorporated periodically. All school staff share responsibility for reinforcing students when they demonstrate the schoolwide expectations. Typically, a schoolwide ticket system (e.g., "Caught being good," "High-fives") is used across all grades and settings (e.g., classroom, nonclassroom). Students are provided with individual feedback when they receive a ticket; however, they also often receive schoolwide acknowledgment when earned tickets are publicly posted or announced. In addition to verbal feedback that is provided to all students, many schools use raffles to provide further reinforcement to select students. Those students who win the raffle might be provided with tangible (e.g., item from the school store) or activity (e.g., invitation to a special lunch) rewards. It is important to note, however, that although the effectiveness of SWPBIS has been demonstrated across several large randomized controlled trials (e.g., Bradshaw, Mitchell, & Leaf, 2010; Horner et al., 2009), the effectiveness of the token component of SWPBIS has not been isolated.

What Behaviors Can Be Targeted?

The first step in implementing a token economy system is to establish the behavioral expectations for which students will be reinforced. In looking at the literature on the use of token economies, students have most typically been reinforced for exhibiting those behaviors that teachers expect to see in the classroom. For example, students might receive tokens for arriving to class on time, facing the front of the room, sitting quietly in their seats, and working on assignments. Reinforcing students in this way for expected behaviors has been shown to successfully decrease disruptive or inappropriate behavior (e.g., O'Leary et al., 1969; Ringer, 1973), increase on-task behavior (e.g., Broden, Hall, et al., 1970), and even improve academic performance (e.g., Birnbrauer, Wolf, Kidder, & Tague, 1965; Boegli & Wasik, 1978; see Table 5.1). However, in reviewing early research conducted on token economies in the 1960s, O'Leary and Drabman (1971) concluded that token economies are most likely to have an effect on nonacademic disruptive behaviors such as being out of one's seat, talking to peers, and turning around in one's chair. In contrast, less work has been done—and

TABLE 5.1. Empirical Studies Examining the Use of Token Economy Systems

Study	Sample	Intervention	Design	Results
Birnbrauer, Wolf, Kidder, & Tague (1965)	8- to 14-year-old students with intellectual disabilities	Token economy	ABA design across five students	Modest improvements in accuracy and work completion during token economy; however, no return to baseline during reversal phase
Boegli & Wasik (1978)	Implemented schoolwide (214 students in grades K–3, 245 students in grades 4–6)	Token economy	AB design across primary and intermediate grades	Notable drop in classroom disruptions; improved reading and arithmetic achievement scores; decrease in number of suspensions
Broden, Hall, Dunlap, & Clark (1970)	Students in grades 7–8 in a special education classroom	Token economy	ABAB within one classroom	Increase in study behavior when token economy introduced
Main & Munro (1977)	Ninth-grade students in general education	Compared praise with token economy	BCBC design	Notable decrease in unacceptable classroom behavior when token economy introduced
Ringer (1973)	Fourth-grade students in general education	Token economy	ABAB within one classroom	Notable reductions in inappropriate behavior when token economy implemented during independent seatwork; results less defined during small-group work

less evidence has been demonstrated—on the effectiveness of token economy systems in improving academic performance.

It is possible to frame behavioral expectations in one of two ways (see Table 5.2 for examples). One possibility is to create a comprehensive list of all specific target behaviors that one expects to see students demonstrate. For example, one teacher might delineate that students are expected to sit quietly, face forward, listen to the teacher, raise their hands to be called upon, and begin working on assignments quickly and quietly. The teacher would therefore administer tokens to students who were observed to be engaging in these particular target behaviors. A second possibility, however, is to frame the expectations more globally. For example, the general expectations in a classroom may be for students to work hard and be nice to others. The teacher would then administer tokens to students when they demonstrated specific behaviors believed to be consistent with the general expectations (e.g., starting work immediately would be a specific example of working hard). If, however, the classroom is within a system that is implementing SWPBIS, the behavioral targets

TABLE 5.2. Examples of Global and Specific Target Behaviors from the Literature

Study	Global target behaviors	Specific target behaviors
Boegli & Wasik (1978)		• Being on time • Having needed materials • Helping others • Completing assigned work
Breyer & Allen (1975)	• Task-oriented behavior	
Broden, Hall, et al. (1970)		• Sitting quietly • Working on assignment
Drege & Beare (1991)		• Using proper language • Showing respect for authority figures
Klimas & McLoughlin (2007)		• Assignment completion
Main & Munro (1977)	• Appropriate behavior	
O'Leary & Becker (1967)		• In seat • Face front • Raise hand • Working • Pay attention • Desk clear
Ringer (1973)	• Appropriate behavior	
Safer, Heaton, & Parker (1981)	• Satisfactory classroom behavior	
Salzberg & Greenwald (1977)	• On-task behavior	

should align with the schoolwide expectations that are routinely taught and reinforced (e.g., "Be safe," "Be respectful," "Be responsible"). Either approach to framing behavioral expectations may be used in a classroom as long as students have a full understanding of how tokens may be earned.

How Should Tokens Be Delivered?

As noted at the beginning of this chapter, tokens can come in various shapes and sizes. For one, tokens may come in the form of objects that can be held by a student, such as plastic chips, stars, marbles, or tickets. Tangible tokens are more often employed with younger children, who can more easily keep track of the number of tokens earned (O'Leary & Drabman, 1971). When using this type of a tangible token system, teachers typically hand the token to the student, who can place it in a bank or other place (e.g., inside one's desk) for safekeeping. Depending on the age and developmental level of the student, however, it may be necessary to carefully consider how and where tokens get stored so that they are not easily lost. For example, in implementing a token system with a kindergarten student with a developmental disability, Klimas and McLaughlin (2007) had the student attach poker chips to a Velcro token board so that the tokens would not get lost and the student could see how much he had earned.

Tokens may also be administered in the form of points or ratings. This type of written feedback tends to be employed more often with older students, given the less conspicuous nature of the recording system (O'Leary & Drabman, 1971). When using points or ratings, it is also necessary to determine where points will be stored. Students may be provided with a card or chart, for example, on which recordings can be made. In a study by Ringer (1973), each student was given a card that was divided into 20 squares. As the teacher was moving around the room during instruction, she would write her initials in one of the boxes and praise the student when he or she was exhibiting appropriate behavior. At the end of the intervention session, those students who had filled up all 20 squares took a trip to the principal's office, where they received praise and a special stamp on their card. O'Leary and Becker (1967), on the other hand, provided each student with a small notebook that was kept on his or her desk. During each lesson, students could earn up to 10 points for demonstrating appropriate behavior, and these points were entered into the student's notebook. One limitation to a ratings-based approach is that the ratings made by teachers may be subjective, given that each student's behavior is not being measured directly (O'Leary et al., 1969). At the same time, however, asking a teacher to conduct more global ratings rather than to reinforce individual instances of desired behavior can also prove to be more feasible, particularly if the size of the class is large.

Regardless of the form in which tokens are distributed, however, it is important that they meet four main conditions. First, you should be able to administer the tokens effortlessly. As such, they should be easily transportable and accessible, and providing them to students should not distract substantially from instruction. Second, tokens should be administered quickly and contingently. If the delay between exhibiting a desired behavior and receiving a token is too long, the student may not understand what he or she had done to receive the token. Third, students should easily understand the value of a token. Explaining the exchange system to an older child or adolescent, who understands how currency works, can be fairly straightforward. However, a more detailed explanation may be necessary for younger children. For example, consistently pairing a point or token with a backup reinforcer when a token system is first introduced will help the student to understand the value of the token.

Finally, it is important that the delivery of a point, token, or ticket be paired with verbal feedback. A token economy system is not meant to be a replacement for positive verbal feedback, but is instead something to be used along with frequent praise and private recognition of good student work. Pairing a token with explicit, positive feedback helps to ensure that the student understands the relationship between the desired behavior and the token reinforcement. For those students who may not be able to fully demonstrate the desired behavior right away, praise should also be provided for approximations of the target behavior in order to provide sufficient motivation (O'Leary & Drabman, 1971). For example, a student who has not been able to complete enough of his or her assigned work to earn a token could be verbally reinforced for getting some portion of the work done. In this way, students will remain motivated to continue to engage in desired behaviors even if they do not receive reinforcement as quickly as their peers.

How Should Rewards Be Incorporated?

One of most critical elements to ensuring a token economy's success is making sure that the available rewards are adequately reinforcing—that is, students need to view the rewards as desirable if the intervention is going to motivate them to change their behavior. For this reason, token economy systems tend to incorporate a variety of possible rewards rather than just one. Having multiple rewards available helps to ensure that there is something within the system that each student finds reinforcing (O'Leary & Drabman, 1971). With the right amount of flexibility, you can put a token price on a range of things that you are willing to let students work toward. Whether it's 5 minutes of extra recess, the answer to one question on a 15-item test, or the chance to help you erase the whiteboard, tokens can have a tremendous amount of flexibility. Having a variety of reinforcers therefore allows Amy to earn chocolate, whereas David gets an hour of video-game time that he can play instead of going to a schoolwide faculty meeting!

Many different types of rewards have been used within the literature; however, these individual rewards generally fall into one of four categories: edible, tangible, activity, or social (see Table 5.3). Edible rewards include small snacks or treats. Tangible rewards are those objects or prizes that a student can possess, ranging from gold star stickers to small toys. An activity reward allows the student to do something or engage in an activity that he or she otherwise would not be able to do. Examples of activity rewards include getting to watch a video at the end of the day or getting 5 extra minutes of recess. Finally, social rewards are those that allow the student to do something *with* someone else. Depending on the student's preference, this could mean getting to have lunch with a teacher or getting to play a game with a classmate.

TABLE 5.3. Examples of Backup Reinforcers

Edible reinforcers	Tangible reinforcers	Activity reinforcers	Social reinforcers
• Candy • Gum • Small snack	• Small toys • Books/comic books • Pencils • Prizes from classroom store	• Five minutes early dismissal to lunch • Ability to change desks for one day • Free time to do art projects, play board games, play with blocks, etc. • Homework pass	• Opportunity to visit the nurse • Opportunity to talk with a friend for 5 minutes • Praise from the school principal • Invitation to a class party

One way to ensure that available rewards are sufficiently reinforcing is to administer a reward preference survey prior to beginning the intervention. A reward preference survey asks students to indicate whether (i.e., yes/no) or rate how (i.e., not at all, somewhat) desirable they believe a potential reward to be. Using data from a reward preference survey, a teacher could then be selective in choosing the items or activities with the highest perceived value. With younger children, it may also be useful to make the rewards more prominent throughout the intervention so as to increase their motivating value. In a study by O'Leary and colleagues (1969), for example, second-grade students were asked to select the prize that they wished to earn before the actual rating period began. In this way, the potential reward was made more salient to the younger children.

It has been suggested that teachers first begin a token economy system using smaller-scale or more activity-based rewards such as stickers or extra free time. If these rewards do not prove to be powerful enough, then larger rewards such as tangibles (e.g., toys) or edibles may be considered (O'Leary, Drabman, & Kass, 1973). The rationale for considering rewards in this way is that research has suggested that it may be easier to successfully fade out an intervention when behavior is being maintained by less powerful, or more natural, rewards.

One final consideration in selecting rewards is the feasibility of the reward choices—that is, it is important that the rewards are not so cost prohibitive or cumbersome that a teacher will be unable to implement them. O'Leary and colleagues (1973) deliberately selected highly feasible rewards that would be available to any classroom teacher when implementing a token economy system across three elementary-level resource classrooms—that is, each point earned could be exchanged for 1 minute of free time, which could be spent painting, playing a board game, playing with blocks, or whatever the student desired. A similar point-to-minute system was used in a study with middle school students in special education (Broden, Hall, et al., 1970); however, each tally mark represented 1 minute that the student could leave early for lunch.

It may also be easier to deliver rewards through a lottery system—that is, rather than using tokens to directly purchase backup rewards, students may use their tokens to participate in a lottery. At the end of each day, each student would receive as many entries into the lottery as the number of tokens earned. A lottery drawing could then be held daily or weekly to select one or more winners from the classroom. Lottery rewards may be known ahead of time or may remain a mystery until the drawing occurs in order to enhance students' motivational interest (see Chapter 6 for a discussion of Mystery Motivator and other randomized reward systems).

Introducing the Intervention

It is advisable to provide the following information when introducing a token economy system to students (see Coach Card 5.3). First, you should provide a rationale for why the token economy is being introduced. Consider either the concerns that you have had about student behavior or which behaviors are desired but not currently being demonstrated.

Second, clearly define the target behaviors and provide a rationale for why these behaviors have been selected. Students must have a clear understanding of what behaviors they are—and are not—expected to exhibit. It may therefore be useful to model what the expected behaviors look like for the class at this time. It is also important, however, that the students understand why you are focusing on these particular behaviors. If there is not a rationale provided, the choice may appear arbitrary. You should be as explicit as possible about how exhibiting these target behaviors will enhance the functioning of individual students or the overall class. Third, the procedures for earning tokens should be made clear. This includes what students need to do to earn tokens (e.g., exhibit one or more target behaviors), when students will be able to earn tokens (e.g., during select periods or throughout the day), and how often tokens will be delivered (e.g., at the end of a period or continuously). Fourth, the function of the tokens or points should be explained. Tokens may be described as a form of currency that can be "cashed in" for things or activities. Fifth, students should be made aware of what types of rewards they can earn. If there are different levels of rewards that require different numbers of tokens, this should be understood. Finally, teachers should outline the procedures for redeeming tokens. For example, some teachers may allow students to exchange their tokens throughout the day, whereas others may choose to limit redemption to only 1 day per week.

VARIATIONS ON THE TOKEN ECONOMY

Successful examples of token economy interventions can be seen within the literature across a wide variety of populations, ranging from general education classrooms to boys whose behaviors were so serious that they required residential treatment services (Mendham & Thorne, 1984). In addition, there are studies supporting token economies with groups of students with intellectual disabilities (e.g., Baer, Ascione, & Casto, 1977), EBDs (e.g., Drege & Beare, 1991), and ADHD (e.g., McGoey & DuPaul, 2000). However, despite the old adage "If it ain't broke, don't fix it," variations on the basic token economy system may prove beneficial in some situations. Two of the more common variations involve the use of response cost and level systems.

Response Cost

Response cost is a behavioral contingency approach in which reinforcers are taken away contingent on inappropriate behavior. One of the response cost strategies that we (sadly!) hear about often in schools is the idea of taking away a student's ability to go to recess if he or she engages in inappropriate behavior. In this situation, something desirable (recess) is being withheld or taken away from the student in the hope that this will make the student less likely to engage in the problem behavior in the future.

Within a standard token economy system, students receive tokens for engaging in appropriate behaviors, while inappropriate behaviors tend to be ignored. Providing tokens to students can give a teacher a great deal of power to recognize positive behavior. In general, this is the best approach—students need to have opportunities to receive recognition for the ideal behaviors they are displaying. However, tokens can also be used as a method for providing disincentives to problematic behavior. Using response cost within a token economy involves providing the student with tokens for engaging in appropriate behaviors, but also taking tokens away contingent on inappropriate behavior. All students typically begin the session with the same predetermined number of tokens. As the day goes on, students' numbers of tokens may go up or down depending on their behavior. However, any tokens that the student still has at the end of class may be exchanged for reinforcers. A flowchart is provided in Figure 5.1 to assist you in designing a token economy system with or without response cost.

In order to illustrate what a token economy involving response cost might look like, we provide a couple of concrete examples. In some cases, all students start out with zero tokens and then can both earn and lose tokens as time goes on. For example, in a study by Drege and Baer (1991), students in an EBD program could earn up to 120 points per day for engaging in appropriate behaviors (e.g., following directions, using proper language, respecting authority figures); however, points were taken away for exhibiting inappropriate behaviors (e.g., swearing, throwing temper tantrums). In other cases, all students start out with a set number of tokens, which are lost when inappropriate behavior occurs. In a study by Fabiano, Pelham, Gnagy, and Burrows-MacLean (2007), this type of approach was used with a group of students who had been identified as having ADHD. Each student began the class period with 100 points but then lost 10 points for each rule infraction. These students then had the opportunity to earn back some of the points lost at the end of the period, as they could earn 25 points for the successful completion of an assignment. Every student

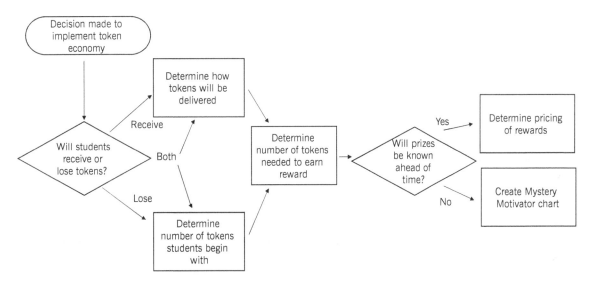

FIGURE 5.1. Flowchart for designing token economy interventions with or without response cost.

who earned a predetermined number of points was allowed to participate in an end-of-the-week activity.

One important caveat to keep in mind when deciding how to implement a token economy involving response cost is that you want to avoid a situation in which a student quickly digs him- or herself into a hole. For example, a teacher may put 10 dashes on the board and remove a dash when a student acts out. We have both observed classes in which all 10 points disappear in the first 5 minutes . . . and the class period lasts another 45 minutes! At that point, the system loses all reinforcing value and it is likely that students will respond with even worse behavior. For this reason, it is extremely important to ensure that students have the opportunity to earn points as well as lose them.

Although several studies have incorporated response cost as one part of a multicomponent intervention (e.g., De Martini-Scully et al., 2000; Zaghlawan, Ostrosky, & Al-Khateeb, 2007), to date only a handful of studies have examined the independent effect of response cost on student behavior. As outlined in Table 5.4, response cost strategies have been

TABLE 5.4. Empirical Studies Examining Use of Response Cost Procedures

Study	Sample	Intervention	Design	Results
Conyers et al. (2004)	Preschool children in a general classroom	Compared response cost and DRO	Alternating treatments design within one classroom	Significant decreases in disruptive behavior when response cost implemented
Drege & Beare (1991)	Students in grades 1–2 in a classroom for students with EBD	Response cost (plus time-out for severe behaviors)	Multiple baseline across three students	Significant decreases in off-task and disruptive behavior when intervention introduced
Iwata & Bailey (1974)	Elementary school students in a special education classroom	Compared response cost and token economy	ABAB within one classroom	No significant differences for behavioral outcomes; work completion somewhat higher in response cost condition
McLaughlin & Malaby (1972)	Students in grades 5–6 in general education	Compared response cost and token economy	BCBC within one classroom	Lower rates of inappropriate verbalizations during token economy condition
Trice & Parker (1983)	10th-grade students in a resource program	Compared response cost and DRL	ABACA design	Immediate decrease in profanity when response cost introduced

Note. DRL, differential reinforcement of low rates of behavior; DRO, differential reinforcement of other behavior.

applied from elementary through high school and across general and special education settings. Findings support the general effectiveness of response cost in decreasing inappropriate behaviors (e.g., Conyers et al., 2004; Trice & Parker, 1983); however, there is also some evidence to suggest that response cost may also improve desired behaviors (e.g., increasing work completion; Iwata & Bailey, 1974). Interestingly, however, one study to directly compare token economy and response cost interventions found stronger effects when the token economy was in place (McLaughlin & Malaby, 1972).

Level Systems

A level system combines a token economy with the behavioral principle of shaping in order to improve student behavior (Cancio & Johnson, 2007). Level systems began in the 1960s within residential and hospital settings, and have subsequently often been used with students with significant behavior problems (see Table 5.5). Students earn points for demonstrating appropriate behaviors in the same way that they do within a traditional token economy; however, the expectations for appropriate behavior—as well as the rewards that students can earn—intensify as the student moves up through different levels of the system. That is, expectations are set fairly low at the initial level; however, the rewards that students can earn are also smaller in nature. Once students are consistently meeting the expectations set at the initial level, they then move up to the second level, where expectations are set a bit higher and students can earn more desirable rewards. Level systems typically incorporate at least four levels and by the time that a student gets to the final level, the goal is that he or she is demonstrating exemplary behavior (Cancio & Johnson, 2007).

TABLE 5.5. Empirical Studies Examining Use of Level Systems

Study	Sample	Intervention	Design	Results
Filcheck, McNeil, Greco, & Bernard (2004)	Preschool classroom	Seven-level system	ABA within one classroom	Decrease in inappropriate behavior when level system implemented; however, no return to baseline when intervention withdrawn
Mastropieri, Jenne, & Scruggs (1988)	High school resource classroom for students with EBD	Four-level system	AB design across 15 students	Decreased talk-outs for 14 out of 15 children; decreased out-of-seat behavior for all 15 students
Mendham & Thorne (1984)	Schoolwide in a residential setting for 7- to 12-year-old boys	Level system	ABAB within one school	Decrease in inappropriate behavior when level system implemented

One of the unique considerations in implementing a level system is that it is necessary to determine what the criteria are for moving between levels. Often, teachers will look at the percentage of possible points earned in order to decide whether the student is ready to move on to the next level. For example, students may need to earn 75% of the possible points for 4 consecutive weeks before they can move on. The criteria for moving down levels must also be specified. For example, students may move down a level if they fail to meet a percentage goal for several weeks or if they engage in a behavior that is considered significantly problematic (e.g., physical aggression).

In addition, it is necessary to determine what rewards are associated with each level of the system. As discussed earlier in this chapter, rewards may be edible, tangible, activity based, or social in nature. The first level might include small rewards such as pencils or snacks, whereas the highest level might include large rewards such as a special lunch or early dismissal. When implementing a level system with students with more significant behavioral concerns, however, levels have often been paired with increasing privileges. For example, a student at level 1 may need to ask permission before leaving his or her seat, whereas a student at level 4 may be able to leave the classroom to get a drink or use the restroom at any time.

As one example, Mendham and Thorne (1984) implemented a schoolwide level system within a residential setting. Students were evaluated in relation to how well they stayed on task during class, followed routines, followed instructions, and played during break. A total of four sequential levels were utilized in this system, with the available rewards ranging from small candies at level 1 up to special privileges, such as watching a video, at level 4. As students moved up the levels, the behavioral expectations not only became more demanding but the reinforcement also became more delayed. For example, an expectation for playtime at level 1 was that the student stayed within bounds, whereas an expectation at level 4 was that the student organized his or her free time productively. In addition, students at level 1 received tokens frequently; however, students at level 4 received tokens only once per week.

Given that the nuances of a traditional level system might be difficult for younger students to fully comprehend, Filcheck and colleagues (2004) modified this type of system for use with preschool students. All students received a shape (e.g., dinosaur, kite) that was initially placed at the middle level on a seven-level chart. If a student exhibited appropriate behaviors, the teacher would provide verbal praise and move the student's shape up on the board. If a student exhibited inappropriate behaviors, he or she would first receive a verbal reminder and then the shape would be moved down on the board if the behavior continued. In order to make the levels salient for young children, the top three levels were represented by sunny faces that became happier as the student moved up the chart. In contrast, the bottom three levels were represented by cloudy faces that became sadder as the student moved down the chart. Approximately two to four times per day, the teacher would provide a group-based reward to all students whose shapes were in the positive (i.e., sunny) levels. The reward, which was often activity based, was selected from a deck of possible reward cards, and those students who earned the reward would engage in the reward activity while their classmates began the next assigned activity. All shapes would then be moved back to the middle, neutral level to begin the next intervention period.

FINAL CONSIDERATIONS:
FIXING PROBLEMS AND FADING THE INTERVENTION

The implementation steps outlined earlier in this chapter are designed to guide you through the process of establishing a token economy system in your own classroom. Nevertheless, implementation does not always go exactly as intended and changes may be needed in order to both bolster effectiveness and increase feasibility over time. In this final section, we outline strategies for dealing with problems as they arise as well as fading the intervention over time.

Troubleshooting: When Token Economy Systems Go Wrong

Token economy systems are designed to be fairly straightforward to implement for teachers and to have broad appeal to a range of students. Nonetheless, problems may arise that serve to reduce the effectiveness of the intervention. Here, we highlight a few of the more common problems that may arise and offer potential solutions for addressing these issues.

Problem 1: Reinforcement Is Sporadic

One reason why a token economy system may fail is because there is insufficient adult supervision (O'Leary & Drabman, 1971). If either the teacher to student ratio is too high, or the teacher does not monitor the classroom sufficiently, many instances of desirable behavior may go unnoticed. If students come to see that they are engaging in appropriate behaviors but are not regularly receiving positive feedback or reinforcement for those behaviors, they may learn that there is no benefit to demonstrating those behaviors. If this potential issue stems from a lack of manpower (i.e., one teacher cannot provide students with feedback frequently enough), one option is to consider employing students to provide feedback to their peers. For example, within the tootling intervention, when students catch their peers doing something good, they are taught to write the "tootle" on a card and submit it to their teacher (Cihak et al., 2009). In a similar manner, students could be provided with tokens that could be given to others only for engaging in the behaviors expected in the classroom. If, on the other hand, the issue stems from a lack of monitoring/supervision, it may be necessary to utilize prompts in order to increase the regularity and frequency with which tokens are delivered. Keeping a set number of tokens in one's pocket may serve as a weighty reminder that tokens need to be delivered, or a variable timer might be used to provide an audible prompt.

Problem 2: The Token Exchange Latency Is Too Long

In some situations, problems may arise when there is too long of a delay between the administration of tokens and the receipt of a reward. The term "temporal discounting" has been used to describe the phenomenon by which the value of a reward decreases as the amount of time until it is received increases (Reed & Martens, 2011). Therefore, for some students, the longer they have to wait to exchange their tokens for a prize, the less motivated they may become to earn tokens. Reed and Martens (2011) examined this phenomenon by implementing a classwide token economy system under two reward conditions. In the first condition, students earned tokens during the class period, which could be exchanged for a reward immediately following the intervention session. In the second condition, earned tokens could be exchanged only at the beginning of the next day (i.e., 24 hours later). Results of this study showed that for students demonstrating high levels of impulsivity, the token economy was more effective when the delay to reward was much shorter.

Problem 3: Rewards Are Priced Incorrectly

It is very important to carefully consider the pricing of rewards, as problems may arise if rewards are either too easy or too difficult to earn. When the price of rewards is set too low (i.e., very few tokens are needed), students may earn rewards very quickly and therefore become satiated. Satiation may result in reduced motivation to engage in desired behaviors because the rewards are no longer seen as motivating. On the other hand, when the price of rewards is set too high (i.e., many tokens are needed), students may feel that success is unattainable. The same thing can happen if the criteria needed to receive a token are too stringent. Both of these situations may lead students to experience learned helplessness and simply give up because they do not feel that it is possible to earn a reward.

Although the pricing of rewards may be a general problem classwide, it is also possible that the pricing system may be inappropriate only for particular students. This may be because it is much easier for some students to meet the behavioral expectations than others. Therefore, rather than using one universal standard for all students, it may be necessary to consider varying the threshold depending on individual students' levels of functioning. In such a case, different reinforcement criteria might be used for particular students. For example, approximations of a target behavior could be reinforced (e.g., talking quietly rather than remaining silent) or warnings could be given before tokens are taken away within a response cost system.

Problem 4: Students Are Hoarding Tokens

Often students will be allowed to carry over earned tokens from one day to the next. In most cases, this will not be a problem; however, challenges may sometimes arise with particular students. For example, a student who knows that he or she already has enough tokens to purchase what he or she wants may choose to misbehave because the student is not motivated to earn additional tokens. This problem was illustrated in a study by Baer et al. (1977), in which the researchers found that one of the students was still able to purchase reinforcers when his behavior was largely inappropriate because he was able to combine a small number of tokens earned that day with other tokens that had been saved up. In this case, the decision was made to institute a rule whereby any tokens not exchanged that day would be forfeited. Another solution might be to put an expiration date on the tokens, such that they cannot be redeemed after a particular date.

Problem 5: Implementation Is Sporadic

Finally, the most common problem may arise if the token economy is not being implemented consistently across time. We have seen situations, for example, in which a token economy system is suddenly removed one day by an exasperated teacher. Typically, this has occurred when the class has been displaying high levels of misbehavior. Not only does this remove a potential behavior management tool, it also violates the trust that students may have with a teacher. Students need to understand that both the expectations for their behavior, and the way in which they will be reinforced for demonstrating appropriate behavior, are both consistent and predictable.

Fading the Intervention

Although a token economy system can be effectively woven into the fabric of a classroom and used throughout the school year, ideally, teacher-administered reinforcement would eventually be replaced with more naturally occurring forms of reinforcement (Drege & Beare, 1991). Two frequent concerns expressed about token economies are (1) the potential cost involved in having to supply ongoing rewards for students and (2) the worry that students may come to believe that they should be rewarded for anything that they do. One way to address both of these potential problems is to begin to fade the intervention after it has demonstrated initial success.

There are several strategies that may be used to fade a token economy intervention. The first option is to gradually reduce the frequency with which tokens are delivered. Whereas it is important when first introducing the intervention to provide students with tokens frequently, over time reinforcement may become more intermittent. One way in which to decrease the frequency of token delivery is to continue to provide students with verbal feedback each time they exhibit a target behavior, but to provide tokens according to an intermittent schedule (e.g., every third or fifth time the behavior occurs) or in a random fashion. Over time, this ratio of positive feedback to tokens may also be increased. Another way in which to decrease the number of tokens administered is to gradually reduce the amount of time during which the intervention is implemented. For example, if the token economy is initially in place throughout the entire school day, you might consider scaling back implementation to particular time periods. Target periods may be selected according to time of day (e.g., implement only in the morning) or in consideration of when behavior continues to be most problematic (e.g., during transitions).

The second option for fading a token economy is to increase the number of tokens needed to purchase particular rewards. In the early stages of implementation, it is important that the "purchase price" for rewards is not set prohibitively high so that all students have a chance of receiving reinforcement. Over time, however, after students have had a chance to experience success with the system, the cost of items might be increased. For example, if the cost of 5 minutes of free time was originally set at five tokens, this criterion might be increased to 10 tokens after several weeks of implementation.

The third option for fading a token economy is to increase the length of time that students have to wait to exchange their points for rewards. Again, when first introducing the intervention, it may be helpful for students to have the opportunity to purchase a reward every day so that there is not a long latency between receiving a token and receiving a prize. As students become more accustomed to the system, however, the opportunity to exchange tokens may be limited to every other day or even once a week.

CONCLUSIONS

Token economy systems have been successfully used in both general and special education settings for nearly a half century. Within these systems, teachers administer either points or tangible tokens to students contingent upon demonstrating expected behaviors, which can later be exchanged for rewards. Token economies may be applied across the age span by carefully considering how tokens will be administered (e.g., plastic chips vs. points written in a log) and what rewards will be most developmentally appropriate (e.g., stickers vs. free time). In some cases, you may consider introducing a response cost component, whereby students can both earn tokens for appropriate behavior and lose tokens for inappropriate behavior. Furthermore, the use of a level system (i.e., pairing a token economy with gradually increasing expectations) may be beneficial in those situations in which higher levels of problem behavior are present.

COACH CARD 5.1.
Preparing to Implement a Token Economy

Steps	Considerations
Determine whether response cost will be incorporated.	• Will students receive tokens for engaging in desired, appropriate behaviors? • Will students lose tokens for engaging in inappropriate behaviors?
Identify the target behaviors.	• Will target behaviors be framed globally (e.g., be kind to others, pay attention)? • Or will specific target behaviors be outlined (e.g., use kind words, raise hand to be called on)?
Determine time period for implementation.	• During what time period are the highest levels of problem behavior typically observed? • Consider starting with a shorter block of time (e.g., 10-minute period) before extending implementation.
Determine how tokens will be delivered.	• Will points be recorded in a notebook or on a whiteboard? • Will physical objects (e.g., tokens, marbles, tickets) be administered?
Determine appropriate rewards for students.	• What types of rewards will students be able to earn (e.g., edible, tangible, activity, social)? • Consider administering a reward preference survey to identify rewards that are sufficiently motivating.
Determine the pricing of rewards.	• Will a certain number of tokens be needed to earn a particular prize? • Will tokens be used as entries into a classroom lottery?
Establish when tokens may be exchanged.	• How long will students have to wait to exchange tokens for rewards? • How often will a reward lottery take place? • Will this occur daily? Weekly?

COACH CARD 5.2. Treatment Integrity Checklist for Implementing a Token Economy

Name: _____   Date: _____

STEPS IN IMPLEMENTING A TOKEN ECONOMY

☐ Review behavioral expectations.

☐ Deliver tokens when expected behavior is observed.

☐ When delivering tokens, explicitly indicate what the student has done to earn the token.

☐ When violations are observed, explicitly remind the student what he or she can do to earn tokens.

☐ Allow students to exchange tokens for rewards *or* enter into a lottery drawing.

If implementing response cost:

☐ Remove tokens when violations are observed.

Total number of steps completed =

Percentage of steps completed =

COACH CARD 5.3.
Steps in Introducing a Token Economy System

Step	Sample dialogue
Provide rationale for introducing token economy.	*As a class, we have been having a lot of trouble using our indoor voices and staying focused during lessons lately. Unfortunately, the reminders that I have given you do not seem to be working. Therefore, we are going to try something new.*
Establish target behaviors and provide rationale for why they are important.	*There are three things that I believe are very important if you are going to learn the most from each class lesson. First, you need face forward in your seat with your eyes on either me or the board. Second, you need to stay in your seat and listen quietly to instruction. Third, whenever I am writing something on the board, you need to be taking notes. If you do all three of these things, not only will you get the most from the lesson but your classmates will be able to pay attention better as well.*
Describe procedures for earning tokens.	*During each lesson, I will be walking around the classroom looking for students who are demonstrating these important learning behaviors. If I see you doing all of these things, you may get one of these tokens. You may not get a token every time that you are demonstrating these learning behaviors but you should have the opportunity to earn at least a few each day.*
Explain purpose tokens serve.	*What can these tokens be used for? Well, you can think of a token like a form of fake money. You can use the tokens to "buy" different things in the classroom.*
Describe available awards.	*Some of the things that you can buy are small so they don't cost as much. Small prizes are things like stickers or 5 minutes of computer time at the end of the day. Other things that you can buy are much bigger so they cost more. Big prizes are things like early dismissal to lunch or a toy from the prize box.*
Describe procedures for redeeming tokens or entering tokens into a lottery.	*At the end of each day, I will open up the "class store." If you want to cash your tokens in for a prize, you can do so then. However, you can also choose to save up your tokens for a larger prize and exchange them later.*

CHAPTER 6

Group Contingencies

Group contingencies may be one of the most powerful and easily implemented classroom management interventions available to teachers. When implemented in a positive frame, they can be used to create healthy, safe, and interactive classrooms. This chapter explores the power of the group contingency by discussing different types, applications, and ways in which group contingencies can be used to improve chaotic classroom settings such as the one described in Box 6.1.

BOX 6.1. Group Contingencies in Action

I (David) stumbled across group contingencies as a new teacher with no previous training. When students acted out, I tried everything that I knew. When I yelled for the first time, the students yelled right back at me saying, "That is not how you are supposed to talk to a lady!" I tried threatening them with demerits—writing poor conduct reports for every infraction that I noticed, and sending students out of the classroom. I issued reprimands. As you are likely not surprised to find out, none of these things worked, meaning they didn't make the behavior any better.

What did work was putting the whole class on silence for 2 minutes (meaning they were not allowed to talk), and extending that for the whole class period if one student broke the rule. In other words, the class responded to negative reinforcement—allowing the students to avoid the pain of not being allowed to talk by convincing them to be silent for 2 minutes. What I found is that students were more willing to work for their peers than for me. I used this as a major component of my classroom management plan.

TYPES OF CONTINGENCIES

Let's begin by returning to the contingencies described earlier in this book. In Chapter 4, we described a contingency as an "if–then" statement that describes what will happen if an individual does something. What is common to any contingency is that it can be broken down into seven components: (1) the behavior of interest, (2) the person responsible for the behavior, (3) when the behavior is supposed to happen, (4) when the behavior will be evaluated, (5) who will receive the reward or punishment, (6) what reward or punishment will be earned, and (7) who will provide the reward or punishment. One of the more familiar contingency examples that might hit home would be when your mother told you that you could have ice cream only if you ate all of your vegetables. This is an example of an individual contingency, in which a reward is provided to an individual based on his or her own behavior. It is also possible to implement a group contingency, in which rewards are provided to an entire group, such as a classroom. Extending the vegetable example, if all of the students in the lunchroom had to finish their vegetables before they could go out to recess (imagine the backlash!), this would represent a group contingency (see Table 6.1 for examples of both individual and group contingencies).

Elliott, Turco, and Gresham (1987) highlighted many of the advantages of group contingencies. First, these interventions are popular among teachers due to their efficiency. Rather

TABLE 6.1. Types of Individual and Group Contingencies

Contingency	What behavior is of interest?	Who is responsible for the behavior?	Who receives the reward/ punishment?	What reward/ punishment is earned?	Who provides the reward/ punishment?
		Individual contingencies			
Individual token economy	Any behavior	One student	One student	Varies	Teacher
Praise	Any behavior	Individual or whole class	Individual, small group, or whole class	Teacher attention	Teacher
Tootling	Prosocial behavior	One student	One student	Praise	Another student
		Group contingencies			
Independent (i.e., classwide token economy)	Prosocial behavior	All students	One student	Varies	Teacher
Dependent	Any behavior	One or more students	All students	Varies	Teacher
Interdependent (e.g., Good Behavior Game)	Any behavior	Whole class	All students	Varies	Teacher

than having to manage multiple behavior plans with different specifications, a teacher needs to recall only one set of rules and expectations. There are also a number of teachers who feel uncomfortable rewarding a subset of the class for good behavior while the rest of the class is not acknowledged. Group contingencies avoid this problem by allowing all students an equal opportunity to earn rewards. Finally, teachers find that group contingencies address not only the behavior of one target student but improve the behavior of nearly all students in a classroom. Because group contingencies encourage students to work together in class, they may help to foster a community of learning. Kelshaw-Leving, Sterling-Turner, Henry, and Skinner (2000) wrote that "this interdependency or intertwining of fates can cause diverse students to encourage or assist each other so that the group can receive reinforcement" (p. 524). This occurs because student behaviors are reinforced not only by the extrinsic reward that is offered by the teacher, but also by increasing the discussions among students and allowing student behaviors to be rewarded by other students' behavior. In other words, these approaches may cue students to behave appropriately and may reinforce ideal behavior for other students (Skinner, Skinner, Skinner, & Cashwell, 1999).

Beyond the practical and philosophical benefits we have outlined, research has also suggested that group contingencies may be one of the most powerful interventions available to teachers. Stage and Quiroz (1997) conducted a meta-analysis of 99 intervention studies designed to decrease disruptive behavior in public education settings. A total of 16 different interventions were identified, ranging from parent training to classroom reinforcement strategies to exercise programs. The largest effect size, however, was found for group contingency interventions ($M = -1.02$). The findings of Stage and Quiroz (1997) have been further supported by several recent reviews of the literature, which have suggested that group contingencies are highly effective in promoting the behavior of both preschool students (Pokorski, Barton, & Ledford, 2017) and school-age children and adolescents (e.g., Little, Akin-Little, & O'Neill, 2015; Maggin, Johnson, Chafouleas, Ruberto, & Berggren, 2012).

When we begin discussing group contingencies, it is important to acknowledge that there are three different types that were first identified by Litow and Pumroy (1975): independent, dependent, and interdependent. These are defined below and in Table 6.2.

Independent Group Contingency: "To Each His or Her Own"

Within an independent group contingency, the same rules apply to all students; however, the contingency is delivered to an individual child based on his or her own behavior. As discussed in Chapter 5, many teachers are reluctant to begin individual behavior plans with individual students for reasons of fairness and time. Independent group contingencies represent an attractive alternative because they allow teachers to treat every child the same way.

Also in Chapter 5, we discussed class- and schoolwide token economies whereby each student receives reinforcement based on the same rules. For example, a teacher may say that a timer is going to go off at an unknown time (remember variable interval schedules from Chapter 2?) and that if a student is on task (has only needed materials on his or her desk, is looking at his or her paper or work) at that time, the student will receive a check-

TABLE 6.2. Types of Group Contingencies

Who must follow the expectations?	Whose behavior do we use for criterion?	Who receives reinforcer?	Example
		Dependent	
One or two individuals	One or two individuals	Entire group	Jason is expected to complete his math assignment. If he does so, the entire class receives an additional 5 minutes of computer time.
		Independent	
Entire group	One or two individuals	One or two individuals	The entire class is expected to complete a math assignment. Each student earns one homework pass if he or she finishes the assignment.
		Interdependent	
Entire group	Entire group	Entire group	The entire class is expected to complete a math assignment. If each and every member of the class completes the assignment, the entire class receives one free question on a test.

Note. From Hulac and Benson (2010). Copyright © 2010 Sage Publications, Inc. Reprinted by permission.

mark on a piece of tape. Then, at the end of the day, every student who gets 20 checkmarks before 3:00 gets an extra 5 minutes to play outside. Token economies are arguably the most recognizable form of an independent group contingency; however, there are other ways in which independent group contingencies may be implemented. For one, it is not always necessary to use secondary reinforcement such as tokens or points. Instead, students may receive the reward immediately after demonstrating the expected behavior. For example, a teacher could say that each student who completes a math assignment with 80% of problems correct gets to work on a math enrichment program on an iPad.

Another variation on an independent group contingency involves providing students with behavioral feedback when they do not meet behavioral expectations. For example, in a study by Axelrod (1973), each student's name was written on the board followed by the numbers 25 down through 1. When a student committed a rule infraction, the highest number was crossed off. The student then received the same number of tokens as the highest number remaining on the board. Although students lose points for breaking the rules within this type of system, it is important to note that they ultimately receive positive reinforcement based on the number of tokens remaining at the end of the day. We have unfortunately also seen many classrooms in which independent group contingencies are being used, but in which they are punishment based (e.g., "If anybody breaks the rules, he or she will receive a demerit"). As discussed in Chapter 4, the problem with this type of system is that students receive feedback regarding only what they should *not* do as opposed to what they *should* do. Independent group contingencies are most effective, however, if the expected behavior is clearly defined, the students believe they can successfully achieve the expectation, and the reward is delivered as promised.

Regardless of the way in which independent group contingencies are implemented, an important distinction is that the individual's reward is not dependent upon the actions of others. As such, independent group contingencies characteristically do not instill peer mediation for contingencies. One exception is a recent study by Dart, Radley, Battaglia, et al. (2016), who designed an independent group contingency that incorporated classroom competition (the classroom password). At the start of each class period, the teacher would announce a classroom password that would be said a certain number of times throughout the period, as well as a prize (e.g., 25 pieces of candy). The students were then responsible for placing an X on a sheet of paper each time the teacher uttered the password. The goal in having students keep a frequency count of the password was that it would help them to better attend to instruction. At the end of the period, the teacher collected the recording sheets and evaluated the accuracy of each student's estimate. Five students were then randomly selected from among those with correct answers to share the prize for the day.

Despite positive empirical evidence (see Table 6.1), independent group contingencies can be both time intensive and difficult to manage given the need to closely monitor the behavior of each student. For these reasons, it may be more practical to consider the use of either dependent or independent group contingencies, in which rewards are based on the behavior of an individual or group of students.

Dependent Group Contingency: "One for All"

Dependent group contingencies refer to situations in which the behavior of an individual, or a small group of individuals, determines the reward that all students receive. For example, if a group of students was misbehaving, and the teacher chose to reward the entire class when those particular students behaved appropriately, this would be considered a dependent group contingency. One of the key advantages of a dependent group contingency system is that it is highly efficient—that is, because it is necessary to only monitor the behavior of select students, this greatly reduces the requirements for data collection (Heering & Wilder, 2006).

One of the first things that must be determined when implementing a dependent group contingency is upon whose behavior the rewards will be based. Drabman, Spitalnik, and Spitalnik (1974) divided all students in a first-grade classroom into four smaller groups and then compared both the effectiveness and acceptability of three different types of dependent group contingencies. Regardless of condition, each student could earn up to 15 points during an observation period for exhibiting appropriate behaviors and each point could be exchanged for 1 minute of free time. Within the first condition, group reinforcement was based on the behavior of the lowest-performing student—that is, all members of the group received the number of points earned by the student who was most disruptive. Within the second condition, group reinforcement was based on the behavior of the highest-performing student. In other words, all members of the group received the number of points earned by the student who was least disruptive. Finally, within the third condition, group reinforcement was based on the behavior of a randomly selected student. Therefore, the teacher randomly selected one student's name from each group and all members of the group received the number of points earned by that student. Results suggested that there were no statistically significant differences with regard to changes in student behavior; however, clear preferences were noted across these three variants. Although students reported liking the system in which rewards were based on the behavior of the highest-performing student in the group, the teacher did not like this option. This was likely because it was possible for students to receive up to 15 minutes of free time when their individual behavior was very poor. The system that received the most favorable ratings from both the teacher and students, however, was that in which rewards were based on the behavior of a randomly selected student. Both the students and teacher found this system to be most equitable, and the teacher also reported that it required the least amount of time and effort.

Successful examples of dependent group contingency systems being used to improve student behavior can be found across both special and general education settings (see Table 6.3). In some cases, the selected students have been made known ahead of time so as to provide motivation. Hansen and Lignugaris/Kraft (2005), for example, implemented a dependent group contingency with junior high school students in a self-contained classroom for students with EBDs. After providing social skills training focused on making positive verbal statements to peers, the teacher explained to the class that they could earn a grab bag reward each day for demonstrating the target behavior. At the start of each day, the names of two students in the classroom would be selected at random and announced publicly. If both of these students made at least four positive statements to peers during the day, the entire class would be able to choose a reward at the end of the day.

One concern in making the selected students known ahead of time, however, is that this can put a high amount of pressure on those students whose behavior determines the reward for the rest of the class (Gresham & Gresham, 1982). These types of situations may result in aggression directed toward those students. To address the issue of pressure being placed on students, Skinner, Williams, and Neddenriep (2004) recommended keeping the person or group upon whose behavior the group reward was being determined a secret from the rest of the class. In a study by Heering and Wilder (2006), for example, one randomly selected row of students was observed each time that a chime sounded at predetermined intervals of approximately 12 minutes. If all students in that row were found to be on task, the class received a point for that interval. Feedback was not provided, however, until the end of the period when the teacher reported the percentage of intervals in which students were found to be on task. If students were on task during at least 75% of the observed intervals, the class received a reward. In this way, the class received feedback about their behavior overall; however, points (or the lack thereof) could not be traced back to particular students.

As another example, Williamson, Campbell-Whatley, and Lo (2009) worked with 10th-grade students in a special education resource classroom to improve overall levels of on-task behavior. The teacher first modeled what on-task behavior looked like and had students

TABLE 6.3. Empirical Studies Examining Use of Dependent and Interdependent Group Contingency Interventions

Study	Sample	Type of contingency	Design	Results
Campbell & Skinner (2004)	Sixth-grade general education classroom	Timely Transitions Game	AB design within one classroom	Large decrease in time spent transitioning
Donaldson, Vollmer, Krous, Downs, & Berard (2011)	Kindergarten general education classrooms	Good Behavior Game	Multiple baseline across five classrooms	Rates of inappropriate behavior decreased when Good Behavior Game implemented
Hawkins, Haydon, Denune, Larkin, & Fite (2015)	High school students in an alternative school for students with EBD	Randomized interdependent group contingency	ABAB design across three classrooms	Large improvements in percentage of students ready to begin class within first 5 minutes
Heering & Wilder (2006)	Third- and fourth-grade general education classrooms	Dependent	Multiple baseline across two classrooms	Improvements in on-task behavior across both classrooms
Kleinman & Saigh (2011)	Ninth-grade history class in urban setting	Good Behavior Game	ABAB within one classroom	Decreases in verbal disruption each time Good Behavior Game introduced
Kowalewicz & Coffee (2014)	K–4 general education classrooms	Interdependent with Mystery Motivator	ABAB changing criterion design across eight classrooms	Improvements in disruptive behavior across all eight classrooms + further reduction noted when criterion changed
Robichaux & Gresham (2014)	Students in grades 1–3 in general education	Interdependent with Mystery Motivator	Multiple baseline across three classrooms	Significant reductions in disruptive behavior across classrooms
Williamson, Campbell-Whatley, & Lo (2009)	10th-grade special education classroom	Dependent	ABAB across six students	Improvements in on-task behavior from baseline to intervention; however, clear reversal noted for only one student

(continued)

TABLE 6.3. *(continued)*

Study	Sample	Type of contingency	Design	Results
Wright & McCurdy (2011)	Kindergarten and fourth-grade students in general education	Compared Good Behavior Game and Caught Being Good Game	ABAC across two classrooms	Both variations effective in reducing disruptive behavior and increasing on-task behavior
Yarborough, Skinner, Lee, & Lemmons (2004)	Second-grade general education classroom	Timely Transitions Game	ABABAB design within one classroom	Large decrease in time spent transitioning

rehearse on-task behaviors while receiving feedback. Every 5 minutes the teacher would then visually scan the classroom and note which students were on task at that moment. At the end of the period, one student's name was pulled from a jar but not shared with the class. If that student met the criteria (four out of five intervals on task), the whole class received a reward (e.g., homework pass, free time).

As we discussed with independent group contingencies, it is important to distinguish between the reward-based dependent group contingencies discussed herein and punishment-based contingencies. Although research evidence supports administering group rewards based on the performance of select individuals, the consequences of punishing all students based on the performance of select individuals are unknown and likely dangerous. The movie *Full Metal Jacket* tells the story of Private Gomer Pyle, who is trying to finish basic training with the Marine Corps. When Private Pyle is caught with a jelly donut in his locker, the frustrated drill sergeant chooses to punish the rest of the group for Pyle's mistake. Although Pyle works harder as a result, he also frustrates his fellow soldiers so much that they retaliate against him. Obviously, this variant of the dependent group contingency would be unethical to use in schools and should not be employed. In this way, careless implementation of group contingencies can create dangerous, hostile situations where the safety of children can be put at risk.

Interdependent Group Contingency: "All for One"

Of the three group contingencies discussed in this chapter, the greatest amount of research evidence exists to support the interdependent group contingency. Within an interdependent group contingency, all students in a group must meet a criterion in order for all students to receive the reward. For example, a teacher may expect that all students enter the classroom, remove their coats and hats, hang up their bags, and be seated at a carpet in the front of the room in 90 seconds. If every student in the class meets that criterion, the entire class may earn an extra 2 minutes of computer time. Because all students are working together to earn a shared reward, there is believed to be greater motivation for students to support one another and work together as a team (Kelshaw-Levering et al., 2000).

Interdependent group contingencies have been successfully used within the literature to improve both student behavior and academic performance (see Table 6.3). In a study by Ling, Hawkins, and Weber (2011), for example, an interdependent group contingency was used to improve engagement during carpet time in a first-grade general education classroom. While seated at the carpet, the class could earn a smiley face if each student was sitting appropriately, keeping his or her hands and feet to him- or herself, speaking only when called on, and paying attention. In contrast, when used to improve academic performance, criteria are typically established in relation to students' work accuracy. Interdependent contingencies have been used to increase assignment grades (Popkin & Skinner, 2003), the percentage of passed quizzes (Sharp & Skinner, 2004), and even homework performance (Theodore et al., 2009).

There are several advantages to using an interdependent group contingency that is based on the behavior of the entire class. For one, it is easier for the teacher to manage because the decision regarding reinforcement is black and white—either everyone receives the reward or no one does. How one criterion is established for the group depends largely on the type of behavior targeted. If the goal is to increase a desired behavior, a minimum criterion for that behavior might be set for each student (e.g., all students must give one another at least two compliments during the day). As one example, Brantley and Webster (1993) established three prosocial expectations for a general education classroom of 25 fourth-grade students: pay attention and finish your work, get the teacher's permission before speaking, and stay in your seat without touching others. Every 45 minutes, a student received a checkmark next to his or her name if that student exhibited two or more prosocial behaviors during an interval. If every student had five of seven checkmarks on 4 of 5 days, the class was rewarded.

If the goal is to decrease an undesired behavior, a threshold could instead be established for each student's behavior (e.g., all students must receive fewer than two reminders to sit quietly) or for the class as a whole (e.g., the class must receive fewer than two reminders to sit quietly). When implementing interdependent group contingency interventions across eight elementary classrooms, teachers in a study by Kowalewicz and Coffee (2014) kept a running tally of disruptive behaviors exhibited by any student. If the total number of disruptive behaviors noted fell below the established criterion, the class received a reward.

In still other situations, however, it may make more sense to compute an average (e.g., the class lines up within 2 minutes on 80% of occasions). In implementing an interdependent group contingency in a self-contained classroom for students with emotional disturbance, Popkin and Skinner (2003) established different goals for performance across three subjects (spelling, math, English). If the average performance across all students met or exceeded the criterion (e.g., 80% accuracy), the class received a reward.

An additional advantage of classwide interdependent group contingencies is that a wider range of rewards can be utilized when reinforcement is administered to everyone. When implementing an independent group contingency, such as a token economy, the use of tangible or edible rewards is often preferred because these rewards can easily be distributed to some but not all students in the classroom. In contrast, it can be very challenging to limit some students' access to activity-based rewards. Providing only particular students with extra recess time or a pizza party, for example, could be difficult for a teacher to manage (Kelshaw-Levering et al., 2000). In addition, it is possible to think more broadly about what activity-based rewards might look like when rewards are made available to the entire class. Skinner and colleagues (1999), for example, offered such creative suggestions as allowing students to attend a special assembly to watch the principal kiss a pig or having teachers in formal attire serve students their lunches!

VARIATIONS ON GROUP CONTINGENCIES

Group contingencies are imminently flexible in that a variety of behaviors can be rewarded at a variety of times in a variety of ways. This next section describes some of the variations of group contingencies that have appeared in the research over the years.

The Good Behavior Game

One of the more popular variations on the interdependent group contingency is what has been called the Good Behavior Game (GBG; Barrish, Saunders, & Wolf, 1969). The GBG varies from a traditional interdependent group contingency in that it incorporates an additional competitive element in which teams of students compete against one another. When the GBG was first developed in 1969, the rules were as such. First, the teacher established several rules, including (1) everybody had to remain in their seat, (2) nobody could sit on top of his or her neighbor's desk, and (3) nobody could talk without permission. Next, the teacher divided the class into two teams. Each team was allotted 10 points, which were represented by 10 dashes on the board. If any member of one team committed an infraction, that teacher erased a dash mark from the board. Finally, at the end of the period, the team with the most points was awarded a prize. Although many subsequent studies have applied these game rules, there is the concern that members of the losing team may respond with anger or disappointment and problem behaviors motivated by jealousy could occur. As a result, other variants have allowed both teams to win if they meet a certain criterion. For example, any teams that have more than 5 points at the end of the day win a reward.

One notable application of the GBG was Kleinman and Saigh's (2011) study within a ninth-grade classroom in New York City. A new teacher with no classroom management training took over a class in the middle of the school year. According to the authors, "students reportedly refused to stay seated, frequently shouted at one another, cursed, and occasionally became involved in physical altercations with classmates. At one point, students reportedly screamed, cursed, and threw objects at the new teacher" (p. 96). When the game was implemented, the teacher divided the classroom into two teams, which were designed to be equal in terms of both number of students and number of students with a propensity to display problematic behaviors. Once the game started, the teacher would respond to a misbehavior by identifying the student as well as describing the infraction. The student then received a point on the board. The team with the fewest points at the end of the day received a piece of candy, and then the team with the fewest points at the end of the week received a pizza or cupcake party. During the implementation phases of the GBG, disruptive behaviors were observed to drop by 90%!

Positive Variations on the GBG

As originally designed by Barrish and colleagues (1969), the GBG is an interdependent group contingency involving response cost. Although response cost is a signal that is useful for communicating to students that they have committed an infraction, it also has some drawbacks. The first is that it fails to communicate to students what they *should* be doing. The second is that it may set up opportunities for students to argue. You probably can easily imagine erasing a point from a team and immediately hearing the claims from students that they did not commit the infraction! Perhaps the most pressing concern, however, is the retaliation that these approaches may bring. If one student was responsible for multiple infractions that caused a team to miss out on a prize, it is possible that others in the class may retaliate against that person. Given these concerns, an alternative approach involves recognizing student behaviors that are prosocial.

Across a small number of studies, the effectiveness of both the traditional GBG and a more reinforcement-based GBG variation have been directly compared. Wright and McCurdy (2011) designed the Caught Being Good Game, in which teachers assign points to teams whose students are following a particular expectation when a silent timer goes off. In a study by Tanol, Johnson, McComas, and Cote (2010), teams began with a clean slate but earned stars for following the rules. Any team that had three or more stars remaining at the end of the 10-minute period received a reward. Across both studies, traditional and positive GBG variants were found to be similarly effective in changing student behavior; however, teachers in the study by Tanol and colleagues (2010) reported a stronger preference for the reinforcement condition due to the fact that it was seen as fostering a more positive environment.

Over the years, variations of the GBG have been successfully used with students across different ages from kindergarten (Donaldson, Vollmer, Krous, Downs, & Berard, 2011) through ninth grade (Kleinman & Saigh, 2011). The GBG has also been used across a range of settings, including general education classes (e.g., Barrish et al., 1969), transitional classes of students with low achievement and highly disruptive behaviors (Johnson, Turner, & Konarski, 1978), specials (e.g., during library; Fishbein & Wasik, 1981), and even in the lunchroom (e.g., McCurdy, Lannie, & Barnabas, 2009). Perhaps most interesting, however, has been the diversity of behaviors targeted using the GBG. Studies include helping residents of a state hospital improve their work output (Lutzker & White-Blackburn, 1979); first- and second graders to increase their toothbrushing frequency (Swain, Allard, & Holborn, 1982); a group of Sudanese second graders to decrease aggression and out-of-seat behaviors (Saigh & Umar, 1983); three classes of high school students identified with emotional difficulties to reduce cursing, inappropriate verbalizations, and out-of-seat behaviors

(Salend, Reynolds, & Coyle, 1989); and upper elementary school students in physical education classes to display more prosocial behaviors during a game of volleyball (Patrick, Ward, & Crouch, 1998). Given demonstrated long-term effects on student development, the GBG has even been referred to as a "behavioral vaccine" (Embry, 2002).

Randomizing Intervention Components

Although group contingencies certainly have the power to make intervention implementation more efficient, there are also some potential limitations to utilizing the same behavioral expectations and rewards for all students in the class. For one, keeping the target behaviors consistent across time may cause problems. In some cases, students may improve with regard to the specific behaviors targeted in the intervention while their behavior in other areas worsens (McKissick, Hawkins, Lentz, Hailley, & McGuire, 2010). Additional problems may result from the use of a single behavioral criterion. If the criterion established for the group proves to be too challenging for particular students, these individuals may see the goal as unachievable and give up on trying altogether (McKissick et al., 2010). Finally, it may be challenging to identify rewards that are sufficiently reinforcing to all students in the group (Kelshaw-Levering et al., 2000). If particular students are not motivated to earn the available rewards, the effectiveness of the group contingency intervention may be significantly reduced. Given these potential limitations, some researchers have recommended the randomization of components within group contingency interventions.

Within the literature, the most popular randomized group contingency intervention has been termed the Mystery Motivator (Rhode, Jenson, & Reavis, 1992). Within the Mystery Motivator, rewards are made available only on certain days and what the actual reward is remains a mystery until it is earned. By not revealing the reward ahead of time, it is believed that students' motivation and interest will be peaked (Murphy, Theodore, Aloiso, Alric-Edwards, & Hughes, 2007). Typically, the classroom teacher marks particular days on a calendar with an "M" using a variable ratio reinforcement schedule. This is done either using an invisible marker or covering up all calendar squares with pieces of paper or Post-it notes. If the established goal for the day is either met or surpassed, that particular calendar square is revealed. If there is an "M" on that day, a reward is randomly selected. Often, cards indicating the available rewards have been drawn from a manila envelope with a large question mark on it (e.g., Kowalewicz & Coffee, 2014). If there is not an "M," the teacher provides the student(s) with positive verbal feedback for a job well-done.

Over the years, Mystery Motivator interventions involving independent, interdependent, and dependent group contingencies have been used with students of different ages and abilities to target a range of outcomes. Successful examples can be found in preschool (e.g., Murphy et al., 2007), elementary (e.g., Robichaux & Gresham, 2014), and high school (e.g., Schanding & Sterling-Turner, 2010). In addition, the Mystery Motivator intervention has been shown to improve both behavioral (e.g., Murphy et al., 2007; Robichaux & Gresham, 2014) and academic (e.g., Madaus, Kehle, Madaus, & Bray, 2003) outcomes.

Several other examples can be found within the literature, however, in which multiple contingency components have been randomized. Group contingency interventions have commonly used different jars (e.g., McKissick et al., 2010), shoe boxes (e.g., Popkin & Skinner, 2003), or envelopes (e.g., Schanding & Sterling-Turner, 2010) in order to randomize the different intervention components. In implementing such an intervention in a second-grade general education classroom, McKissick and colleagues (2010) randomized the target behaviors (e.g., out-of-seat behavior, talking out, disrespect), behavioral criteria (i.e., one to four behavioral occurrences), and available rewards (e.g., small tangibles, free time at the end of class) and found notable increases in student engagement as a result. Popkin and Skinner (2003) used a similar type of intervention to improve performance on in-class assignments in a middle school self-contained classroom. In this case, randomizing the performance criterion (e.g., 90% accuracy in spelling) and rewards (e.g., extra computer time, playing games) helped to improve the daily grades obtained by students in spelling and mathematics.

Jones, Boon, Fore, and Bender (2008) modified the basic dependent group contingency to create the Mystery Hero intervention. The goal of the intervention was to decrease the number of verbally disrespectful behaviors occurring in a middle school resource classroom. At the start of each period, the classroom teacher would randomly select the name of one student (i.e., the Mystery Hero) and place this name in an envelope. In a second envelope, the teacher would place a randomly selected reward for the day (i.e., the Mystery Reward). If at the end of the period, the Mystery Hero had reduced his or her number of inappropriate verbalizations from the previous day, the entire class would receive the Mystery Reward and the Mystery Hero would receive public verbal reinforcement (e.g., "Jose did such a nice job of speaking respectfully to each of you today that he has earned everyone in the class a homework pass"). However, if at the end of the period the goal was not met, no public statement was made. Rather, the teacher met privately with the student to provide feedback and encouragement regarding future behavior.

Kelshaw-Levering and colleagues (2000) implemented an ABACBC design in order to investigate the effectiveness of randomizing different components of a group contingency intervention. During the B phase, rewards were randomly selected from a jar, as is typical in a Mystery Motivator intervention. During the C phase, four different jars were used in order to randomize all components of the intervention. Slips of paper in the first jar were labeled with different target behaviors of interest and slips in the second jar were labeled either "individual" or "group" to indicate the type of contingency in place. When an individual contingency was in place, a slip was drawn from the third jar, which contained the names of all of the students in the class. Finally, the fourth jar contained slips of paper indicating the different rewards available.

The Timely Transitions Game

As discussed in Chapter 3, one time of the day that problem behavior is more likely to occur is during a transition (Arlin, 1979). This is because transitions are times when expectations for students are more ambiguous and when less supervision is typically afforded. Establishing a step-by-step routine for what students should do during transitions therefore removes any ambiguity and makes the expectations for student behavior clear and predictable. To address problems with transition, Campbell and Skinner (2004) created a variation on an interdependent group contingency, called the Timely Transitions Game (TTG). First, the teacher explains the expectations for the students during the transition and posts these in the front of the classroom. Next, appropriate transition behaviors are practiced and students receive corrective feedback if necessary. Once the expectations are well understood, the teacher explains that the class can earn a reward if the amount of time that it takes to transition is equal to, or less than, a criterion that will be randomly drawn each day. During each day of intervention, the teacher then times the students to see how long the transition took. If the actual time spent transitioning is no more than the randomly drawn criterion, the class receives 1 point toward a larger reward. In a study by Yarborough, Skinner, Lee, and Lemmons (2004), daily points came in the form of letters, which could be used to spell out a reward (i.e., P-A-R-T-Y). Although research on this type of intervention is somewhat limited, studies have reported substantially faster and more orderly transitions across elementary (e.g., Yarborough et al., 2004), middle (e.g., Campbell & Skinner, 2004), and high school (e.g., Hawkins, Haydon, Denune, Larkin, & Fite, 2015) settings.

FINAL CONSIDERATIONS: FIXING PROBLEMS AND FADING THE INTERVENTION

Having described the many different ways in which group contingencies may be structured in the classroom, we now turn to discuss how to troubleshoot problems that may arise as well as how to fade a group contingency intervention over time.

Troubleshooting

Although group contingency interventions may be flexibly constructed in order to best meet the demands and characteristics of your local setting, unanticipated problems may arise in the process of implementation. Within this section, we draw your attention to a few of the more common problems that may surface and offer suggestions for how these problems may be addressed.

Problem 1: The Criterion Set Is Not Appropriate

Regardless of the type of contingency system implemented, the criterion for gaining or losing points needs to be not too easy and not too hard. Finding this "Goldilocks point," however, can be a challenge for teachers. Our suggestion is that teachers always first err on the easy side. If students find something new that is too difficult, they are apt to give up quickly. Once students have experienced some success with the system, the bar can then be raised concerning behavioral expectations. If implementing an interdependent group contingency, it is important to keep in mind that it may sometimes be difficult for students to achieve the criterion given the composition of the teams—that is, teachers may accidently make the teams unfair by including too many students who display inappropriate behaviors in one group. It is important that all students feel like they have a chance to earn a reward, and it may be useful to ensure that teams are balanced with regard to students who typically behave as expected and those who may do so less frequently.

Problem 2: Individual Students Seem to Be Sabotaging the Group Reward

We all know that there are some students who may find acting out reinforcing—and this does not necessarily change just because a group contingency is put into place. In fact, some students may even seem to enjoy the fact that their acting-out behavior caused their teams to lose points. These challenges may occur frequently, but there are several ways of addressing individual students who are trying to ruin it for the group. For example, if one student commits too many rule violations, that student could be excluded from the reinforcer if his or her team won that week (Medland & Stachnik, 1972). The problem, however, with excluding a disruptive student from the contingency altogether is that these are often the students who most need behavioral supports in place. Therefore, another alternative is to place the student who is disrupting the intervention on their own independent group contingency. The student should be eligible to receive some type of reward—though this will sometimes look different from the larger class reward—and should be able to rejoin his or her team with improved behavior. Third, rather than deducting points for infractions, the focus of the intervention could instead be shifted to reinforcing appropriate behavior. It has been suggested that students are more likely to band together to encourage one another when appropriate behaviors are targeted (Skinner et al., 1999).

Problem 3: Students Are Retaliating against One Another

As noted earlier in this chapter, the use of dependent or interdependent contingencies may result in a high amount of pressure being placed on students (Tingstrom, Sterling-Turner, & Wilczynski, 2006). For example, a student who loses points for the rest of the group or class may become the subject of the wrath of other students. There are two potential ways to handle this problem. First, the teacher may provide explicit instruction to the other students in the class regarding how to respond to an offending student if another student causes the rest of the group to lose points. For example, rather than yelling at the student or groaning about the loss of points, students could be taught to provide corrective feedback for past behavior and encouragement for future behavior to their classmates. Second, as noted above, teachers may also apply a rule whereby if one team member is responsible for a certain number of points, he or she would not be counted as part of the team that day.

Problem 4: Other Students Feel That It Is Unfair to Be Losing Out on a Reward When One Student Misbehaves

This last problem is more philosophical than the other problems are, and really has to do with our understanding of fairness. All students deserve the things that they need. In general, this refers to a safe place to learn, the opportunity to receive an excellent education, and activities that promote their physical, cognitive, and social growth. When we hear this concern, we often have to ask ourselves whether the child has really been harmed by not receiving an extra pizza party, an extra 5 minutes of recess, or an extra homework pass. In such situations, we have to say that the answer is no. However, if the reinforcer is something that the students need—such as access to any part of the curriculum or opportunities to move and exercise—then the intervention should be considered unethical and should not be implemented.

Using Randomization to Solve Multiple Problems

Earlier, we discussed how randomization could be used to enhance group contingencies. They can also be used to solve several problems that may crop up. For example, some students may not find the group reward equally motivating. In those circumstances, it is appropriate to utilize a Mystery Motivator or to randomize the reinforcers using envelopes, jars, or invisible ink (Kelshaw-Levering et al., 2000). As we mentioned earlier, there may also be some students for whom a predetermined criterion is too high. To address this problem, many teachers choose to randomize the criterion. For example, a teacher may have an envelope with the percentage of correct responses that the whole class needs to average to receive a reward. In the envelope are numbers between 50 and 80%. This way, students know that there is a chance that the criterion is accessible to them. (Note: As the class begins to show improvement, some of the lower numbers can be taken out of the envelope and replaced with higher numbers!) Randomizing the criterion may also help those students who stop working when the criterion is met. For example, a student may realize that he or she has already completed 60% of the problems on a worksheet and may decide that he or she does not need to do any more work. If the criterion is unknown to the student, and the possibility of a 90% criterion is in the envelope, the student would likely continue working to make sure he or she does not fall behind the criterion.

Fading the Intervention

Ideally, students would come to class prepared to work and would need no extrinsic behavioral supports; however, we know that that is not always reality. Group contingencies can be incredibly helpful in bringing student behavior to an expected level of functioning; however, in the long term, we would prefer for students to be able to display appropriate behavior without external supports. In order to move toward this expectation, we need to consider options for fading these interventions.

When considering how to fade an intervention, it is worth revisiting what we learned about schedules of reinforcement in Chapter 2. When we are first learning a new behavior, reinforcement needs to occur frequently or even continuously. This way, we learn quickly what behaviors will be rewarded and which ones will not. However, creating behaviors that are sustained requires the use of variable reinforcement schedules whereby the behavior is reinforced less frequently. Thus, having students work for larger rewards—but providing those larger rewards less frequently—may help students begin to regulate their own behaviors. Rather than giving students an opportunity for reinforcement every 5 minutes, for example, a teacher may slowly increase that interval to 6, 7, or even 10 minutes. The slower the increase, the more likely students will not notice the difference.

Another approach involves raising the criterion over time. When starting a new intervention, teachers want students to be successful, and they may set a low bar so that students "win" the game. For example, a teacher may initially determine that the class will earn a reward if 75% of students earn 75% or more on their homework assignments. After the class consistently meets that criterion, however, the teacher may make the criterion slightly more challenging by requiring that 75% of students earn 80% or more on their homework assignments. Again, a slow increase in the criterion will again be less detectable, but will help students to rely less on the intervention over time.

A final option may involve increasing the number of target behaviors or settings over time. In this way, the expectations for student behavior gradually become more challenging and students must therefore put forth greater effort in order to earn established rewards. For example, a group contingency intervention may initially focus on ensuring that the students sit quietly during whole-class instruction; however, once this goal has been achieved, important classroom behaviors such as asking questions and participating in group discussion may be added to the list of behavioral expectations. In addition, once success with the intervention is demonstrated during whole-class instruction, the group contingency could be extended to other instructional periods and settings during the day as well.

CONCLUSIONS

When we started our discussion of reinforcement in Chapter 4, we highlighted a fairly simple contingency:

> If Beatrice's desk is clean at the end of the day, Beatrice will receive a homework pass from the teacher.

Because this is a book about managing entire classrooms of students, however, we want to think about developing group contingencies that are both efficient and able to support a range of students at the same time. It is probably easiest to invoke a group contingency that can be applied in one fell swoop, such as the following:

> If everybody in the class turns in a math assignment with 80% accuracy, the whole group gets a Frisbee.

However, you can probably identify many problems that may arise:

- What if some students can't do the assignment?
- What if a student fails to complete the assignment with 80% accuracy and ends up causing everybody to lose their Frisbee?

- What if students don't care about Frisbees?
- What if the teacher does not want to track the behavior of all students?
- What if students work hard on their math, but slough off on their other assignments?
- What if students stop working after they get 80% correct?

Thankfully, there is not just one way to implement a group contingency, but many different options and configurations available (see Table 6.4 on page 120 for a comparison and Coach Cards 6.1–6.5 for implementation guidance). Your challenge is finding the one that will work best in your own setting. Keep in mind, however, that although group contingencies provide an effective means of reducing student misbehavior and allow a teacher to spend more time on instruction, teaching students behavioral skills is still critical. Group contingencies are methods to support student behavior, but do not provide a substitute for teaching. One method that has useful implications for improving both behavioral and academic skills involves self-management—a process that helps to internalize the behaviors that we want students to demonstrate. This is the focus of the next chapter.

TABLE 6.4. Comparing Implementation of Various Group Contingency Interventions

Steps	Whole-class contingency	Good Behavior Game	Caught Being Good Game	Good Behavior Game with reinforcement
Identify the target behaviors.	Usually only positive reinforcement	Response cost only—designed to reduce problem behaviors	Positive reinforcement only	Response cost and positive reinforcement
Determine whose behavior rewards will be based upon.	Individuals randomly drawn from a "hat"	Anybody in the class on one of two teams	Anybody in the class on one of two teams	Anybody in the class on one of two teams
Determine criteria for receiving prizes.	If everybody whose name is drawn from the hat has met the criteria	A team has a certain number of points remaining on the board. Or: The team with the most points	A team has a certain number of points remaining on the board. Or: The team with the most points	A team has a certain number of points remaining on the board. Or: The team with the most points
Determine whether any components will be randomized.	*Reminder*: For all interventions, both rewards and criterion may be randomized!			
Divide the classroom into teams.	The whole class is typically the team in these situations.	Divide the class into two equal teams.	Divide the class into two equal teams.	Divide the class into two equal teams.
Determine the criteria for earning and/or losing points.	Criterion may be assignment completion, assignment accuracy, or ability to ignore one student's problematic behavior.	Any infraction results in a point loss.	When a random interval timer goes off, the teacher looks to see whether all students are meeting the expectation and awards points accordingly.	A mixture of random interval timer and point loss for infractions.
Determine time period for the game.	*Reminder*: We recommend starting with a 15-minute time period. Then work your way to periods of the day that are especially difficult.			

COACH CARD 6.1. Steps in Introducing a Group Contingency with Response Cost

Step	Sample dialogue
Provide rationale for introducing group contingency intervention.	*Class, today we are going to play a game. This game is going to help decrease the amount of time we spend talking while we work on our assignments. It is important that we cut down on the amount of time that is spent talking because it is taking away from the time that we have available to learn.*
Establish target behaviors and provide rationale for why they are important.	*There are a few particular behaviors that have become problematic in the classroom. These behaviors are problematic because they make it difficult to learn at the same time. These are the behaviors that we should not see:* *1. Being out of our seat without permission.* *2. Having other materials on our desks.* *3. Talking when we need to be working silently.*
Explain how teams/targets will be established.	**Interdependent GC:** *At the start of each week, I will divide you into three teams. You will work with your team to follow the rules each day.* **Dependent GC:** *Each day, I will randomly select the name of a student (or group of students) out of this jar. This student will be the Mystery Student for the day* **or** *this team will be the Mystery Team for the day.*
Describe procedures for earning points.	**Interdependent GC:** *Each day I will put 10 dashes on the board for each team at the start of the period. If I see a member of your team breaking one of the class rules, your team will lose one dash.* **Dependent GC:** *Each time that this timer goes off, I will look to see whether the Mystery Student/Team is breaking any of the class rules. If so, the entire class will lose one dash.*
Explain criteria for receiving prizes.	**Interdependent GC:** *At the end of the day, each team that has at least seven dashes remaining will earn the daily reward: an extra 5 minutes to play on the playground.* **Dependent GC:** *At the end of the day, if there are at least seven dashes remaining, the entire class will earn the daily reward: an extra 5 minutes to play on the playground.*

COACH CARD 6.2. Treatment Integrity Checklist for Implementing a Group Contingency Intervention with Response Cost

Teacher: _____ Date: _____

Observer: _____ Activity: _____

STEPS IN IMPLEMENTING A GROUP CONTINGENCY INTERVENTION WITH RESPONSE COST

☐ Review behavioral expectations and goal for earning reward.

☐ Select student/team (**if implementing dependent group contingency**).

☐ Signal to students that game is about to begin.

☐ Begin the interval timer (if applicable).

☐ Remove tokens when violations are observed.

☐ When violations are observed, explicitly remind the student what he or she can do to earn tokens.

☐ Determine whether the goal is met for the day.

☐ Administer reward if earned.

Total number of steps completed =

Percentage of steps completed =

Step	Sample dialogue
Provide rationale for introducing group contingency intervention.	*Class, today we are going to play a game. This game is going to help increase the amount of time that we spend quietly working on our assignments. Having a quiet work environment is important because it allows other students to focus and to get more of their work done.*
Establish target behaviors and provide rationale for why they are important.	*There are a few ways that you can demonstrate to me that you are working quietly. These include:* *1. Facing forward in your seat.* *2. Raising your hand if you need to ask a question.* *3. Keeping your eyes focused on your work.*
Explain how teams/targets will be established.	**Interdependent GC:** *At the start of each week, I will divide you into three teams. You will work with your team to earn points each day.* **Dependent GC:** *Each day, I will randomly select the name of a student (or group of students) out of this jar. This student will be the Mystery Student for the day* **or** *this team will be the Mystery Team for the day.*
Describe procedures for earning points.	**Interdependent GC:** *If I see a member of your team demonstrating one of the expected behaviors, your team will earn a point.* **Dependent GC:** *Each time that this timer goes off, I will look to see whether the Mystery Student/Team is demonstrating the expected behaviors. If so, the entire class will earn a point.*
Explain criteria for receiving rewards.	**Interdependent GC:** *At the end of the day, each team that has more than 10 points will earn the daily reward: an extra 5 minutes to play on the playground.* **Dependent GC:** *At the end of the day, if there are at least 10 points on the board, the entire class will earn the daily reward: an extra 5 minutes to play on the playground.*

COACH CARD 6.4. Treatment Integrity Checklist for Implementing a Group Contingency Intervention with Reinforcement

Teacher: _____   Date: _____

Observer: _____   Activity: _____

STEPS IN IMPLEMENTING A GROUP CONTINGENCY INTERVENTION WITH REINFORCEMENT

☐ Review behavioral expectations and goal for earning reward.

☐ Select student/team (**if implementing dependent group contingency**).

☐ Signal to students that game is about to begin.

☐ Begin the interval timer (if applicable).

☐ Deliver points when expected behavior observed.

☐ When delivering points, explicitly indicate what the student(s) has/have done to earn the point.

☐ When violations are observed, explicitly remind the students what they can do to earn points.

☐ Determine whether the goal is met for the day.

☐ Administer reward if earned.

Total number of steps completed =

Percentage of steps completed =

COACH CARD 6.5. Steps in Introducing the Good Behavior Game

Step	Sample dialogue
Provide rationale for introducing the Good Behavior Game.	*Class, today we are going to play a game. This game is going to help increase the amount of time that we spend quietly working on our assignments. Having a quiet work environment is important because it allows other students to focus and to get more of their work done.*
Establish target behaviors and provide rationale for why they are important.	*There are a few ways that you can demonstrate to me that you are working quietly. These include:* *1. Facing forward in your seat.* *2. Raising your hand if you need to ask a question.* *3. Keeping your eyes focused on your work.*
Explain how teams will be established.	*At the start of each week, I will divide you into two teams. You will work with your team to earn points each day.*
Describe procedures for earning points.	*If I see a member of your team demonstrating one of the expected behaviors, your team will earn a point.*
(Optional) Describe procedures for losing points.	*If a member of one team violates one of these class rules—profanity, touching another person, or yelling out without permission—that team will lose 1 point.*
Explain criteria for receiving rewards.	*At the end of the day, each team that has more than 10 points will earn the daily reward: an extra 5 minutes to play on the playground.*

CHAPTER 7

Self-Management

Up until this point in the book, we have focused on intervention strategies that are directed by the classroom teacher. Whether providing behavioral feedback, delivering tokens, or managing a group contingency system, primary responsibility for both intervention development and implementation is retained by adults in the classroom. This clearly makes sense from a practical standpoint, in that the classroom teacher is used to a managerial role—managing lesson plans, assessments, individual personalities, and even the classroom environment—on a daily basis. Philosophically speaking, however, it has been argued that the use of teacher-directed interventions ultimately means that student behavior remains externally—rather than internally—managed (Gross & Wojnilower, 1984). As a result, students may not learn the skills needed to regulate their own behavior in future contexts.

Given these concerns, one potential alternative involves shifting responsibility for intervention components from the teacher to the student. Within the literature, the term "self-management" has been used to refer generally to those interventions in which students are expected to play a more active role in the modification of their own behavior (Briesch & Briesch, 2016). Those interventions falling under the umbrella of self-management, however, have been found to vary widely with regard to what components are included and how procedures are carried out. In fact, in a review of the literature, Briesch and Chafouleas (2009) identified a total of 16 different intervention configurations across 30 studies of behavioral self-management.

Despite variations in the literature, the basis of all self-management interventions is *self-monitoring*. Outside of the classroom, many of us engage in self-monitoring on a regular basis. If you have ever used an activity-tracking device to record the number of steps you took, or a food journal to keep track of what you have eaten, you have engaged in self-monitoring. Self-monitoring involves systematically observing and recording instances of a predetermined target behavior. When applied to classroom situations, students might be asked to mark down each time they make an off-topic comment during classroom instruction or each time that they raise their hand appropriately. In order to build a more compre-

126

hensive self-management intervention, this basic self-monitoring component is often supplemented with additional components such as an evaluation of performance, assessment of rating accuracy, administration of points or rewards, and/or monitoring of performance over time (Briesch & Briesch, 2016).

Different explanations have been put forth as to why self-management may be effective in changing behavior. One explanation is that keeping track of one's behavior may lead to behavior change due to what has been called the principle of reactivity (Nelson & Hayes, 1981). Think about how your teaching changes when your supervisor comes in to watch you. Most of us become more aware of the things that we are doing well, as well as the things that we are probably supposed to be doing but do not do. This refers to the reactivity phenomenon, whereby a behavior changes when somebody watches it. Usually when we think about reactivity, we think about individuals acting differently in the presence of observers. However, reactivity can also occur if you are the only one in the room—that is, the simple act of paying closer attention to your own behavior can cause it to change. McFall (1970) described this phenomenon by explaining that "nearly everyone has had the experience of becoming self-conscious about his behavior and, as a result, experiencing a change in that behavior. For example, if a person's attention is drawn to the way he walks, holds his hands, or swings a golf club, it often makes it difficult for him to perform these activities naturally" (p. 140).

Kanfer (1970), on the other hand, offered a different explanation for how self-management works, depicting the process as requiring more conscious participation on the part of the individual. Within this model, the individual receives feedback about his or her behavior through self-monitoring, self-evaluation, and self-reinforcement phases. After observing one's own behavior in the self-monitoring phase, this observation is compared to some preestablished goal or standard in the self-evaluation phase. Depending on whether one's actual behavior exceeds or falls below the goal or standard, either self-reinforcement or punishment occurs in the final phase. This self-reinforcement or punishment then plays a role in changing future behavior. For example, within the classroom, a goal set for a particularly mobile student might be that he or she should not get out of his or her seat more than twice during a class period. After receiving some training, the student keeps a tally of each time that he or she gets out of his or her seat (i.e., self-monitoring). At the end of the period, the student compares the tally with the preestablished goal of two instances of out-of-seat behavior (i.e., self-evaluation). If his or her tally falls at or below two for the period, the student takes a short motor break before returning to his or her work (i.e., self-reinforcement). If the motor breaks are sufficiently reinforcing, it is believed that the student will be more motivated to remain in his or her seat in the future.

IMPLEMENTING SELF-MANAGEMENT TO SUPPORT STUDENT BEHAVIOR

Beginning in the 1970s, many studies were published supporting the effectiveness of self-management in changing student behavior in school-based settings. In order to synthesize this ever-expanding literature base, several systematic reviews and meta-analyses have recently been conducted of the self-management literature. Roughly 20 years ago, Stage and Quiroz (1997) highlighted the effectiveness of self-management in their meta-analysis of behavioral interventions designed to decrease disruptive behavior in classroom settings. Self-management was found to be one of the most effective interventions conducted in public education settings, with a reduction in problem behavior of nearly 1 full standard deviation across 30 single-case- and group-designed studies. More recently, meta-analytic reviews have found similarly strong effects for those studies conducted in elementary general education settings (Busacca, Anderson, & Moore, 2015; percentage of nonoverlapping data = 90.49%) as well as for those single-case studies conducted more generally irrespective of grade level or setting (Briesch & Briesch, 2016; percentage of all nonoverlapping data = 88.70%, phi = 0.93).

Most of these reviews have largely focused on the effectiveness of self-management interventions when carried out with individual students. However, there are situations in which the same problem behavior has been identified for multiple students in a similar setting. Here, it is more efficient to apply the same strategy to the group rather than create multiple individualized plans that may compete for already limited resources such as instructional time (Mitchem & Young, 2001). Use of self-management as a classwide intervention also affords the added benefit of teaching skills related to independence and personal responsibility to *all* children rather than solely those children identified as having particular behavioral needs (Miller, Strain, Boyd, Jarzynka, & McFetridge, 1993). Given that meta-analytic reviews have found strong effects both for students with disabilities and also their typically developing peers across both general and special education settings (Briesch & Briesch, 2016; Busacca et al., 2015), these findings suggest great promise for the use of self-management at the classwide level.

Empirical evidence in support of the use of classwide self-management extends back to the 1970s as well (e.g., Ballard & Glynn, 1975; Glynn & Thomas, 1974; Glynn, Thomas, & Shee, 1973); however, there has been renewed interest in this intervention approach in recent years (Briesch et al., 2013; Chafouleas, Hagermoser Sanetti, Jaffery, & Fallon, 2011; Denune et al., 2015; Hoff & Ervin, 2013; Trevino-Maack, Kamps, & Wills, 2015). As outlined in Table 7.1, studies have been conducted across diverse populations to target a range of behaviors using various procedures. Given that there is not one "right" way to implement a self-management intervention, our aim in this chapter is to highlight the range of applications that do exist so that you may be able to design an intervention configuration that best fits your situation. We begin by describing some of the important considerations that go into designing any self-management intervention and then follow with specific discussion of those modifications that can be used to enhance feasibility of implementation at the classwide level (see also Coach Cards 7.1 and 7.2).

Is Self-Management Right for Everyone?

The first question that you may be asking yourself is whether self-management is an intervention that would be appropriate for your particular students. Over the years, self-management interventions have been shown to be effective in improving the behavior of a

TABLE 7.1. Empirical Studies Examining Use of Classwide Self-Management

Study	Sample	Intervention	Design	Results
Briesch, Hemphill, & Daniels (2013)	Seventh-grade students in general education	CWSM + DGC	Multiple baseline across two classrooms	Moderate improvements in on-task behavior
Chafouleas, Hagermoser Sanetti, Jaffrey, & Fallon (2012)	Eighth-grade students in general education	CWSM + IGC	Multiple baseline across three classrooms with embedded changing criterion design	Large decrease in off-task behavior; less notable improvements in engagement and preparedness
Denune et al. (2015)	Sixth-grade students with EBD	Compared IGC and IGC + CWSM	ABCBC design within one classroom	CWSM did not enhance effectiveness of IGC alone
Hoff & Ervin (2013)	Second-grade students in general education	CWSM	Multiple baseline design across three classes	Moderate decrease in off-task behavior
Mitchem, Young, West, & Benyo (2001)	Seventh-grade students in general education	CWPASM	Multiple baseline design across three classes	Large increases in on-task behavior
Trevino-Maack, Kamps, & Wills (2015)	10th- and 11th-grade students in remedial reading course	CWSM + TE	ABAB design across three classes	Moderate improvements in active engagement

Note. CWPASM, classwide peer-assisted self-management; DGC, dependent group contingency; IGC, interdependent group contingency; TE, token economy.

wide range of students. First, although self-management interventions have most commonly been employed with students in the late elementary grades, they have been shown to be equally effective across a wide range of age and grade levels (Briesch & Briesch, 2016). In fact, successful examples can be found ranging from the preschool (Connell, Carta, Lutz, et al., 1993) to the high school (Trevino-Mack et al., 2015) level. Although the core elements of a self-management intervention (e.g., training in behavioral definitions, self-observation, self-recording) remain consistent regardless of the student's age, the way in which these intervention steps are carried out must be made developmentally appropriate. For example, within early education settings, it is likely that self-management components will need to be more heavily adult directed given the developmental skills of young children (Holland, Malmberg, & Gimpel Peacock, 2017). As we move through this chapter, we therefore highlight specific ways in which self-management interventions may be adapted for use with students at different grade levels.

In addition, self-management interventions have also been found to be effective for both students with and without exceptionalities. One population with whom self-management interventions have frequently been used is those students with ADHD. A recent meta-analysis found self-management interventions to be highly effective in both increasing appropriate and decreasing inappropriate behaviors among students with ADHD (Reid, Trout, & Schartz, 2005). Additionally, DuPaul, Eckert, and Vilardo (2012) found that cognitive behavioral interventions involving self-management strategies produced significantly larger effect sizes (effect size = 3.31) than those interventions involving basic reinforcement or punishment (effect size = 2.40) when used with students with ADHD. Multiple self-management studies have also been conducted with students with autism spectrum disorder (ASD). In their meta-analytic review of 11 studies conducted with students with ASD, Lee, Simpson, and Shogren (2007) found that self-management interventions were effective in promoting appropriate behavior and that effectiveness did not differ as a function of student age (e.g., preschool vs. school age), target behavior (e.g., increase appropriate, decrease inappropriate), intervention components (e.g., self-monitoring vs. self-management), or materials utilized (e.g., paper and pencil vs. tokens). Although these results suggest great promise for supporting classrooms of students with diverse needs, it is important to keep in mind that the majority of studies to date with students with disabilities have been conducted in special education settings. Given the suggestion that self-management may be an effective way of promoting the inclusion of students with disabilities, it appears that more research is needed to examine effectiveness in general education settings.

What Behaviors Can Students Self-Monitor?

When it comes to what behaviors can be targeted within a self-management intervention, most of the evidence that we have exists for a limited number of target behaviors. Findings have been consistent across meta-analytic reviews, with the overwhelming majority of studies targeting individual students focused on increasing on-task behavior and a smaller percentage focused on decreasing problem behaviors (Briesch & Briesch, 2016; Bruhn, McDaniel, & Kreigh, 2015; Busacca et al., 2015). When applied classwide, self-management has been shown to increase on-task behavior when used across both general (e.g., Briesch et al., 2013) and special education settings (e.g., Denune et al., 2015). Some research also exists to suggest that asking students to monitor their on-task behavior may also lead to significant improvement in work completion (Merrett & Blundell, 1982). In addition, successful examples of the use of self-management to reduce disruptive behaviors have also been noted when students have been taught to monitor behaviors such as inappropriate verbalizations (e.g., Davies & Witte, 2000) and rule-following behavior (e.g., Hoff & Ervin, 2013).

Although classwide interventions have focused largely on engagement, disruption, and work completion, a wider range of behaviors have been targeted when implementing self-management as an individualized intervention. In a study by Stahmer and Schreibman (1992), for example, self-management was used to teach children diagnosed with ASD appropriate play behaviors (e.g., driving a toy car instead of sucking on it or throwing it). Whereas Strain, Kohler, Storey, and Danko (1994) taught students with ASD how to initiate peer interactions and appropriately respond to requests from peers, Sainato, Goldstein, and Strain (1992) used self-management to teach preschool students facilitative strategies (e.g., how to invite a friend to play) that they could use to increase the participation of students with ASD in play activities. Across both studies, strategy training alone did not lead to increases in strategy usage; however, the introduction of self-recording (i.e., having the child mark yes or no, depending on whether a particular strategy was used successfully) resulted in significant increases in strategy usage across both studies. General education teachers may therefore consider the use of self-management strategies to support the generalization of social skills taught in the classroom.

What Should Self-Recording Look Like?

Just as there are many different possible target behaviors for use within a self-management intervention, there are also numerous ways that those target behaviors may be recorded. Specifically, what self-management looks like can differ substantially depending on the population and target behavior of interest. Selecting the best means of recording first involves determining what about the behavior is of the most interest. As we discuss in the next chapter, behaviors can generally be classified as either events (i.e., clear beginning and end, of similar duration) or states (i.e., semicontinuous, difficult to count). Because event behaviors are ones that can be counted, the most straightforward means of recording is to provide students with a blank form such as the one provided in Figure 7.1 (see also Form 7.1 for a blank form*), and to ask them to keep a tally of how frequently the behavior occurs. As one example, in a study conducted with high school students at risk for dropping out of school (Gottman & McFall, 1972), students were taught to self-record instances of speaking during class discussion in order to promote classroom engagement. One of the advantages of frequency counts is that they are easy for students to learn and useful when the rate of behavior is of interest (Foster, Laverty-Finch, Gizzo, & Osantowski, 1999).

In some cases, however, what may be of interest is whether the behavior occurs rather than how frequently it occurs. If you think over the course of a school day for a few minutes, you can probably easily come up with a list of expectations for students that they simply either meet or don't meet: arriving to class on time, having necessary materials, turning in homework, writing down assignments. For these types of behaviors, keeping a frequency count would not make sense because it is simply a dichotomous (i.e., yes or no) decision. Instead, such yes or no behaviors may best be recorded using a checklist. For example, Wood, Murdock, and Cronin (2002) worked with four middle school students who had been expelled from their home school due to significant disciplinary issues. These students were provided with a 10-item checklist that they were to complete once during an academic period. The checklist items spanned a range of appropriate academic behaviors, including whether the student followed the teacher's directions and whether he or she participated in classroom discussions. An example of a self-monitoring form utilizing a checklist format is provided in Figure 7.2 (see also Form 7.2 for a blank form).

---

*All blank forms appear at the ends of chapters, following the coaching cards.

Name: Joanne   Date: April 12

Activity: Social Studies   Time: 10:30–11:15

Instructions: Mark an X in the box each time that you:					
#1: Call out without raising your hand			**#2:** Talk to a neighbor without permission		
X	X	X	X	X	
X	X				

FIGURE 7.1. Self-monitoring frequency of disruptive behaviors.

Name: Joanne   Date: April 15

Activity: Social Studies   Time: 10:30–11:30

Did I . . . ?	Yes	No
Arrive to class on time?	✓	
Bring my notebook to class?		✓
Bring appropriate writing instruments?	✓	
Hand in my completed homework?		✓
Write down the homework assignment?	✓	

Number of Yes Checks __3__ ÷ Total Checklist Items __5__ = __60__ %

FIGURE 7.2. Self-monitoring dichotomous behaviors.

When the behavior(s) of interest are ones that cannot easily be counted or checked off, however, alternative ways of evaluating the behavior(s) must be used. Perhaps the most popular method of recording state behaviors such as classroom engagement has been through the use of interval recording. As we discuss further in Chapter 8, interval recording involves observing and recording one or more target behaviors at predetermined periods of time. For example, in a study by Rooney, Hallahan, and Lloyd (1984), students in a general education second-grade classroom were provided with individual recording sheets and asked to assess (i.e., yes or no) whether they were paying attention each time that a tone sounded. An example of a form that could be used for interval recording involving dichotomous decisions is presented in Figure 7.3 (see also Form 7.3 for a blank form). When working with individual students, self-observing and recording intervals have occurred as frequently as every minute (e.g., Dunlap et al., 1995; Edwards, Salant, Howard, Brougher, & McLaughlin, 1995) or every 5 minutes (e.g., Hoff & DuPaul, 1998; Rock & Thead, 2007). In order to maintain feasibility within a classwide intervention context, however, it is likely that longer intervals (e.g., 10–15 minutes) will be more appropriate.

Alternatively, both state and event behaviors may be assessed using a rating scale format. Rather than recording individual instances of a behavior, an overall judgment is made at the end of a block of time or day. In a study by Hoff and Ervin (2013), students in a second-grade classroom were taught to rate how well they, as well as the class overall, followed the classroom rules. Students used a 5-point scale to self-assess at the end of each class period, wherein a rating of 1 represented that several rules were broken and a rating of 5 represented that all rules were perfectly followed. An example of an interval recording form utilizing a rating scale format is provided in Figure 7.4 (see also Form 7.4 for a blank form). One of the key advantages of using a rating scale is that it is less intrusive to the func-

Name: Joanne   Date: April 15

Activity: Social Studies   Time: 10:30–11:30

Instructions: Each time that you hear the timer, record whether or not you were paying attention to instruction.

Paying Attention	Not Paying Attention
×	
	×
	×
×	
×	
×	
×	
Total: 5	**Total:** 2

5/7 = 71% on task

FIGURE 7.3. Self-monitoring dichotomous state behaviors.

Name: Joanne   Date: April 15

Activity: Social Studies   Time: 10:30–11:30

Instructions: Each time that you hear the timer, record how well you were paying attention to instruction.

Rating Form
How well was I paying attention? 0 = not at all 1 = somewhat 2 = totally
0   (1)   2
0   1   (2)
(0)   1   2
0   (1)   2
0   1   (2)

Earned Points __6__ ÷ Total Points __10__ = __60__ %

FIGURE 7.4. Self-monitoring using a rating scale.

tioning of the classroom because frequent assessments do not need to be made. Rather than pulling out forms intermittently throughout class to conduct ratings, students can instead conduct a single summative rating at the end of class. At the same time, one of the key disadvantages of using a rating scale is that retrospective ratings are more prone to error. Because the behavior is not recorded at the time that it occurs, there is a greater likelihood for recollections to be distorted.

Finally, in some situations, it may be possible to directly record the permanent products of a target behavior. Within clinical applications, adults have been taught to self-record a wide range of variables from the number of miles walked in a day to the number of cigarettes left in a pack (Foster et al., 1999). Within school-based settings, however, the most common application of this has been self-recording of work completion (i.e., performance). A student, for example, may be asked to record the number of math problems completed by the end of class or the number of pages read in a story. Within the literature, however, there has been a debate surrounding the differential effectiveness of teaching students to self-monitor attention (SMA) versus self-monitor performance (SMP), which has received ongoing attention.

Monitoring Attention versus Performance

Over the years, researchers have sought to determine whether academic and behavioral gains made when students are monitoring their attention are similar or different from gains made when monitoring performance variables (e.g., accuracy, productivity). The structure of these two approaches is very different in that students monitoring attention typically receive intermittent prompts to self-observe and record. See Figure 7.5 for an example depicting the distinction between SMA and SMP. Although cueing has sometimes been used within SMP (e.g., Lloyd, Bateman, Landrum, & Hallahan, 1989), students monitoring performance more typically conduct one summative self-evaluation at the end of a period (e.g., Harris, Graham, Reid, McElroy, & Hamby, 1994; Reid & Harris, 1993). Some authors have argued that attention is necessary to ensure academic performance (Hallahan & Lloyd, 1987), and therefore is the most important and relevant variable to target. The opposing argument, however, has been that increasing attention will not necessarily lead to improvements in academic achievement and that observed on-task behavior is not necessarily correlated with actual cognitive engagement (Treiber & Lahey, 1983).

Researchers have compared SMA and SMP during spelling (Harris et al., 1994; Reid & Harris, 1993), math (e.g., Lloyd et al., 1989, Maag, Reid, & DiGangi, 1993), and writing (e.g., Harris et al., 1994) tasks. Neither approach has been found to be consistently superior in improving on-task behavior (e.g., Harris, Friedlander, Saddler, Firzzelle, & Graham, 2005; Harris et al., 1994), and effects on productivity have been shown to vary depending on the target population. For example, studies conducted with students with specific learning disabilities suggested that SMP resulted in higher levels of academic productivity than

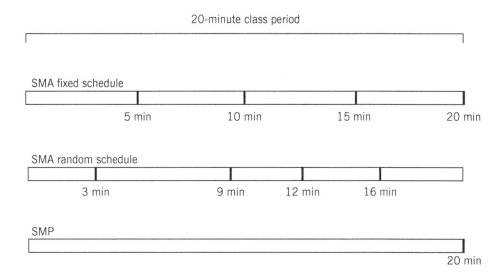

FIGURE 7.5. Monitoring attention (SMA) versus performance (SMP). SMA would likely occur multiple times throughout a 20-minute class period. For example, every 5 minutes, a student may be prompted to record whether or not he or she was paying attention at the time prompted. SMP would more likely occur at the beginning or end of a 20-minute class period. For example, at the end of a 20-minute class, the student may record the number of multiplication problems he or she completed during the class. SMA may be done utilizing either a fixed or a variable schedule. A fixed schedule would be the student being prompted to self-record after a passage of time that is the same throughout the period. A variable schedule would be the student being prompted to self-record after a passage of time that may be different between each prompt.

SMA (Harris, 1986; Reid & Harris, 1993), whereas the opposite was found in one study conducted with students with ADHD (Harris et al., 2005). Rafferty and Raimondi (2009) therefore suggested that "because students with [learning disabilities] are generally characterized by their academic deficits and students with ADHD are partially characterized by their attentional deficits, self-monitoring the corresponding target may make intuitive sense" (p. 282).

Limitations to each method have been noted by both students and researchers. It has been suggested that SMA may be detrimental to academic achievement given that students must split their focus between the assigned work and rating task (Reid & Harris, 1993). On the other hand, students have expressed concern with regard to the fact that recording the number of words written or problems completed may be overly time-consuming (e.g., Harris et al., 1994; Lloyd et al., 1989). Given the fact that limited differences have been identified between SMA and SMP, it stands to reason that use of SMA may be preferable to both teachers and students given its relative simplicity (Reid, 1996). However, our review of literature makes clear that no one method is best for all situations. Selection of the specific pieces of a self-management package should be determined based on careful consideration of the particular situation.

Should Student Ratings Be Externally Evaluated?

Within the literature, there are several examples of studies in which teaching students to simply observe and record their own behavior led to significant improvements in their classroom functioning (e.g., Levendoski & Cartledge, 2000; Prater, Hogan, & Miller, 1992). Such findings seem to be consistent with the reactivity explanation for self-monitoring discussed early on in this chapter—that is, students may change the way that they behave simply by way of being asked to think about their behavior more frequently. One potential challenge of this approach, however, is that it may be necessary for some students to have self-monitoring prompts or reminders continuously in place in order for reactivity to occur.

One alternative approach is to incorporate an evaluation component into the self-management intervention. As discussed previously, Kanfer (1970) theorized that self-management is most successful and sustainable when behavior is not only monitored but also evaluated and reinforced. This is because the individual can use the evaluative feedback to make conscious and deliberate changes to future behavior. There are two types of evaluation that are commonly used in self-management interventions: comparison of ratings to a predetermined goal to assess performance or comparison of ratings to an external standard to assess rating accuracy. Within the first approach, the classroom teacher typically sets an ambitious yet achievable goal for ratings based on the student's current level of performance and then assesses whether this goal has been met each day. For example, the goal for a student who is currently calling out 10 times during literacy instruction might initially be to have no more than seven call-outs during the same instructional period. At the end of each literacy block, the teacher would then meet with the student to review his or her recording sheet and determine whether the daily goal was met. Within the second approach, the focus is more on promoting accurate assessment on the part of the student. A goal would first be set for the accuracy of student ratings (e.g., need to be within two tally marks of the teacher's ratings) and then the teacher and student would both record the number of call-outs during the literacy block. At the end of the period, the teacher would then meet with the student to compare recording sheets and determine whether the accuracy criterion was met. Alternatively, a combination of the two evaluative procedures may be used, whereby the student receives points based on his or her absolute performance (i.e., comparison to predetermined goal); however, bonus points can also be earned for accurate assessments.

Although incorporating an evaluation component is believed to lead to more sustained behavioral change (Kanfer, 1970), it is important to keep developmental appropriateness in mind when structuring a debriefing meeting—that is, when the adult meets with the student to review his or her ratings, typically some level of discussion occurs surrounding the ratings made (regardless of whether points or tokens are actually assigned). In these situations the adult may, for example, ask the student to identify examples of when he or she was engaging in appropriate behavior, therein providing validation for the ratings. It has been suggested, however, that asking younger children to validate their ratings may introduce unnecessary cognitive and/or communicative demands (Sainato, Strain, Lefebvre, & Rapp, 1990). As a result, it becomes necessary for the adult to provide the child with a greater degree of performance feedback than is typical in applications with older children. For example, let's say that there is a young child who often plays alone during free time because he or she does not use words to communicate with others. A self-management intervention could be set up in which the student is asked to self-assess how well he or she used words with others during free time using a scale with three faces (e.g., smiling, neutral, frowning). Rather than asking the student to provide specific examples of how he or she communicated with his or her peers, the adult may need to keep anecdotal notes over the course of the rating period that can be used to support or refute the student's ratings when they meet to compare and discuss ratings.

Unfortunately, little is known about the independent effect of self-evaluation on student behavior given that reinforcement is nearly always paired with the evaluation component. Two studies conducted in the 1970s, however, found that self-evaluation did not result in significant behavioral change until contingent reinforcement was introduced (Santogrossi, O'Leary, Romanczyk, & Kaufman, 1973; Turkowitz, O'Leary, & Ironsmith, 1975), suggesting that the goal comparison may not be effective in and of itself. For this reason, it may be necessary to consider use of a reward component if evaluation is to be used.

Should Rewards Be Incorporated?

Once the target behaviors and recording methods have been determined, the next question that inevitably arises is whether it is important to include a reinforcement component—that is, should students receive external rewards for positive ratings or for rating themselves accurately? Use of rewards within a self-management intervention can provide students with additional motivation to change their behavior, so long as the rewards are seen as sufficiently desirable (see Chapter 5 for a discussion of rewards and reward preference surveys). Similar to the use of token economies and group contingencies, it is also important to ensure that the criteria for earning rewards are reasonable so that the student sees success as something that is achievable. This means both setting a reasonable goal for behavior that the student has a chance of meeting and ensuring that the student does not have to wait an inordinate amount of time to receive the reward.

As one example, Trevino-Maack and colleagues (2015) combined self-management with token economy procedures for use with high school students across three remedial reading classes. During class, students recorded whether or not they completed four tasks that were believed to be critical to improving their grades: entering information in their daily planner at the start of class, taking notes, completing assigned work, and completing a reading log. Each student could earn 1 point daily for each task completed and a bonus point was possible at the end of the week if four reading logs had been completed. Points were exchanged for tickets, which the students could use to exchange for small prizes (e.g., small snack) or save up to earn larger prizes (e.g., lunch coupon). Substantial improvements were noted in students' levels of active engagement across all three classrooms examined.

To date, mixed results have been found when investigating the effectiveness of reinforcement within the self-management literature. Within those studies that directly compared self-monitoring and self-monitoring plus reinforcement (e.g., Gansle & McMahon, 1997; Maag, Rutherford, & DiGangi, 1992), incremental effects of reinforcement were noted. However, a recent meta-analysis found that those self-management studies that did not use reinforcement demonstrated significantly larger effect sizes than those studies that did use reinforcement (Briesch & Briesch, 2016). It therefore appears that additional research is warranted in order to explore the role of reinforcement when implementing self-management at the classwide level.

Introducing the Intervention

Given the number of variations that may be used, it is important to highlight the following information when introducing a self-management intervention to students (see Coach Card 7.3). First, as is true of all of the interventions we have described throughout this book, it is important to provide a rationale for why the intervention is being introduced. This allows the teacher to clarify any concerns and justify the introduction of something new. Second, a rationale should also be provided for what specific behaviors will be targeted and why. Simply telling students that a behavior is problematic is often not sufficient to ensure behavior change. Rather, teachers should explain what behaviors students should demonstrate and how exhibiting those behaviors will help them to succeed academically or socially. Third, one should explain the procedures that students will use to self-monitor their behavior. This includes what recording will look like and how often it will occur. Fourth, if students are to earn points through their self-ratings, this system should be explained. Points may be administered to individual students, such as in a token economy, or points may be administered to groups of students, such as in interdependent and dependent group contingencies. Finally, if rewards are to be used, the procedures for earning rewards should be explained. For example, will students be able to exchange points for rewards or will accumulated points be used to work toward a larger prize?

ENHANCING THE FEASIBILITY OF CLASSWIDE IMPLEMENTATION

Despite the fact that self-management interventions have been promoted as less logistically burdensome for teachers than traditional contingency systems, it is important to keep in mind that these interventions nevertheless require the commitment of both teacher motivation and resources in order to be successfully implemented. When moving to the use of self-management at the group or classwide level, feasibility becomes a more pressing concern— that is, the idea of trying to keep track of multiple monitoring sheets or find a way to provide feedback to students on the accuracy of their ratings can quickly become overwhelming. Luckily, small adjustments to the intervention procedures can result in large improvements with regard to feasibility. Next, we describe a few of the variations on self-management interventions that may help to promote usability when applying strategies classwide.

Modifications to Recording Procedures

One of the biggest challenges in implementing self-management classwide is the sheer amount of paperwork that can be involved. If each student is charged with completing a rating form, the teacher then has to manage many different pieces of paper throughout the day. One alternative to using traditional paper-and-pencil means of recording behavior is to teach students to use signals (e.g., raising hand) in order to indicate performance of a skill. For example, one of the classroom expectations for middle school students in a study by Briesch and colleagues (2013) was to maintain their SLANT (Sit up, Lean forward, Ask questions, Nod your head, Track the speaker) throughout instruction. Students were taught to self-assess their SLANT by holding their thumbs up (i.e., perfect SLANT), thumbs sideways (i.e., not perfect but demonstrating some behaviors), or thumbs down (i.e., poor SLANT) each time that a timer buzzed. In this way, teachers may quickly scan the group and provide brief verbal feedback to each student with regard to the accuracy of his or her assessment without needing to deal with individual recording sheets.

Moving away from paper-and-pencil methods of recording may be particularly useful when implementing self-management with younger students. For example, transitioning between activities was identified as problematic in a study conducted in an early intervention preschool setting (Connell, Carta, Lutz, et al., 1993), and therefore students were taught transition skills as well as how to rate their own transitioning behavior on a daily basis. In order to make the self-rating feasible for a population of 4-year-olds, students were instructed to raise their hand if they had engaged in a targeted behavior (e.g., putting things where they belong, putting on a jacket) during the transition. Each student's self-assessment was then compared with the teacher's assessment during a group debrief and students were given either praise or corrective feedback based on the accuracy of their self-assessments. Across other applications, preschool students have also been taught to move a bead on a string (Shearer, Kohler, Buchan, & McCullough, 1996) or place a foam disk into a container (Strain et al., 1994) each time that a specific social interaction strategy was used.

Modifications to Evaluation Procedures

Another aspect of self-management implementation that can become challenging when applied classwide is the use of evaluation procedures. As discussed earlier in this chapter, although an evaluation component is not essential, often the classroom teacher meets with the student to discuss the ratings that have been made and to provide a reward for desirable performance. Although these individual meetings can be accomplished fairly quickly, the total amount of time needed can become unwieldy when multiplied by 20 or 30 students in a classroom. For this reason, one of two modifications have typically been made to evaluation procedures when implementing self-management classwide.

Consider Evaluating Behavior at the Group Level

One option for enhancing feasibility may be to have students monitor their behavior in groups rather than having students individually monitor their own behavior. In implementing a self-monitoring system with a third-grade classroom, Davies and Witte (2000) used the natural seating layout of the classroom as a way to assign students to groups. A team chart was then placed at the center of each table, which contained three quadrants (green, blue, red) and five dots. Whenever a student on the team made an inappropriate verbalization, that student was instructed to move one dot from the green to the blue quadrant. If any instances of inappropriate verbalizations were not recorded in this way, the teacher would instead move a dot to the red quadrant. In order to ensure that students were supportive rather than critical of one another, the teacher discussed what an appropriate reaction to a moved dot would look like and provided feedback to individual students whose reactions were deemed inappropriate.

Classwide self-management may also be made more manageable by pairing self-monitoring with reinforcement strategies that rely on group attainment of a preset goal, such as found in group contingencies (see Chapter 6). Here we provide specific examples of how self-management may be integrated within all interdependent and dependent group contingency systems.

Within an interdependent group contingency, all students in a class are organized into smaller groups. If each person in the group receives a rating that is at or above the goal (e.g., 80% correct), then all members in the group receive the reward (e.g., pajama party after 10 days of meeting goal). Chafouleas and colleagues (2010) used this approach with three eighth-grade classrooms. Students were taught to self-evaluate the degree to which they were prepared for class, engaged in instruction, and completed their homework at the end of each class period using an 11-point Direct Behavior Rating (DBR) scale (i.e., 0 = not at all, 10 = totally). The classroom teacher then met with each student to briefly review his or her ratings and to determine the degree to which the student ratings matched those of the teacher. Students received individual points based on both their absolute performance and the accuracy (i.e., correspondence with teacher ratings) of their ratings, which they then combined with the points of their teammates (i.e., group of three to five students) to derive an average team score. If at the end of the week the team's cumulative score met or exceeded the predetermined criterion, the entire team received reinforcement.

Denune and colleagues (2015) similarly combined self-monitoring with an interdependent group contingency intervention in order to improve the engagement and disruptive behavior of middle school students with EBD in an alternative school setting. The group contingency component was modeled after the Good Behavior Game, wherein after the class was divided into smaller groups, the teacher reviewed the classroom rules with the students and explained that they could earn rewards at the end of class for meeting a randomly selected goal. Roughly every 10 minutes, the students were instructed to record (i.e., yes or no) whether they were staying seated, using respectful language, paying attention, and completing their work at the same time that the teacher evaluated these student behaviors. The teacher then drew a percentage criterion of possible points earned (e.g., group earned at least 75% of possible points) from a paper bag at the end of the period. Each team whose points exceeded the criterion would then earn a mystery prize (e.g., snacks, small tangibles), which was randomly drawn from a second paper bag.

Within a dependent group contingency, in contrast, whether or not the group receives the reward is based upon the behavior of select individuals. When combined with self-management, this means that group rewards could be based on the ratings obtained by individual students or the accuracy with which individual students rated themselves. Because the behavior of only a few students is monitored and "counts" toward earning the group reward, both motivation to rate accurately and the feasibility to complete procedures are potentially enhanced. This option was recently utilized in the study previously described by Briesch and colleagues (2013) within a middle school general education classroom. Each time the buzzer sounded, the teacher rated the behavior of three students sitting at a predetermined, but randomly selected, table. The class then received 1 point for each match between the teacher's rating and the student's rating, for up to 3 points per interval. In order to avoid potential stigmatization, the teacher reported the number of points that the class had received each interval but did not announce which table had been selected for evaluation.

Consider Use of Peer-Assisted Self-Management

Another option for enhancing the efficiency of classwide applications of self-management involves utilizing peers to provide a check on the accuracy of self-monitoring results. Mitchem, Young, West, and Benyo (2001) developed the classwide peer-assisted self-management (CWPASM) program, which combines elements of classwide peer tutoring (Delquadri, Greenwood, Whorton, Carta, & Hall, 1986) and self-management. In Mitchem et al.'s (2001) study, all students in a seventh-grade language arts classroom were assigned a peer partner and these pairs were randomly assigned to one of two classroom teams. Students were then taught to rate their own rule-following behavior as well as the behavior of their assigned partner using a 4-point scale. Each time that a tone sounded (approximately every 10 minutes), students compared their ratings with their partner's. If ratings matched, each student received the number of points assigned by their partner as well as a bonus point for the pair. If ratings were off by 1 point, each student simply received the points assigned by his or her partner. In those cases in which a larger discrepancy was identified between ratings, however, no points were assigned. To make sure the student pairs were being honest, a "mystery match" component was introduced, by which the teacher secretly observed one pair from each team on a given day and then compared his or her ratings with those self-assigned. Matches identified between student and teacher ratings resulted in 10 bonus points for the student pair. Results of a multiple baseline design suggested significant increases in the overall level of on-task behavior in the classroom following implementation of CWPASM. Taken together, promising options for enhancing the feasibility of classwide application of self-management strategies are available and warrant consideration when multiple individuals could benefit from intervention supports.

FINAL CONSIDERATIONS: FIXING PROBLEMS AND FADING THE INTERVENTION

Having outlined both the rationale and procedures for implementing self-management strategies classwide, in this final section we focus on what to do when problems arise and how to begin to fade the intervention as time goes on.

Troubleshooting

Although things may go wrong when implementing any classroom intervention, the potential for problems to arise may be somewhat greater when implementing self-management interventions. This is due to the fact that responsibility for implementation no longer rests solely in the hands of the classroom teacher. Next, we outline a few of the more common problems that may arise and present potential solutions for addressing them.

Problem 1: Students Are Not Rating Accurately

One problem that may be encountered is that of students not rating their behavior accurately. This issue was illustrated by Lloyd and Hilliard (1989), who found that student ratings were highly inaccurate when compared with ratings conducted by external observers (mean on task = 99% for student ratings, 56% for observer ratings). The authors referred to this as the "Yes, I've cleaned up my room phenomenon," in that the students claimed that their behavior was much better than it actually appeared. Disagreements regarding assessments may lead to tension between the classroom teacher and student that can appear difficult to resolve. One way in which to promote more accurate assessments on the part of students may therefore be to provide rewards contingent upon the accuracy of ratings. In the same study by Lloyd and Hilliard (1989), there was a significant increase in actual on-task behavior as well as rating accuracy (mean on task = 95% for student ratings, 91% for observer ratings) when students received reinforcement for maintaining at least 80% accuracy with teacher ratings. Such results seem to suggest that the accuracy of student ratings may be questionable in the absence of external evaluation.

Within the literature, there are several examples of studies in which rating accuracy has been emphasized. In some cases, students have earned points solely based upon the accuracy of their ratings (e.g., Peterson, Young, Salzberg, West, & Hill, 2006). However, more typically, students have earned points based on both the magnitude and accuracy of their own self-ratings (e.g., Barry & Messer, 2003; Rhode, Morgan, & Young, 1983). In a study by Hoff and Ervin (2013), for example, the teacher compared her rating of the class to the class rating generated by the students at the end of each period. The class received a bonus point for a perfect match, kept the points earned on the rating scale for a 1-point discrepancy, and earned no points if the discrepancy was 2 or more points.

Problem 2: Self-Monitoring Appears to Be Too Cognitively Demanding

Many of the examples of self-management that we have focused on throughout this chapter may be more relevant to older students. Those students who are younger or have developmental delays may struggle to understand what behaviors are being targeted or to independently evaluate their own behavior. Fortunately, there are several available options for extending self-management use to younger populations. First, pictures can be used to increase the saliency of target behaviors and to facilitate evaluation. Several studies have utilized pictorial posters in which particular strategies (e.g., sharing with a friend; Sainato et al., 1992) or steps involved in performing a skill (e.g., stop what you're doing—clean up materials—move to assigned seat; Connell, Carta, & Baer, 1993) are depicted and hung on the classroom wall. The form used for self-monitoring then consisted of a smaller version of each of the posters rather than utilizing words to describe the behavior. Sainato et al. (1990) extended the use of pictorial representations by photographing the target children demonstrating appropriate on-task or waiting behavior. In this way, each child's form therefore contained a self-modeling example. Second, the use of pictures may also help to make the rating scale more interpretable. Whereas older students are better able to discriminate between values on a Likert-type scale (e.g., 1 = not following classroom rules, 5 = perfectly following classroom rules), interpretation of this type of scale is much more challenging for a younger child. Alternatively, use of a smiley face scale facilitates a more accurate rating, and could be easily converted to a numerical scale to assist in summarization and interpretation (see Figure 7.6).

Rating Form			
How well did I play with my friends?			
Recess	☹	☺	☺
Centers	☹	☺	☺
Lunch	☹	☺	☺

FIGURE 7.6. Example of a self-monitoring form for use with younger students.

Problem 3: Students Become Overly Focused on, or Distracted by, Self-Monitoring

Although we wish for students to become more reflective regarding their behavior through use of a self-management intervention, there exists a risk that students may become distracted by, or overly focused on, the self-monitoring process. As one example, a student may have difficulty shifting his or her attention back to assigned work after completing his or her ratings. Another example might be a student who is fixated on the clock or on his or her intervention materials in anticipation of the next rating period. There are a couple of ways to address this type of problem should it arise. First, it may be important to consider reducing the frequency with which ratings are conducted. If the student is being asked to self-monitor quite often, this may make it difficult to maintain focus on regular classroom activities. By observing and recording one's behavior only once or twice a period, however, this would allow for longer uninterrupted periods of time between rating occasions. It is also important to maintain a variable interval so that the students do not know when the timer will go off. A second consideration would involve making changes to the intervention materials. For example, if having a self-monitoring card on a student's desk proves to be too much of a distraction, use of hand signals may be a preferred alternative. Finally, make sure the target behavior is one that is incompatible with clock watching or other types of distracted behavior.

Fading the Intervention

As with the other interventions that we have discussed in this book, even interventions that prove to be highly successful cannot be implemented forever. Rather than abruptly removing an intervention, self-management interventions should be gradually faded over time in order to increase the likelihood of sustained behavioral change. Although several of the fading strategies discussed in previous chapters also apply here (e.g., reduce the frequency with which rewards are earned, increase the threshold for earning rewards), there are some strategies that are unique to self-management applications.

One of the first options for fading a self-management intervention is to consider changes to how the monitoring component is conducted. In those situations in which one behavior has been monitored on a frequent basis (e.g., rating how well students were paying attention every 5 minutes), the number of times that a student is asked to self-monitor may be reduced over time. For example, monitoring may be reduced to every 10 minutes, then every 20 minutes, and eventually may occur only once at the end of an instructional period. On the other hand, in those situations in which multiple behaviors are evaluated using a checklist approach, it may be possible to abbreviate the rating task as time goes on. For example, rather than asking the student to individually assess whether each specific behavior occurred (e.g., "Did I arrive to class on time?"; "Did I bring my books to class?"), he or she might instead be asked to provide one global assessment of class preparation (e.g., "Was I prepared for class today?").

A second option for fading use of self-management is to gradually move from the use of teacher-determined to student-determined rating periods. Most often, students have been cued regarding when to conduct self-assessments through the use of a teacher-delivered prompt (e.g., verbal, buzz of a timer). However, over time, students may be charged with the responsibility for determining when ratings should occur. For example, after removing an external prompt, students could be instructed to keep an eye on the clock and to remember to rate their own behavior at least twice an hour. In a study by Prater, Joy, Chilman, Temple, and Miller (1991), fading of rating prompts was gradually reduced until students were eventually told simply to record their behavior "only when they thought about it" (p. 170).

Finally, if the classwide self-management intervention involves comparing teacher and student ratings, this component may prove overly burdensome over time due to the time that is required for regular check-ins to occur. It is therefore important that this matching component be faded. One way in which to fade a matching component is to move toward the use of random spot checks. For example, the accuracy of students' ratings may be checked only once or twice in a given day. It is important, however, that the timing of the spot checks remains a mystery to the students, so that they are not able to anticipate when greater care should be taken with their ratings. When the classroom teacher feels confident that the students are self-assessing their own behavior with a high degree of accuracy, the matching component may be discontinued entirely, such that evaluation is based on self-ratings alone.

CONCLUSIONS

Use of self-management strategies is believed to be advantageous both because they reduce the implementation demands placed on classroom teachers and promote personal responsibility among students. Although there is a much deeper evidence base supporting the use of self-management interventions with individual students, an increasing number of studies focused on classwide applications have been noted in recent years. This growing evidence base has suggested that classwide self-management may be used successfully to both promote appropriate behavior (e.g., engagement) and decrease inappropriate behavior (e.g., classroom disruption). In order to ensure that self-management interventions are maximally feasible, it may be necessary to consider incorporating group contingencies or utilizing peers as intervention agents.

COACH CARD 7.1. Preparing to Implement Classwide Self-Management

Steps	Considerations
Identify the target behaviors.	• Do you wish to increase a desirable behavior (e.g., paying attention, participating in class)? • To decrease a problem behavior (e.g., calling out, out of seat)?
Determine time period for implementation.	• Will students self-monitor throughout the day? • During a particular instructional block?

Determine what method students will use to self-record.	• Can the target behavior be counted?
	• Are there permanent products that can be evaluated?
	• Or is use of interval recording most appropriate?
	  ○ If so, how frequently will students be asked to record their behavior (e.g., every 10 minutes, once at the end of an instructional block)?
	  ○ If so, what type of prompt will be used to signal when it is time to record (e.g., teacher prompt, timer)?

Determine how behavior will be recorded.	• Will students use a paper-and-pencil monitoring form to record behavior? • Will hand signals be used to communicate ratings?
Determine whether a group contingency will be used.	• Will students self-monitor independently? • Will students be divided into teams for the purpose of self-monitoring?
Determine whether/how feedback will be delivered.	• Will students be evaluated based on rating accuracy and/or actual performance? • Will students receive verbal feedback regarding their performance? • Will feedback be delivered in the form of physical objects (e.g., tokens, marbles, tickets) or points for desired behavior? • Will feedback be provided by the teacher or other classmates?
Determine appropriate rewards for students (if applicable).	• Will students be able to exchange points or tokens for rewards? • Will these rewards be administered at the individual or group level?
Determine criteria for exchanging points (if applicable).	• How many points will be needed to earn a prize(s)? • Will these values change over time?
Determine when points may be exchanged (if applicable).	• Will students be able to exchange points/tokens for rewards every day or less frequently?

COACH CARD 7.2. Treatment Integrity Checklist for Implementing Classwide Self-Management

Teacher: _____   Date: _____

Observer: _____   Activity: _____

STEPS IN IMPLEMENTING CLASSWIDE SELF-MANAGEMENT

☐ Provide students with necessary rating materials (if applicable).

☐ Review behavioral expectations.

☐ Set timer to signal student when to observe (if needed).

☐ Ensure students complete self-ratings.

☐ Complete teacher ratings (if applicable).

If implementing CWSM with feedback and rewards:

☐ Provide performance feedback (verbally or in form of points/tokens).

☐ Provide students with rewards if earned (if applicable).

Total number of steps completed =

Percentage of steps completed =

COACH CARD 7.3. Steps in Introducing Classwide Self-Management

Step	Sample dialogue
Provide rationale for introducing classwide self-management.	*I've noticed that many of you have been off task this past week. This makes it hard to cover the important material that will be on our final exam. To help all of us be better prepared as you can be, we are going to try something new for these last few weeks.*
Establish target behaviors and provide rationale for why they are important.	*We use acronyms to help us remember lots of different things. [Provide examples if needed.] Today we are going to learn a new acronym that is designed to help you remember what it means to be engaged in class. The acronym is SLANT. First, the S stands for sit up. You want to make sure that you are sitting up straight in your chair—not slouching down or with your head on the desk. Second, the L stands for lean forward and listen. If you are turned around in your seat or talking to your neighbor, you are demonstrating to me that you are not listening. Third, the A stands for ask questions. Asking questions shows me that you are paying attention and thinking about the material. Fourth, the N stands for nod your head. When you nod your head yes or no, you are helping me know whether you are understanding what we are talking about or whether you need more information. Finally, the T stands for track the speaker. This means that whenever someone is speaking—whether it is myself or one of your classmates—you should direct your eyes toward that person. This shows the person that you are paying attention to what is being said. If you are doing all of these things, then it shows me that you are engaged in what is going on and ready to learn.*
Describe self-management procedures.	*For these last few weeks of class, I am going to challenge you to become more aware of what your behavior looks like in class by rating your own behavior. Each day when you come into class, I am going to remind you of what it means to have an appropriate SLANT and then set a timer. Each time that the buzzer goes off, I want you to rate your own SLANT. If you think that you have a really good SLANT (you're doing all five things perfectly), then you should give me a thumbs-up. If you caught yourself with a pretty bad SLANT (e.g., turned around in your seat, talking to your neighbors), then you should give me a thumbs-down. If your SLANT wasn't perfect (e.g., sitting up in seat but not listening attentively), you should stick out your thumb to the side. You won't know when the buzzer is going to go off, but it will happen a few times during each class.*
Explain how students will earn points (if applicable).	*Each time that you guys rate your own SLANT, I am also going to randomly pick one table to rate as well. I'm not going to tell you which table I picked until after you show me your rating. If I pick your table and your rating matches mine, the class will get a point. That means that each time that the buzzer goes off, the class could earn up to 4 points. Remember that by doing all five things (SLANT), you're showing me that you are engaged so there shouldn't be any arguments about ratings. If you choose to argue about a point, the class will not get any points for that rating period and will have to wait until the next beep.*
Describe how rewards may be earned (if applicable).	*Each day I will record the number of points that the class earned on the board as well as the number of points that the class **could have** earned. If at the end of the week, the class has earned at least 80% of the points possible, everyone will earn a small surprise the next Monday. If we can keep that average up until the end of the trimester, then we will have a class party to celebrate the end of the year and exams.*

Self-Monitoring Form (Frequency)

Name: _____ Date: _____

Activity: _____ Time: _____

Instructions: Mark an X in the box each time that you:					
#1:			#2:		

_____

Self-Monitoring Form (Checklist)

Name: _____ Date: _____

Activity: _____ Time: _____

Did I . . . ?	Yes	No

Number of Yes Checks _____ ÷ Total Checklist Items _____ = _____%

Self-Monitoring Form (Interval Recording)

Name: _____   Date: _____

Activity: _____   Time: _____

Time	Behavior	Yes	No

Self-Monitoring (Rating Scale)

Name: _____   Date: _____

Activity: _____   Time: _____

Time	Behavior	Rating 0 = not a problem 1 = somewhat of a problem 2 = a problem 3 = a major problem			
		0	1	2	3
		0	1	2	3
		0	1	2	3
		0	1	2	3
		0	1	2	3
		0	1	2	3
		0	1	2	3

PART IV

STRATEGIES FOR ENHANCING IMPLEMENTATION AND EFFECTIVENESS

CHAPTER 8

Collecting Classwide Data

The subsequent chapters in this book are designed to provide you with practical, evidence-based strategies that you can use to support positive student behavior in the classroom. Although knowing *what* you can do to effect change in classroom settings is certainly important, knowing whether or not what you did actually worked is of critical importance as well. Data are an important piece of everyday life in schools. Teachers use data to make decisions about what type of supports particular students may require, what changes are needed to instruction, and to measure student growth. The goal of this chapter is to help you identify the data collection method that makes most sense for the behavior you are looking to change *and* also fits well within your daily routines. After guiding readers through the process of identifying a target behavior and determining how best to measure it, we review strategies for collecting and evaluating data to determine intervention effectiveness.

IDENTIFYING THE TARGET OF MEASUREMENT

Although the strategies outlined in this book are designed to support the behavior of *all* students in a classroom, there are actually two levels at which we may choose to collect data. In schools, we are most often accustomed to making student-level decisions—that is, data are collected for individual students and used to make decisions in order to promote the success of that particular student. Classwide interventions (see Chapters 5–7), however, have the dual advantage of being able to support the behavior of both individual target students *and* the larger student body as well. In some situations, although a strategy or intervention is applied classwide, data collection may be limited to one or more individual students because it is the behavior of these students that is of greatest interest. However, data may also be collected at the group level in order to determine the overall effectiveness of a classwide intervention or may be advantageous if the behavior of multiple students is of interest—that is, collecting data at the group level reduces the burden on the data collector (who is often the already busy classroom teacher!) because it is not necessary to manage multiple data collection plans (Krasch & Carter, 2009).

IDENTIFYING THE PROBLEM

After we have determined whose behavior is of interest, the next step is to identify which particular behavior(s) we wish to assess. Although it may be obvious to us that a problem exists, it can sometimes be difficult to pinpoint precisely what that problem is. Before we can move forward in collecting data, it is essential that we identify the target behavior. Target behaviors are those behaviors that we are interested in changing and they can be either desirable or undesirable. Desirable target behaviors reflect those things that we want to see increase (e.g., class participation), whereas undesirable target behaviors reflect those things that we want to see decrease (e.g., side conversations with classmates). When we use the term "behavior," we mean those things that students do that can be both observed and measured. Pushing another student or getting out of one's seat are behaviors that can be both observed and measured. It is important to distinguish behaviors from traits or internal states, which require some level of inference to assess. For example, a student may be described as hardworking or lazy, honest or sneaky, or outgoing or shy. Generally speaking, if you can easily put the word "is" in front of the problem (e.g., he or she is overactive, he or she is deceptive), it is probably a trait. Similarly, internal states are not behaviors. When a student is feeling anxious or angry, these are things that cannot be reliably observed by an outside individual. However, we might notice that a student's face turns red, veins pop out in his or her neck, or that the student speaks more quickly and loudly. In the first column of Table 8.1, we have listed a number of common teacher concerns that cannot be explicitly observed or measured. To the right of each general concern are more specific observable, measurable indicators that would serve as appropriate measurement targets.

Once we have identified an appropriate target behavior, we next need to operationally define it. Operational definitions are written using observable, measurable terms, leaving no room for individual interpretation of what might be meant by a particular term. When a student is described as exhibiting "hyperactive behavior," what comes to mind? A student who is bouncing up and down in his or her seat and drumming on the desk? Out of his or her seat and talking to peers? Calling out answers and making distracting noises during lessons? All or none of these examples may capture exactly what we are thinking of when we hear the term "hyperactive behavior." Creating an operational definition therefore allows us to communicate to others exactly what we mean when we use a particular term.

There are several characteristics of strong operational definitions that are important to note (see Box 8.1). The first is that a strong operational definition should include both examples of what the target behavior is and non-examples of what the target behavior is not. Providing examples and non-examples helps to clarify which types of behaviors should "count" and which ones should not. Consider a situation in which we are interested in measuring disruptive behavior and define disruptive behavior as "any verbal or motor behavior that interferes with the ability of the teacher to teach or other students to learn." Including examples and non-examples can help to clarify the boundaries of when a behavior would

TABLE 8.1. Identifying Appropriate Target Behaviors

General teacher concern	More specific target behaviors that can be observed and measured
Student is aggressive.	Calls other children names. Hits other children. Pushes other children. Threatens other children.
Student is disruptive.	Calls out. Drums on desk. Gets out of seat without permission. Makes noises.
Student is anxious.	Complains of being sick. Turns in incomplete assignments. Doesn't speak in class. Fidgets.
Student is lazy.	Doesn't follow directions. Submits incomplete homework. Takes a long time to get out materials. Turns in incomplete assignments.
Student is hyperactive.	Fidgets. Gets out of seat. Plays with objects. Talks with classmates.

be considered problematic versus when it might be acceptable. To illustrate this point, the behavior of talking to peers might be considered an example of disruptive behavior when it occurs during instruction or when students are expected to work independently. In contrast, talking to peers might be perfectly acceptable (i.e., non-example) if it occurs during group work or during designated free time. Making these distinctions clear within the operational definition can reduce later anxiety when it comes to judging what does or what does not constitute the target behavior.

BOX 8.1. Characteristics of a Strong Operational Definition

A strong operational definition should:

- Include both examples (i.e., what the behavior is) and non-examples (i.e., what the behavior is not).
- Pass the "stranger test" (i.e., a complete stranger could read your definition and know what to observe).
- Pass the "dead-man test" (i.e., behavior could not be demonstrated by a dead man).

The second characteristic of a strong operational definition is that it should be able to pass the "stranger test." In other words, if a stranger walked into your classroom and read the operational definition, he or she would be able to reliably determine when the target behavior was occurring. A definition that passes the stranger test is one that spells everything out rather than leaving specific terms up to individual interpretation. Noncompliance, for example, may be a relevant problem behavior for a particular student; however, noncompliance can take on many forms. Although the term may bring to mind the image of a student standing with arms crossed and aggressively refusing to do what was told, there are more mild versions of noncompliance that we may also wish to capture such as laying one's head on the desk rather than beginning work. The stranger test ensures that the operational definition we create is adequately specific and interpreted similarly by different individuals.

Finally, strong operational definitions should pass the "dead-man test," in that the target behaviors are not only observable but also involve movement (Hosp, Howell, & Hosp, 2003). In other words, target behaviors should be those things that a dead man could not do. Often behaviors that fail to pass the dead-man test are those that tell us what a student does *not* do. Take, for example, the target behavior of "sits on the rug without bothering others." This behavior would fail to pass the test because a dead man could certainly refrain from bothering others just as long as the target student. In this case, a better target might be one that illustrates what the student should be doing when sitting on the rug (e.g., sits quietly with legs crossed and eyes toward the front of the room).

DETERMINING THE DIMENSION OF INTEREST

Once a target behavior has been identified and defined, the next step is to classify the behavior according to type. All behaviors can generally be classified as either event or state behaviors (see Table 8.2). Event behaviors are those that have a clear beginning and end, and are generally of a similar length (Saudargas & Zanolli, 1990). This means that it is fairly obvious to even a casual observer when the student first begins to engage in the target behavior and when the target behavior is over. Event behaviors can also be thought of as those that easily lend themselves to being counted. For example, because it would be fairly easy to count the number of times that a student raises his or her hand or shoves a classmate, these would be classified as event behaviors.

State behaviors, on the other hand, are those that vary in duration and are difficult to count (Saudargas & Zanolli, 1990). Student engagement is one clear example of a state behavior. It is not uncommon for student engagement to ebb and flow throughout an instructional period. For example, a student may be engaged in instruction for 2 minutes, stare off into space for 30 seconds, reengage for 1 minute, and then talk to a neighbor for a minute and a half. If we were to count the number of times that this student was engaged during this 5-minute period of time, the resultant value (i.e., 2) would have little meaning. Rather, there are additional dimensions of state behaviors that must be considered in order to paint a descriptive picture of what has occurred.

TABLE 8.2. Differentiating between Event and State Behaviors

Event behaviors	State behaviors
Characteristics	
• Clear beginning and end	• Difficult to count
• Generally of similar length	• Vary in duration
Examples	
• Asking questions	• Academically engaged
• Calling out	• Interacting with peers
• Hitting a peer	• Talking to classmates
• Noncompliance	• Tantrumming
• Raising hand	• Tapping pencil
Recording methods	
• Duration	• Momentary time sampling
• Frequency count/rate	• Partial interval sampling
• Latency	• Planned activity check
• Percentage of opportunities	• Whole-interval sampling
• Scatterplot	

In some cases, it may not be immediately obvious whether a target behavior should be considered a state or an event. In such a situation, it is necessary to examine the nature of the behavior and the regularity with which it is occurring in order to make this determination. Consider, for example, the target behavior of inappropriate verbalizations, which is defined as "any verbalization that is not directly related to classroom instruction or disrupts classroom activities." If the primary concern was that a student blurted out answers during whole-class instruction, this type of inappropriate verbalization would lend itself to being counted—that is, if each blurt-out was brief (e.g., "Wait!"; "I know!"; "Oooh! Oooh!"), and these interjections did not occur so frequently as to make counting difficult, inappropriate verbalizations could be considered an event behavior. If, on the other hand, the student's inappropriate verbalizations consisted mainly of tangential conversations with classmates, this might be more difficult to count—that is, the student may make a quick side comment to a student across the aisle on one occasion and then engage in a longer conversation with his or her immediate neighbor. Because simply counting the number of times that the student talked would not accurately reflect how often the behavior was occurring, inappropriate verbalizations would best be considered a state behavior in this situation.

Event Recording

If we have decided that a behavior is an event behavior, it is then necessary to determine exactly what about the behavior we are most interested in assessing. There are several different dimensions of a behavior that may be of interest. The first is *frequency*, or how often the behavior is occurring. We may be interested, for example, in how often a student raises his or her hand to answer a question or pushes another student on the playground. Keeping a tally of the number of times that the behavior occurs is certainly the easiest way to measure frequency. Using this approach, the observer simply makes a tally mark each time that the target behavior occurs (see Figure 8.1). This form of data collection is easy to implement, in that it does not require training or specialized forms. It is important, however, that both the number and frequency of target behaviors is manageable so that data collection does not become unwieldy. Keeping count of the number of times that students call out answers without raising their hands may be reasonable, whereas counting the number of times that students raise their hands to answer a question could quickly become all-consuming! A tally can be kept using a paper-and-pencil log; however, the log must be easily accessible so that the recording of behavior does not disrupt the regular classroom. If this type of recording is found to be too cumbersome, alternate methods of maintaining a frequency count should be considered. Common methods that have been used in classroom settings include moving rubber bands from one wrist to the other, moving paper clips from one pocket to the other, or clicking a golf counter each time that the target behavior is observed.

One important consideration when it comes to using frequency count data is that the time frame for data collection must be kept consistent if data are to be directly comparable across days. Imagine, for example, that you were interested in collecting data on calling-out behavior during the morning meeting. On day 1, you noted six instances of calling out and on day 2 you noted four instances. It would appear that the behavior was more problematic

Instructions: Mark a tally each time the behavior occurs.

Behavior	Frequency
Calling out	
Raising hand	

Instructions: Cross out a number each time the behavior occurs.

Calling Out	Raising Hand
15	15
14	14
13	13
12	12
11	11
10	10
9	9
8	8
7	7
6	6
5	5
4	4
3	3
2	2
1	1

FIGURE 8.1. Examples of event recording sheets.

on day 1; however, this would be assuming that the same amount of time elapsed. If, on the other hand, the morning meeting lasted only 20 minutes the first day and 40 minutes the second day, these data would tell a different story. In situations in which the overall observation period is not consistent across time, it is necessary to calculate a *rate of behavior*. The rate can easily be calculated by dividing the number of instances of a behavior by the total number of minutes in the observation period. Using the data above, the rate of calling-out behavior for day 1 would be 6/20, or 0.30 call-outs per minute. For day 2, the rate would be 4/40 = 0.10 call-outs per minute. Calling out clearly occurred more often on day 1 than day 2 when the overall length of the morning meeting is taken into account!

An additional consideration when recording the frequency with which a behavior occurs is whether the behavior is what can be termed as "opportunity dependent"—that is, can the behavior occur an infinite number of times during the recording period or is it dependent on something else happening? One simple example of an opportunity-dependent behavior is raising one's hand to answer a question. If we simply recorded the number of times that a student raised his or her hand during math instruction and found that the answer was zero, two possibilities exist. The first is that the student was given multiple opportunities to answer questions; however, he or she chose not to raise his or her hand at all. The second is that the student did not raise his or her hand to answer a question because no questions were actually posed. Clearly, zero hand raises would be considered much more problematic in the first scenario than the second, and therefore information is needed to clarify this. In those situations in which the target behavior is believed to be opportunity dependent, a *percentage-of-opportunities* metric can be calculated by dividing the number of times that the behavior actually occurred by the number of opportunities there were for the behavior to occur. For example, if directions were provided to a student on five occasions and he or she followed the directions only once, the percentage of opportunities on which the student followed directions would be 1/5, or 20% of opportunities. Other examples of opportunity-dependent behaviors include noncompliance, saying "Please" or "Thank you," and responding appropriately to requests to play.

Tallies can be fairly easy to keep and provide useful information regarding the frequency with which a behavior occurs during a specific period of time. If one is interested, however, in understanding how the behavior looks across multiple periods in the day, this is best accomplished using what is called a *scatterplot*. A scatterplot can be used to better understand when problem behavior is occurring and to identify any potential patterns related to its occurrence. Typically, each column represents a different day of the week and each row represents a different time period during the day. Time periods should be determined in consideration of what the behavior is and how frequently it is believed to occur. A 10-minute time period may be appropriate in one situation, whereas an hour block may make more sense in another. It may also make the most sense to divide the day into activity blocks (e.g., morning meeting, literacy, writing) based on daily transitions. Each time that the target behavior occurs, the teacher is asked to record it within the appropriate time period. If more than one target behavior is of interest, different markers may be used to represent each target behavior within the scatterplot. Figure 8.2 illustrates how a scatterplot might be used to record calling out and out-of-seat behavior within a particular classroom.

Instructions: Place an X in the box each time that a student calls out. Place a O in the box each time that a student gets out of his or her seat without permission.

	Monday	Tuesday	Wednesday	Thursday	Friday
8:00–8:30	X	X X	O X X	X	X X X
8:30–9:00	O		O X X	O X X	O X
9:00–9:30		O X	X	X	O
9:30–10:00	O O	O O O	O O	O	O O X X
10:00–10:30			X	O X	X
10:30–11:00	X	O X		O	O X
11:00–11:30			O O X	O X	O O
11:30–12:00	O O O	O O	O O O	O O X	O O O
12:00–12:30		X	X	X X	X X X
12:30–1:00	O X			O	X
1:00–1:30	X		O X	X	X X
1:30–2:00		O X	X	X X	O O X
2:00–2:30	O O	O O O	O O	O O O	O O O O

FIGURE 8.2. Example of a scatterplot.

One of the central advantages of a scatterplot is that the graphic depiction allows you to quickly identify any patterns that may be occurring with regard to the target behavior. In looking at Figure 8.2, for example, it appears that students are out of their seats (O) most frequently during the blocks of time from 9:30 to 10:00, 11:30 to 12:00, and 2:00 to 2:30. Given that each of these time blocks immediately precedes a break in the schedule (i.e., snack, lunch, dismissal), it seems that the students may benefit from inserting a motor break (i.e., scheduled opportunity to move around) in the middle of each instructional block. Although there is not a clear pattern within each day with regard to calling-out behavior, it does appear that the behavior becomes more frequent as the week progresses. This information may also be useful in intervention planning, suggesting that more intensive behavioral supports may be necessary near the end of the school week. A blank scatterplot recording form is provided in Form 8.1.

Although with some event behaviors we are most interested in how often they occur, in other cases what may be of greater interest is for how long the behavior occurs, or duration. We may, for example, be interested in knowing how long a student's tantrum lasts or the amount of time that a student spends wandering around the room during classroom instruction. Duration is most typically measured by starting a timer when the behavior begins and then stopping it when the behavior ends. When describing duration data that have been collected across multiple occasions, these data are most often summarized and reported with regard to the average length (e.g., On average, Jill's tantrums lasted 6 minutes) or range observed (e.g., Jill's tantrums were observed to last anywhere from 2 to 25 minutes).

One additional way of looking at the timing of a target behavior is to examine latency. Although duration looks at how long the behavior occurs, latency is a measure of how much time elapses before a behavior is initiated. For example, we may be interested in knowing how long it takes for a student to take out his or her textbook. In this case, latency would be measured by starting a timer when the instruction was given to take out the textbook and stopping it when the student actually took the textbook out. Latency data may be summarized in a similar manner as duration data, such as by reporting the average latency or range of latency periods.

State Recording

State behaviors, which cannot be easily counted or timed, are best estimated using interval recording procedures. Interval recording procedures involve observing and recording one or more target behaviors at predetermined periods of time. We begin by breaking down an overall observation period into smaller chunks. When interval recording is used by external observers, these chunks are typically less than a minute (e.g., 10 seconds, 15 seconds, 30 seconds); however, if participant observers (e.g., teachers) are asked to record behavior, longer intervals (e.g., 1 minute, 5 minutes) will likely be needed in order to ensure feasibility. Next, we choose one of three types of recording procedures: whole-interval, partial-interval, or momentary time sampling. Within whole-interval sampling, the target behavior is recorded as present only if it was observed during the entire interval. Within partial-interval sampling, the target behavior is recorded as present if it was observed at any time during the interval. Finally, within momentary time sampling, the target behavior is recorded as present if it was observed at a particular point in the interval (e.g., within the first 3 seconds of the interval). Typically, interval recording procedures have been used to estimate the level of behavior for an individual target student. The number of intervals in which the behavior was observed is divided by the total number of intervals and then multiplied by 100% in order to obtain an overall estimate of occurrence. For example, if a target behavior was observed during 10 out of a total of 20 intervals, the percentage of occurrence would be 50%. An example of an interval recording sheet is presented in Figure 8.3 (see also Form 8.2 for a blank form).

Because it does not matter whether the behavior occurred for 1 second or 20 seconds within a 30-second interval, partial-interval sampling has been noted to potentially over-

Instructions: At the start of each interval, record whether the class is on task (+) or off task (−). If any disruptive behaviors occur during the remainder of the interval, place a mark (+) in the Behavior #2 column.

Time	Behavior 1 On task	Behavior 2 Disruptive	Notes
10:00–10:10	+	+	
10:10–10:20	+	+	
10:20–10:30	−	+	Multiple students talking to neighbors.
10:30–10:40	+		
10:40–10:50	−	+	Bill told a joke, students laughing.
10:50–11:00	−	+	A few students continue to laugh.
11:00–11:10	+		
11:10–11:20	−	+	Students turned around to look where noise came from.
11:20–11:30	+	+	
11:30–11:40	+	+	
11:40–11:50	−	+	Juan asked what was for lunch, students whispering.
11:50–12:00	−	+	Students looking at clock, turned around in seats.
Percentage of Intervals Observed	6/12 = 50%	10/12 = 83%	

FIGURE 8.3. Example of an interval recording sheet.

estimate the frequency of a behavior (Powell, Martindale, & Kulp, 1975; Powell, Martindale, Kulp, Martindale, & Bauman, 1977). In contrast, whole-interval sampling has been noted to potentially underestimate the frequency of a behavior. This is because if a behavior occurred for 28 of the 30 seconds in an interval, for example, it could not be recorded as present. Just as the first two beds that Goldilocks found in the forest were too hard and too soft but the third one was just right, momentary time sampling is said to strike a more desirable balance between the underestimation of whole-interval sampling and the overestimation of partial-interval sampling. Within momentary time sampling, a behavior is recorded as present if it occurs at the beginning or end of an interval (e.g., first or last 3 seconds). As long as the target behavior is not one that occurs at a very low or very high rate, studies have shown momentary time sampling to provide the most representative estimate of behavior (e.g., Brulle & Repp, 1984; Murphy & Goodall, 1980; Powell et al., 1975, 1977). As an additional benefit, because the behavior needs to be observed for only a few seconds during the interval, the demands placed on the observer are also greatly reduced.

Within the school-based literature, there are many examples of interval recording procedures also being used at the classwide level; however, many of these studies have utilized very short intervals, thereby limiting the feasibility of such approaches for classroom teachers. For example, in some cases, observers have rotated among the students, observing and recording a different student's behavior during each 10- to 30-second interval (e.g., Chafouleas et al., 2012; Lannie & McCurdy, 2007). Another possibility involves dividing the classroom into smaller groups and assessing the behavior of the entire group at predetermined times (see Figure 8.4). Sutherland and colleagues (2000; Sutherland, Alder, & Gunter, 2003), for example, divided target classrooms into quadrants and then rotated between observing

Time	Group	All students in group on task?	Notes
10:00–10:10	1	+	
10:10–10:20	2	+	
10:20–10:30	3	−	Side conversations
10:30–10:40	1	−	Turned around in seat
10:40–10:50	2	+	
10:50–11:00	3	+	
11:00–11:10	1	−	Head down on desk
11:10–11:20	2	+	
11:20–11:30	3	+	
11:30–11:40	1	−	Staring out window
Percentage of Intervals Observed		6/10 = 60%	

FIGURE 8.4. Example of a recording sheet for observing groups of students.

each of these four groups of students in random order. At the end of each 1-minute interval, the class received credit for being on task only if *all* members of the target quadrant were simultaneously on task.

One interval recording procedure that may be of greater utility to classroom teachers managing competing demands is the Planned Activity Check (PLA-Check; Risley & Cataldo, 1973). At predetermined intervals, an observer scans the room and records the number of students engaging in a specific target behavior. This number is then divided by the total number of students present and multiplied by 100% to generate a percentage of students engaged in the target behavior. An overall average for the observation period can then be estimated by computing an average across all intervals observed (see Figure 8.5, Form 8.3 for a blank form, and Box 8.2 for a case example). Although some studies have used fairly short intervals (e.g., 15 seconds; Raspa, McWilliam, & Maher Ridley, 2001), recent evidence has suggested that increasing PLA-Check intervals up to 5 minutes may not meaningfully decrease the overall accuracy of observational estimates (Dart, Radley, Briesch, Furlow, & Cavell, 2016). The blank interval rating form provided in Form 8.4 for use in conducting PLA-Check assessments was adapted from Krasch and Carter (2009). By filling in the box that corresponds with the number of students demonstrating the target behavior during each interval, one can easily see any patterns that emerge with regard to problem behavior throughout the day. Furthermore, by rotating the page 90 degrees and connecting each of the filled-in boxes with a line, you get a quick graph of what student behavior looks like throughout the day.

Rating-Based Tools for Assessing Event and State Behaviors

All measurements exist on a continuum with regard to the directness of measurement, or how close in time measurement occurs to the actual occurrence of behavior. The methods described above offer the distinct advantage of being highly direct methods of assessment.

Instructions: At the end of each 5-minute block, scan the classroom and record the number of students observed out of their seats without permission.					
	Monday	**Tuesday**	**Wednesday**	**Thursday**	**Friday**
10:00–10:05	/ 25 =	/ 25 =	/ 25 =	/ 25 =	/ 25 =
10:05–10:10	/ 25 =	/ 25 =	/ 25 =	/ 25 =	/ 25 =
10:10–10:15	/ 25 =	/ 25 =	/ 25 =	/ 25 =	/ 25 =
10:15–10:20	/ 25 =	/ 25 =	/ 25 =	/ 25 =	/ 25 =
10:20–10:25	/ 25 =	/ 25 =	/ 25 =	/ 25 =	/ 25 =
10:25–10:30	/ 25 =	/ 25 =	/ 25 =	/ 25 =	/ 25 =
Average for Literacy Block					

FIGURE 8.5. Example of a Planned Activity Check recording sheet.

BOX 8.2. Case Example:
Using Observational Data to Monitor Performance

After returning from a professional conference, Mr. Chun decides to implement a classwide token economy system with his third-grade students. He knows that it is important to collect outcome data in order to determine whether the intervention is working, but he is not sure of the best way to do this. Given that his main goal is to reduce the number of side conversations that are taking place during class time, he considers how to best monitor this behavior. Although it would be straightforward to keep a running tally of the number of side conversations observed, Mr. Chun realizes that this will not account for the fact that these conversations vary widely in length. For example, whereas one student may make a quick comment to his or her neighbor, another pair of students may engage in a lengthier back-and-forth dialogue. In addition, he questions the feasibility of keeping a tally, given the constant vigilance that would be necessary in order to scan the room for offenders.

Given the complexities inherent in counting side conversations, Mr. Chun next considers use of an interval recording procedure. In order to ensure that interval recording will be practical to use on a daily basis, he decides to use a Planned Activity Check procedure. Mr. Chun decides to begin the intervention during language arts and sets a vibrating timer to buzz at 5-minute intervals throughout the instructional block. When the buzzer goes off, he scans the room to count the number of students engaged in side conversations with their peers and records this number on the form below. At the end of the period, he then calculates an overall percentage for the day by summing the total number of students observed talking and dividing by the number of students in the classroom (20) times the number of observation intervals (6), or 120. This allows him to track the percentage of students engaging in side conversations on a daily basis in order to assess the effectiveness of the intervention over time.

Instructions: At the end of each 5-minute block, scan the classroom and record the number of students engaging in side conversations with their peers.

	Monday	Tuesday	Wednesday	Thursday	Friday	Week
10:00–10:05	6	2	0	1	3	
10:05–10:10	2	0	1	3	0	
10:10–10:15	5	5	2	0	0	
10:15–10:20	4	0	2	0	0	
10:20–10:25	3	8	4	2	0	
10:25–10:30	0	0	2	2	2	
Average	20/120 students = 17%	15/120 students = 13%	11/120 students = 9%	8/120 students = 7%	5/120 students = 4%	10% weekly average

Direct assessment tools are those for which the recording of behavior occurs in close proximity to the actual behavior. Assessment procedures become more indirect as they become more removed in time from the actual occurrence of behavior. Although some degree of accuracy is sacrificed when individuals are asked to provide their perspectives on target behaviors at a later date and time, these procedures do help to maximize feasibility and therefore may be preferred within the context of busy classrooms.

There are several rating-based tools that classroom teachers may use to assess student behavior in the classroom. The first option is what has been called Direct Behavior Rating (DBR). DBR involves the rating of a predetermined, operationally defined behavior at the end of a predetermined block of time (e.g., math instruction, school day; Chafouleas, Riley-Tillman, & Sugai, 2007). Ratings have most typically been conducted using a Likert-type scale consisting of six (e.g., Volpe & Briesch, 2012) to 11 (e.g., Chafouleas et al., 2010) gradients. For example, a teacher might be asked to rate the percentage of time that a student was academically engaged during math instruction using a 0–10 scale. Although the use of Likert ratings is similar in format to completing a comprehensive rating scale such as the Behavior Assessment System for Children (BASC-3; Reynolds & Kamphaus, 2015), use of DBR requires that the ratings be conducted based on a more discrete block of time (e.g., during an instructional period rather than over a period of 1–2 months).

DBR has most commonly been used to monitor the behavior of individual students; however, extensions to the classwide level have also been noted. In a study by Riley-Tillman, Methe, and Weegar (2009), the classroom teacher rated the overall engagement of the entire classroom at the end of each silent reading period across baseline and intervention phases. Engagement data were simultaneously collected using systematic direct observation in order to provide a check on the validity of the obtained data. When data obtained from both sources were graphed, similar findings were demonstrated using visual and numerical analysis. Examples of DBR forms that may be used with both older and younger classrooms can be found in Figure 8.6. and a case example is provided in Box 8.3 (p. 170).

Whereas DBR has typically been used to estimate the percentage of time that a target behavior occurred, performance-based behavioral recordings may be used when frequency is not what we are most interested in. For example, Likert-type ratings may be used to estimate duration or intensity (Steege & Watson, 2009). When creating a performance-based behavioral recording form, each point of the Likert scale should be clearly defined (see Figure 8.7, p. 171). In a study by Steege, Davin, and Hathaway (2001), for example, staff in a group-home setting used a 5-point Likert rating scale to rate stereotypic behavior in three individuals with autism. The 5 points on the Likert scale were designed to correspond with the number of minutes during which the behavior was observed (e.g., 1 = 1 second to 2 minutes 59 seconds, 2 = 3 minutes to 5 minutes 59 seconds, 3 = 6 minutes to 8 minutes 59 seconds). A very different example of performance-based behavioral recording was developed by Iwata, Pace, Kissel, Nau, and Farber (1990) in order to assess damage to surface tissue caused by self-injurious behavior. Three-point Likert-type scales were used to estimate both the number of wounds present (e.g., 1 = one wound, 2 = two to four wounds) and the severity of those wounds (e.g., 1 = local swelling only, 2 = extensive swelling). A blank performance-based behavioral recording form is provided in Form 8.5.

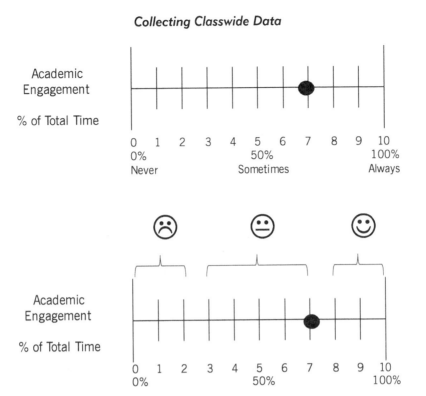

FIGURE 8.6. Example DBR scales for use with older and younger students.

Permanent Product Data

Although observational or rating-based methods can provide us with important information as to what effects the intervention has had on key outcomes of interest (e.g., engagement, disruptive behavior, productivity), we acknowledge the fact that collecting these types of data also involves an investment of resources—that is, beyond the time and materials needed to implement the intervention itself, additional energies are needed to collect new data in order to evaluate intervention effectiveness. There is, however, an alternative approach to monitoring progress that can help to reduce the demands on busy classroom teachers: use of permanent product data.

Permanent products, or extant data, are those naturally occurring sources of data that already exist in the environment. Some of the most common classroom-based examples of permanent products are those of an academic nature: quiz or test grades, completion of assignments, and submission of homework, to name just a few. Because teachers tend to maintain a lasting record of these outcomes of interest, such as in a grade book, these data can be harnessed in order to evaluate student progress rather than needing to collect new information. Permanent products may also be used, however, to monitor behavioral performance over time in response to classwide intervention.

The key to identifying potential permanent products for use in monitoring classwide interventions is to consider what tangible, lasting records of behavior result from implementation of the intervention. In other words, at the end of the day, what records of student behavior are you left with? One intervention that most easily lends itself to the evaluation of permanent

---

BOX 8.3. Case Example:
Using Direct Behavior Rating to Monitor Performance

Mrs. Bindra had been successfully using a token economy in her second-grade classroom for several years, but this year she has made a big move to teach fifth grade. Given that a major part of her job this year involves preparing her students to transition to middle school, she would like to put an intervention in place that promotes a greater level of personal responsibility and accountability for classroom behavior. She therefore decides to implement a classwide self-management intervention, wherein all students will complete a checklist at the start of the day to self-assess how prepared they are for class. Specifically, each student will indicate whether he or she (1) put belongings away in the closet, (2) placed completed homework in the appropriate bin, (3) took out an appropriate writing utensil and paper, and (4) began quietly writing his or her daily reflection by the time that the bell rang.

Although she could theoretically monitor these preparatory behaviors at the individual student level, Mrs. Bindra is concerned about the amount of time that this would take each morning. She would like for the daily check to take no more than a couple of minutes, so as not to distract from the morning routine. She therefore decides to complete a classwide rating of behavior using DBR. As students are preparing for class each morning, she will circulate around the room making mental notes of how many students have not successfully completed the checklist items. She will then use a 5-point DBR scale (i.e., 0 = no students completed, 1 = some students completed, 2 = roughly half of the students completed, 3 = many students completed, 4 = all students completed) to rate each checklist item.

Daily DBR: Classroom Preparation					
Put belongings away	0	1	2	3	4
Submitted homework	0	1	2	3	4
Took out materials	0	1	2	3	4
Quietly began reflection	0	1	2	3	4
				Total Points:	

---

product data is a self-management intervention—that is, because students typically evaluate their behavior and record it on a piece of paper, these monitoring sheets may be collected and used to track performance over time. If students were self-monitoring the number of talk-outs in class, for example, the average number of talk-outs per class period could be calculated each day and monitored to determine whether sufficient progress was being made.

In some cases, however, permanent records of performance may not be automatically generated through implementation of the intervention. It may therefore be necessary to explicitly add a step to incorporate permanent product recording. Consider, for example, implementation of a classwide token economy intervention. Although the number of tokens earned each day could certainly be used to monitor performance over time, teachers may not always know how many tokens each student has earned if the students are responsible for holding on to them until they wish to redeem them for a reward. A permanent product could easily be generated, however, by keeping a central log of the number of tokens earned each day. Similarly, if student performance is evaluated in relation to a goal at the end of each day when implementing a group contingency intervention, the only record of performance may be whether or not the goal was met. A more detailed picture of student performance could be generated, however, by recording the number of points each group earned on a daily basis and tracking this number over time (see Box 8.4 for a case example).

Certainly, the key advantages of using permanent product data relate to applied feasibility. The fact that additional data do not need to be collected beyond what was already generated through the intervention means fewer demands on both time and resources. There are, however, some disadvantages to the use of permanent product data that should be noted. Whereas observational and rating-based measures can be tailored to capture different aspects of behavior that may be of interest, permanent products are fixed in nature. As a result, you are limited to knowing about only certain aspects of student behavior and cannot necessarily dig below the surface. Knowing how many tokens a student earned in a given day, for example, does not tell you what types of behaviors the student displayed to earn those tokens or how many opportunities for earning tokens the student might have actually missed. It is therefore important to design permanent product recording logs to include all of the information believed to be pertinent to answering those questions of most interest. Finally, there are some permanent products such as grades and behavioral attendance that may naturally change over the course of a semester. For example, many classes start with assignments that are reviews or are very basic, and then the work becomes progressively more difficult as the curriculum becomes more demanding and abstract. Thus, there may naturally be a worsening in student classwork. Similarly, with behavior, there are many schools where student behavior during the early fall is reasonably good, but behavior problems and office discipline referrals increase as the school year progresses. If such change occurs, it may make evaluating classroom behaviors more challenging. Comparison with other classes may be appropriate in these situations.

Rating Key		
0 = Julia's tantrum lasts < 1 minute	0 = Vocal only, not directed at others	
1 = Julia's tantrum lasts 1–2 minutes	1 = Vocal only, but directed at others	
2 = Julia's tantrum lasts 2–3 minutes	2 = Vocal + physical, does not affect others	
3 = Julia's tantrum lasts 3–4 minutes	3 = Vocal + physical, disturbs others	
4 = Julia's tantrum lasts > 4 minutes	4 = Vocal + physical, injures others	
Time Period/Activity	**Duration**	**Intensity**
Morning meeting	2	2
Literacy stations	0	1
Recess	3	4

FIGURE 8.7. Example of a performance-based behavioral recording form.

BOX 8.4. Case Example:
Using Permanent Product Data to Monitor Performance

Ms. Cisneros is concerned about the performance of her sixth-grade students in period A, and believes that these academic problems stem from the level of noise and activity in the classroom. After consulting with the Student Support Team, Ms. Cisneros decides to implement a group contingency with response cost aimed at reducing disruptive behavior. She divides the class into four teams for the purpose of playing a game. At the start of each period, she puts 5 points in each team's "point bank" on the whiteboard and reminds the class of the "four keys to mathematical success": (1) look at the board, (2) listen quietly, (3) take notes, and (4) ask clarification questions. If any member of the team violates one of the four classroom expectations, 1 point is taken away from that team's total. At the end of the week, those teams with 20 or more points on the board are excused from having to do the weekend homework assignment.

At the end of the first week of implementation, Ms. Cisneros sits down with one of her colleagues from the Student Support Team to discuss any problems that may have arisen. She reports that the students have been excited about the intervention and appear motivated to earn the weekend homework pass. When they move to review the student outcome data, however, they come to realize that there is only one data point for the week—the number of points remaining in each team's point bank—which is written on the whiteboard. In discussing this further, Ms. Cisneros and her colleague decide that it would be helpful to have a daily record of performance as well in order to better understand how student behavior fluctuates throughout the course of the week. Together, they draw up a simple recording sheet so that Ms. Cisneros can enter the number of points that each team has remaining on a daily basis. She will keep the recording sheet inside of her grade book and then graph the average number of points earned by each team on a daily basis in order to draw a more detailed picture of student performance in response to the intervention.

Group Contingency Point Log: Period A				
	Team 1	Team 2	Team 3	Team 4	Class Average
Monday					
Tuesday					
Wednesday					
Thursday					
Friday					

COLLECTING AND EVALUATING DATA
TO DETERMINE INTERVENTION EFFECTIVENESS

Collecting Data

Determining which data collection method to use can be similar to settling on the perfect color of paint for your living room. After laying out all of the options side by side, you may feel yourself drawn to one in particular. The more you sit with that option, however, the more questions may arise (e.g., Will it be too dark? Will it clash with the furniture?). You may even go out and buy a sample of paint to test out in a small corner of the room before deciding that another shade would be better. Lots of time and brain power goes into selecting the perfect paint; however, once that decision is made and you can finally breathe in a sigh of relief, you realize that the work of actually painting the room is still ahead of you.

Once you have selected a data collection method that strikes the right balance between precision and feasibility, it is time to lay out a plan for how the data will actually be collected. Among the questions that need to be answered at this stage are when and how often data collection will occur. If the intervention that you wish to evaluate is being implemented only during a particular time of day (e.g., during literacy instruction, during classroom transitions), this makes the question of when data will be collected very straightforward. If, however, an intervention is implemented over a large portion of, or throughout, the school day, it will be necessary to make some choices. When using data collection methods that are fairly quick and simple to carry out, it may be possible to divide the overall schedule into smaller chunks (e.g., corresponding to different subjects or instructional activities) and to collect data throughout the school day. On the other hand, if the data collection method is one that would be too cumbersome to use continuously, specific time periods or settings might be prioritized and targeted for data collection.

The next step is to collect some data before the intervention is put into place in order to obtain an estimate of baseline performance. The idea of baseline data collection is one that may strike some people as counterproductive. After all, if we know that there is a problem and have identified something that may work to alleviate that problem, why wouldn't we want to put it into place right away? There are at least a couple of reasons why collecting data in the absence of intervention can be incredibly important. First, baseline data are needed in order to verify that there is, in fact, a problem that warrants action. If we are going to invest our time and efforts into carrying out an intervention plan, we first want to know that such efforts are needed. Collecting baseline data can therefore help to confirm whether the hunch that we have about a behavior is a correct one. Second, baseline data are needed in order to set appropriate goals for intervention. If we do not have a concrete sense of what behavior looked like prior to intervention, there will be no way to tell for sure whether or not our efforts have been successful.

The next question that inevitably arises is one of how long baseline data should be collected before an intervention can be put into place. Unfortunately, there is no magic number of days or data points that are needed; rather, decisions must be made by considering elements of each individual situation. The general rule, however, is that data should be collected until they demonstrate a predictable pattern of behavior (Kratochwill et al., 2010). When the pattern of behavior is predictable, this allows us to estimate what behavior would probably look like in the future if we chose not to intervene. If you look at Figure 8.8, you will see two very different patterns of responding. The graph on the left represents responding that is highly variable; it is therefore very difficult to predict what the student's behavior will look like the next day. The graph on the right, however, depicts behavior that is steadily increasing. If we had to guess what the student's behavior would look like the next day, we would have a fair guess as to what to expect. Generally speaking, fewer data points will be needed to derive a general sense of baseline performance when estimates of behavior are highly consistent, whereas a greater number of data points will be necessary when data are highly variable.

The final determination is how long an intervention should be implemented before a decision regarding student response can be made. As with the collection of baseline data, there are no hard-and-fast rules regarding the number of data points that should be collected while an intervention is in place. In fact, common recommendations are that an intervention should be implemented for a period of time that would be considered "reasonable" in order to see an effect, or for long enough to be able to say with confidence that the intervention was or was not effective. When more concrete guidelines have been put forth, individuals and organizations have generally endorsed a range of time. For example, the RTI Action Network (Metcalf, n.d.) suggests that a decision regarding student response to intervention may be made after 6–12 weeks, assuming that the intervention has been implemented consistently and weekly data are available. Regardless of the implementation time frame selected at the outset, however, it is critical that data are monitored in an ongoing fashion in order to determine whether the intervention is showing promise or if changes may need to be made to the plan.

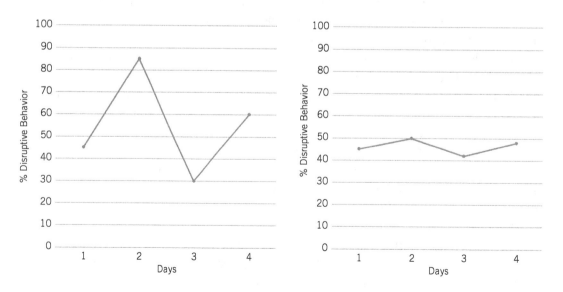

FIGURE 8.8. Examples of data demonstrating high and low variability.

Evaluating Data

Although collecting progress monitoring data surely involves heavy lifting, the work is not over once the data have been entered into a spreadsheet or computer program! Rather, it is important that we actually look at the data in order to determine whether or not the intervention has been effective. There are two primary approaches that can be used to evaluate intervention effectiveness: employing visual analysis or calculating a quantitative measure of effect size.

Visual Analysis

When using visual analysis, a determination is made as to whether behavior improved substantially from baseline to intervention by visually examining a graph. Although this approach may sound fairly simple, there is more to visual analysis than simply "eyeballing it." Three primary strategies are typically used—either in isolation or combination—to visually analyze single-case data (see Figure 8.9). The first thing that can be examined is whether there is a change in the degree of *variability* in the data. This is sometimes referred to as the "bounce" in the data, or how much the values vary from day to day. In most cases, it is desirable for behavior to become less variable over time. For example, if a student's level of engagement in classroom instruction was found to vary from 35% one day to 75% the next day, we would want engagement levels to be more consistently high. In some cases, however, an increase in variability may be seen as a good thing. Often this is true when the baseline level of a behavior is consistently very low (e.g., consistently close to zero). In such a case, seeing a few spikes in the data would actually be considered a positive finding.

The second thing that can be examined when using visual analysis is whether there is a change in the *trend* of the data. Trend refers to the slope of the data, or the direction in which the data are going. When data appear to be going up over time, this represents a positive trend. When data appear to be going down over time, this represents a negative trend. If the data appear to be going neither up nor down, this represents a flat, or zero, trend. The greater the change over time, the steeper the trend will be. The presence of trend implies that there is a gradual change in the target behavior over time. For example, if a student receives social skills instruction, we would expect the student to demonstrate a greater number of prosocial behaviors as the total number of sessions increases. It is important to note, however, that in some cases an immediate change in behavior may be more likely than a gradual change. The introduction of a token economy, for example, may result in behavior change as soon as appropriate behavior is reinforced. In such cases, examining the immediacy of change (i.e., how quickly the effect occurs subsequent to introduction of the intervention) may make more sense than examining trend.

The third thing that can be examined when using visual analysis is whether there is a change in the *mean level* of the behavior from baseline to intervention. When an intervention is put into place in order to decrease a problem behavior, we want to see that the average level of the behavior decreases from baseline to intervention. In contrast, when

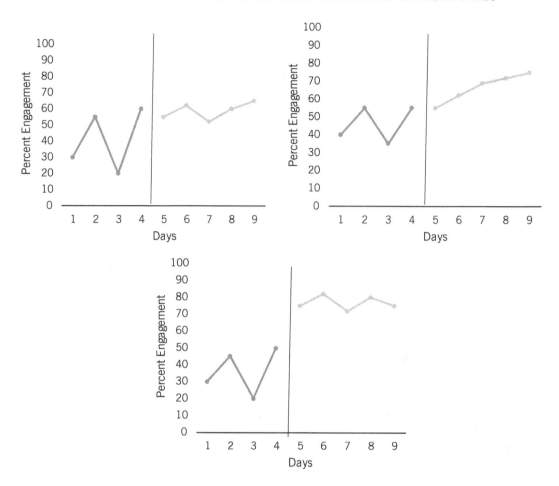

FIGURE 8.9. Demonstrating changes in variability, trend, and level.

the goal is to increase the degree to which a desirable behavior is present, we want to see that the average level of the behavior increases from baseline to intervention. Although examining change in the mean level of behavior can provide useful information, it is important to keep in mind that the greater the variability or trend in the data, the less meaningful the mean value becomes. This is clearly illustrated by considering that the mean of four highly variable data points gathered during intervention (20%, 90%, 10%, 100%) would be 55%.

Although there are three aspects of the data that *may* be analyzed, this does not mean that one *should* necessarily analyze all three. Instead, it is important to consider what about the behavior you would expect to change after implementing the intervention. If, for example, baseline data highlighted a great degree of variability in classroom engagement from one day to the next, you might look to see whether the intervention helped to stabilize the student's behavior such that he or she consistently maintained engagement at a particular level (i.e., change in variability). If, on the other hand, classroom engagement was found to be consistently low during baseline, it might be more meaningful to examine whether changes occurred in level (i.e., overall increase in mean level of engagement) and/or trend (i.e., from zero trend to increasing trend).

Because a detailed overview of using visual analysis to examine single-case data is beyond the scope of this chapter, interested readers are referred to Kratochwill and Levin (2014) and Riley-Tillman and Burns (2009) for an in-depth discussion of this topic.

Basic Metrics for Quantifying Effect Size

Visual analysis has generally been considered to be the "gold standard" for analyzing time-series data, given the assumption that two people should be able to look at a graph and agree that an effect is there if the effect is truly present. Research conducted over the past several decades, however, has suggested that raters may not be as consistent in their agreement concerning visual effects as one might be led to assume (e.g., Jones, Weinrott, & Vaught, 1978; Ottenbacher, 1990). As a result, an increasing number of researchers in the fields of psychology and education have begun to calculate effect sizes in single-subject research, therein focusing on the practical significance of results (Brossart, Parker, Olson, & Mahadevan, 2006). It has been suggested that quantitative analysis of single-subject data may be particularly useful when the baseline data are unstable, or when the researcher cannot predict the effects of a treatment (Parker et al., 2005). In recent years, numerous effect size estimators have been developed by researchers in the fields of education and psychology; however, many require sophisticated statistical expertise or software. In this chapter, we therefore limit our review to those effect size estimators that can be calculated by hand and easily interpreted by school-based professionals: percentage of nonoverlapping data (PND) and percentage of all nonoverlapping data (PAND).

PERCENTAGE OF NONOVERLAPPING DATA

Of all of the effect size metrics that have been proposed for use with time-series data, the PND metric has been around the longest and is perhaps the easiest to calculate. PND looks at potential overlap between data points collected in the baseline and intervention phases, and represents the proportion of intervention data points that exceed those data points observed during baseline (Scruggs & Mastropieri, 2013). In order to calculate this percentage, one must first identify the level (i.e., y-coordinate) of the "best," or most extreme, baseline data point. Determining the best data point, however, requires consideration of the nature of the target behavior. If the target behavior is one that is problematic or undesirable, lower is better (i.e., lower levels of disruptive behavior or aggression). However, if the target behavior is one that is positive or desirable, higher is better (i.e., higher levels of prosocial behavior or engagement). Once the best baseline data point has been identified, the next step is to count the number of intervention data points that represent improvement beyond the best point during baseline. This number represents the number of nonoverlapping data points. The number of nonoverlapping data points is then divided by the total number of intervention data points and multiplied by 100% to obtain the PND. Interpretive guidelines for PND have suggested that percentages above 90% represent strong effectiveness, percentages between 70 and 90% represent effectiveness, percentages between 50 and 70% represent questionable effectiveness, and percentages below 50% represent a lack of effectiveness (Scruggs & Mastropieri, 1998).

PERCENTAGE OF ALL NONOVERLAPPING DATA

One of the commonly noted drawbacks of PND has been the fact that it is highly influenced by extreme data points—that is, even if the overwhelming majority of baseline data points represent an undesirable level of behavior, one particularly good data point would mean that the PND would be 0%. The PAND metric was therefore proposed as an alternative to PND that is less dependent on individual data points (Parker, Hagan-Burke, & Vannest, 2007). PAND represents the percentage of nonoverlapping data points between phase changes, which in this case is defined as the "minimum number [of data points] that would have to be swapped across phases for complete score separation" (Parker et al., 2007, p. 197). An additional advantage of PAND is that it can be translated to a Pearson's phi coefficient, which may be more easily interpreted given that it is a "bona fide effect size" (Cohen, 1988, p. 223). At the same time, however, it is important to note that the use of PAND is recommended only in those cases in which a minimum of 20 data points have been collected.

In order to calculate the PAND, the first step involves identifying the minimum number of data points that you would need to swap across phases in order for there to be no overlap between phases. This number is then divided by the total number of data points and multiplied by 100% in order to obtain a percentage (i.e., PAND). Once the PAND has been calculated, the next step is to create a 2×2 contingency table (see Figure 8.10). First, the percentage of baseline data points to total data points is entered at the bottom of column 1, in the space marked by the letter E. Second, the percentage of intervention data points to total data points is entered in the bottom of column 2, in the space marked by the letter F. Third, the percentage of overlapping data points (i.e., $1 - $ PAND) is divided by 2 and the resultant value is entered in cells B and C. Finally, the values for cells A and D are determined by subtracting C from E and B from F, respectively. After all cells in the 2×2 table have been populated, phi can then be calculated using the formula $(a / [a + c]) - (b / [b + d])$. Imagine, for example, that you collected 5 data points during baseline, 10 during the intervention phase, and that the PAND value was 60%. You will see in Figure 8.10 how a phi coefficient of 0.09 would be calculated using this information. Interpretative guidelines put forth by Cohen (1988) suggest that a phi coefficient less than 0.30 is considered negligible, 0.30–0.49 is small, 0.50–0.69 is moderate, and 0.70 or above is strong.

Determining Next Steps

Once visual analysis has been conducted, or quantitative measures of effect calculated, the ultimate decision regarding intervention effectiveness must be made. If the data suggest that the intervention was effective in changing student behavior, there are a couple

A	B
E – C	(1 – PAND) / 2
C	**D**
(1 – PAND) / 2	F – B
E	**F**
% of data points in baseline	% of data points in intervention

A	B
13	20
C	**D**
20	47
E	**F**
33	67

$$[13/(13+20)] - [20/(20+47)] = .39 - .30 = .09$$

FIGURE 8.10. Contingency table for converting PAND to phi.

of options that we may consider. In those cases in which the intervention was not overly burdensome to implement, and therefore could easily be maintained over a longer period of time, it may make most sense to keep the intervention in place as is. In this situation, the old adage "If it ain't broke, don't fix it" could certainly apply. For example, after implementing a token economy system for several weeks, the systems and procedures may become naturally integrated into the framework of the classroom. In such a case, it would make most sense to simply keep doing what one has been successfully doing. If, however, implementation has been challenging and is not seen as sustainable, it may make more sense to look for ways in which to scale back the intervention. Implementation may be limited to certain times of the day or reinforcement may be delivered less frequently moving forward. Regardless of the modifications made to the system, however, it is important to continue to collect outcome data intermittently (e.g., once every week as opposed to once every day) in order to ensure continued effectiveness.

If, however, it appears that the intervention has not been successful, it is important to acknowledge that the absence of a positive intervention effect can signify one of three things. One possibility is that the intervention was not implemented in the way that was intended (i.e., with fidelity; see Chapter 9). If fidelity data show that the intervention was not implemented with the frequency or intensity required, troubleshooting should first focus on putting consultative supports in place to raise fidelity. If, however, fidelity data show that the intervention was implemented as intended, the second possibility is that the intervention was of insufficient intensity. As we discuss in Chapter 10, there are several ways in which we may intensify an intervention to better meet the needs of one or more students. It may therefore be useful to test such modifications in order to see whether intervention effectiveness is enhanced. The third option, however, is that the intervention simply was not effective. Even those interventions that have been rigorously evaluated in order to be classified as "evidence based" may not be well aligned with the needs, skills, or other unique characteristics of an individual student. In such a case, an alternative intervention may be warranted.

CONCLUSIONS

No matter how well researched the intervention, or seemingly perfect the fit, we cannot know with certainty that it was an effective choice without collecting outcome data. As we have outlined in this chapter, there are several different strategies that may be used to monitor intervention effectiveness. Whereas direct observation methods provide us with data that tend to be more objective and therefore accurate, collecting these data may be more time- and resource intensive. Rating-based tools, on the other hand, may be less burdensome to use but are also subject to a greater degree of subjectivity. Regardless of the method used, it is important that data are collected both prior to and during implementation in order to determine intervention effectiveness. Either visual analysis or quantitative effect size metrics may be used to support decision making when unsure of whether an intervention should be kept in place or discontinued.

Blank Scatterplot

Instructions:					
	Monday	Tuesday	Wednesday	Thursday	Friday

Blank Interval Recording Form

Date: _____   Time: _____

Instructions:			
Time	Behavior 1	Behavior 2	Notes
Percentage of Intervals Observed			

Planned Activity Check Recording Sheet

Classroom: _____

Date: _____   Start Time: _____   End Time: _____

Instructions: At the start of the observation, record the total number of students present during the observation. Then, at the start of each interval, scan the classroom and count the number of students who are observed to be off task.

Total Number of Students Present: _____

Time	Behavior		Total Number of Students	Percentage of Students
		÷		
		÷		
		÷		
		÷		
		÷		
		÷		
		÷		
		÷		
		÷		
		÷		
		÷		
		÷		
		÷		
		÷		
		÷		
		÷		
		÷		
		÷		
		÷		
		÷		
		÷		
		÷		
	Average Percentage of Students			

Blank PLA-Check Form

Instructions:	
Interval	**Number of Students Engaged in Target Behavior**

Blank Performance-Based Behavioral Rating Form

Rating Key			
0 =			
1 =			
2 =			
3 =			
4 =			
Time Period/Activity	**Target Behavior:** _____	**Target Behavior:** _____	**Target Behavior:** _____

CHAPTER 9

Assessing Intervention Integrity

We have big ideas about classroom management. By reading the first eight chapters of this book, we hope that you have come away with the positive belief that these interventions can be effective in changing student behavior and that they are practices that you can feasibly implement. The previous chapters have focused on heuristics and practices that have empirical support behind them. Unfortunately, even the best intervention will fail to support student behavior if it is not implemented as intended. Consider a child who has been prescribed some form of medication to address symptoms of ADHD. For students with ADHD, a consistent medication regimen can be considered a best-practice intervention to help reduce the number of acting-out behaviors while subsequently increasing the amount of time spent on task. Unfortunately, many of these students take the medications erratically, which means their behavior can also become erratic. If a child is not taking the medication as designed, does that mean the medication itself is ineffective? Of course not. In fact, an improper medication regimen is one of the principal concerns for many physicians.

The same is true for many of the practices that we described earlier—if the intervention is not implemented as designed, behavior may not improve. In other words, it is not enough to prescribe a behavioral intervention—instead we need to consider whether interventions *can be* implemented as intended and whether they *are* being implemented as intended. Whether an intervention is implemented as intended has been referred to within the literature as treatment integrity, treatment fidelity, treatment adherence, procedural reliability, and treatment plan implementation (Gresham, 2009). For simplicity within this chapter, we use the term "treatment integrity." Treatment integrity is critically important to intervention evaluation. If no changes in student behavior are seen, knowing the level of treatment integrity can help us to understand whether the lack of response is simply due to a lack or absence of treatment. This knowledge is particularly important when making high-stakes special education classification decisions based upon response-to-intervention data—that is, we do not want to judge a student as nonresponsive to intervention efforts and in need of more intensive services if the reason for nonresponse is a lack of treatment fidelity. Said differently, if we aren't doing the right thing in the right way, then we are in error—not the children. It should come as no surprise that research has found that student outcomes improve as intervention integrity improves (Gresham, Gansle, Noell, Cohen, & Rosenblum, 1993; Noell, Gresham, & Gansle, 2002; Noell et al., 2005; Sterling-Turner, Watson, & Moore, 2002). If positive changes in student behavior do occur, knowing the level of treatment integrity can help us to understand whether the effects are due to the intervention or to other outside factors.

Although we cannot sit with and coach each of you through the implementation of every strategy and intervention discussed in this book, we can make recommendations for things you can do to make sure you are implementing with integrity. This is why it is important to devote a chapter to discussing the importance of treatment integrity and the ways in which it may be promoted and monitored. After all, simply knowing that particular classroom management strategies are effective does not mean that we as educators will change our practice (Fixsen, Naoom, Blase, Friedman, & Wallace, 2005; Noell et al., 2005). We highlight the different available methods for treatment integrity assessment (e.g., permanent product review, direct observation) as well as recent literature related to effective strategies for promoting intervention integrity.

ASSESSING TREATMENT INTEGRITY

How to Assess Treatment Integrity

Within a given day, there are a seemingly endless number of tasks that a classroom teacher must manage. There is attendance to be taken, homework to be checked, lessons to be delivered, behavior to be regulated—the list goes on. It comes as no surprise that, with all of the other things that teachers have to do in the classroom, it can be difficult to also monitor treatment integrity. In fact, research has shown that there is a tendency for teachers to overestimate adherence to intervention plans when asked to report on implementation (Noell et al., 2005). In a study of nearly 30 teachers, for example, teachers were asked to estimate their adherence to behavioral intervention plans for individual students (Wickstrom, Jones, LaFleur, & Witt, 1998). Although the teachers themselves reported that they had followed the plans with a high degree of integrity, direct observations demonstrated that 100% of the teachers were actually implementing the interventions with less than 10% integrity. In fact, the average level of integrity was only 4%! These results suggest that simply asking someone if he or she is implementing something is not sufficient. Instead, it is important that we conduct a deliberate and purposeful assessment of treatment integrity. This is accomplished through three steps of operationally defining the intervention, selecting an appropriate method of measurement, and estimating the level of implementation.

Operationally Defining the Intervention

The first essential step in assessing treatment integrity is to operationally define the intervention. As we've talked about throughout this book, operational definitions are important when implementing classroom interventions in order to promote a shared understanding of the target behaviors. In much the same way, operationally defining the intervention helps to affirm what steps are considered critical to intervention implementation. Operationally defining an intervention first involves conducting a task analysis. Whenever we have a big task or project ahead of us in everyday life, an effective strategy to ensure that it gets done is to break it down into a number of smaller steps. When planning a wedding, for example, the number of things that need to be done may at first feel completely overwhelming. In planning dinner, there are caterers to be hired, seating arrangements to determine, response cards to send out, and so on. However, sitting down and writing out a list of all of the individual tasks that need to be accomplished can help to ease anxiety and provide a game plan for what needs to happen and when.

Task analyzing an intervention similarly helps to provide a road map for implementation. Something to keep in mind, however, is that there is often one set of steps that must be completed prior to implementing an intervention and one set of steps that must be completed during the intervention. The preparatory set of steps is assessed only once at the outset of the intervention. This includes steps such as selecting the target behaviors and determining what rewards will be used. The active implementation steps, on the other hand, are assessed on a daily basis. These include steps such as reminding students of the expectations and administering points and rewards. Throughout the previous chapters, we have provided coach cards that address both the preparatory and active implementation steps needed to effectively implement a particular intervention. In Table 9.1, we provide an additional example of how these steps would be delineated for the Good Behavior Game (GBG).

In some cases, we may be fortunate to find that a component checklist already exists, particularly when using a packaged intervention. If not, we must start by identifying the first essential step needed to implement the intervention (e.g., provide a rationale for why the intervention is being implemented) and then follow by adding on subsequent steps (e.g., teach students what the behavioral expectations are, post expectations at the front of the classroom). Because it can be easy to overlook a small but important step (imagine how your birthday cake would turn out if you forgot to add the baking powder!), it can be helpful

TABLE 9.1. Assessing Integrity of the GBG Prior to and during Implementation

Preparatory steps (one time)	During implementation (daily)
• Identify the target behaviors. • Communicate the target behaviors to students. • Determine the criteria for losing points. • Determine the criteria for receiving prizes. • Determine appropriate prizes for students. • Determine a time period for the game.	• Divide the classroom into two or more equal teams. • Reset board to collect points for the session. • Begin the interval and remove points from each team. • Review number of points at the end of the session and record on data sheet. • Announce winner. • Administer appropriate reward.

to ask a colleague who is familiar with the intervention to read over your checklist to see whether anything is missing.

Methods of Treatment Integrity Measurement

Once you have outlined the steps of the intervention, the next step is to determine how integrity will be measured. There are three main approaches that are used to assess integrity: direct observation, self-report, and permanent product recording. As is true of most things, there are both unique advantages and limitations to the use of each. Selecting an appropriate method involves balancing the accuracy of assessment with concerns related to practical feasibility.

At one end of the spectrum is an approach that is highly accurate but often more limited in terms of feasibility: direct observation. The use of direct observation involves having someone other than the primary implementer enter the classroom in order to observe implementation. The primary advantage of using direct observation is that it produces highly accurate estimates of behavior given the use of an objective observer. There are, however, a couple of limitations to the use of direct observation as well. One is that it requires additional manpower beyond what is available in the classroom. Additionally, there is potential for a reactivity effect, in which the person being observed changes his or her behavior due to the presence of an observer—that is, when a teacher knows his or her implementation is being monitored, he or she may be more likely to implement the intervention with integrity than under typical circumstances.

At the other end of the spectrum is self-report. The use of self-report involves having the implementer retrospectively indicate the degree to which an intervention was implemented as intended. The feasibility of this method is very high, given that it is quick to do and does not require any external resources. Related, there is also a much lower chance for a reactivity effect, given that the teacher is the one doing the recording. At the same time, however, this is often the least reliable method. As we discussed previously, there is a good deal of research that suggests that teachers tend to overestimate their degree of treatment integrity.

Somewhere in between direct observation and self-report is permanent product recording. Permanent products are data that already naturally exist in the classroom environment. Because there is no need to collect any additional information beyond that which is typical during implementation, the use of permanent products is more feasible than direct observation. Additionally, because implementation behavior is recorded in close proximity to the time at which it occurs, use of permanent products tends to result in a more accurate estimate of implementation than self-report. To assess permanent products, each step of the intervention should ideally result in a tangible outcome that can be reviewed at a later time (see Figure 9.1 for an example of a permanent product checklist for the GBG). Self-management interventions, for example, easily lend themselves to the use of permanent product recording because the monitoring card serves as a record of whether the intervention was actually carried out. One potential problem, however, is that not all interventions necessarily lend themselves to permanent products (Noell, 2007). The use of behavior-specific praise is one example for which there would not necessarily be a record of teacher behavior.

Intervention Step	Permanent Product	Present (Y/N)?
Divide classroom into two or more equal teams.	List of teams documented.	
Reset board to collect points for the session.	N/A	
Remind students of the GBG rules.	N/A	
Begin the interval and remove points from each team.	Documented loss of points on board.	
Review number of points at the end of the session and record on data sheet.	Total points for each team recorded on data sheet.	
Announce winner.	N/A	
Administer appropriate reward.	Awarded prize recorded on data sheet.	

FIGURE 9.1. Example of a permanent product recording sheet for the GBG.

Estimating Integrity

After selecting a method of recording, the next step is to determine how integrity will be calculated (see Table 9.2). When most of us think about treatment integrity, we think about it as a dichotomous (i.e., yes or no) question—that is, we pose the question of whether something was either implemented or not implemented. This is what is commonly referred to as adherence. One way that we can assess adherence is to calculate the percentage of total intervention steps that were carried out. Each step of the plan that was identified in operationally defining the intervention could be included in a checklist, with steps checked off as they are completed. Dividing the percentage of steps successfully completed by the total

TABLE 9.2. Available Options for Assessing Treatment Integrity

What is measured	How measured	How reported
Adherence	Was the intervention implemented (yes/no)?	• Percentage of total intervention steps completed within 1 day • Percentage of days on which each intervention step was completed
Quality of delivery	How was the intervention implemented?	• Qualitative rating of how well the intervention was implemented (e.g., 1–5 scale)
Participant responsiveness	How engaged were the participants?	• Qualitative rating of how engaged and responsive participants were (e.g., 1–5 scale)

number of steps would then provide a percentage of treatment integrity for that particular session. These daily percentages, in turn, could be averaged in order to provide an estimate of overall treatment integrity. Although understanding the overall level of treatment integrity can be helpful, in some situations we may be more interested in how often particular intervention components are implemented. In this situation, we might instead calculate a percentage within components but across days.

However, Dane and Schneider (1998) suggested that other dimensions of intervention implementation may be important to both consider and monitor as well, including the quality of delivery and participant responsiveness. When we talk about the quality of delivery, we are more interested in *how* the intervention is implemented than *whether* the intervention is implemented. Think back, if you will, to your own days in school and remember your favorite teachers. Chances are that their demeanor was cheerful and that they were enthusiastic about the subject matter. If you were lucky, their own excitement for learning was contagious and rubbed off on you in a way that even made learning trigonometry enjoyable. Throughout class, they maintained a perfect Goldilocks pace that was neither too slow nor too fast. Now imagine substituting one of those teachers—who was full of energy and enthusiasm—with what we will call a "robot teacher." The latter teacher delivers instruction in a very dry and matter-of-fact way. Rather than looking excited about the material, the teacher looks fairly bored or maybe even put out by the task. He or she fluctuates between moving through lessons at a tortoise's pace and speeding through explanations such that everyone is left behind. Even if both of these teachers get through the prescribed lesson by the end of the class period, who are you likely to learn more from? For most of us, we are likely to be more engaged—and therefore ultimately get more out of instruction—when the quality of implementation is high. Simply assessing whether or not the intervention was delivered therefore misses this important aspect of treatment fidelity. Quality of delivery is perhaps most easily assessed using a qualitative rating. For example, an observer might be asked to rate on the quality of delivery on a scale from 1 to 5, where 1 represents delivery that was choppy, inconsistent, and/or unenthusiastic, whereas 5 represents delivery that was fluid, consistent, and highly enthusiastic.

Participant responsiveness is an additional aspect of treatment integrity that is often ignored. This concept refers to the degree to which those individuals receiving the intervention are engaged in the process. Although we would assume that participant responsiveness would be higher when the quality of implementation is high, it is important to keep in mind that this is not always necessarily true. Depending on the student's mood, health, or other outside factors, he or she may be distracted and have difficulty attending to the intervention at hand. If a student spent the entire intervention session with eyes closed and head down on the desk, we would not expect that student to gain much from the intervention— even if each component was delivered precisely and with as much enthusiasm as possible! Similar to quality of delivery, participant responsiveness is best assessed using a qualitative rating. For example, a student who was totally unengaged in, or resistant to, the intervention might receive a rating of 1, whereas a student who was enthusiastically participatory might receive a rating of 5.

What Degree of Integrity Is Enough?

Do you remember the amazing findings we discussed in Chapter 1 with regard to the decreases in aggressive behavior seen when the GBG was implemented in the Baltimore public school system (Kellam et al., 1994)? After the researchers stopped working with the school and providing implementation supports, the school began implementing the same intervention on their own with a variety of students. Unfortunately, the results of those interventions were not nearly as powerful. The reason? It appears that the lack of support and coaching was a critical feature lacking in the school's independent implementation.

One of the questions that often arises in any discussion of treatment integrity is what level of integrity is considered sufficient. We can all agree that little to no treatment integrity should be considered a bad thing, whereas high to perfect treatment integrity should be aimed for. The question, however, is what to do with integrity that is somewhere in between. In the world of education, we often fall back on the magical value of 80%. We want the reliability of a test to be at or above .80, we want 80% of students to be appropriately served with Tier 1 interventions, and we want to see 80% agreement between two observers assessing student behavior in the classroom. Often this desirable value of 80 has been extended to the assessment of treatment integrity as well, with guidelines stating that 80% or greater integrity is necessary in order to judge implementation as sufficient.

One of the problems inherent in the assessment of treatment integrity is that simply establishing one common criterion level is unlikely to work for all situations. One reason why a universal criterion does not work is because typically all intervention components are not equally important. Positive effects may still be seen, for example, if the three components judged most critical are implemented perfectly but the teacher struggles to implement seven of the components that are more minor in nature (Pipkin, Vollmer, & Sloman, 2010). When we talk about "critical components," we are referring to those pieces of an intervention that are believed to be necessary in order to bring about a desired outcome (Sutcliffe, Thomas, Stokes, Hinds, & Bangpan, 2015); in other words, the "active ingredients." In some cases, the developers of an intervention may lay out very clearly what they believe the critical components to be. For example, there may be existing research to suggest that omitting particular pieces of the intervention does not noticeably affect desired outcomes. In other cases, however, it may be necessary for the user to make his or her best guess regarding which components are critical, drawing from either the research or personal experience with the intervention.

Using the GBG as an example, the intervention is believed to result in positive behavior change because students (1) are explicitly taught behavioral expectations, (2) receive contingent feedback regarding their performance, (3) receive reinforcement for meeting established goals, and (4) are motivated by the competitive element of the game. These would, therefore, be considered the critical components of the intervention. It is possible to add other components or to make stylistic changes to how those critical components are carried out; however, these types of changes would not be considered critical (i.e., believed to be primarily responsible for behavior change). For example, a teacher implementing a variation of the GBG may recognize that the teams are not equal, and work harder to recognize the good behavior of the "weaker" team in an effort to make sure the members of the team do not suffer from learned helplessness and decide the game is unwinnable. As long as both teams receive regular feedback and the opportunity to earn rewards, such a modification would be fine. Another teacher may start out implementing the GBG using a randomized reward, but then come to realize that students really find an extra 5 minutes of recess to be most reinforcing. In this situation, the decision to change the nature of the reward would not be considered a modification to the critical components.

Another reason why establishing a universal criterion for treatment integrity value may not make sense is because different students may require different levels of integrity. In examining the effects of treatment integrity on math performance, for example, Noell et al. (2002) found that some students performed well when the intervention was implemented exactly as planned, whereas other students performed similarly well when integrity was much lower. Finally, different levels of treatment integrity may be necessary at different stages of implementation. Higher levels of treatment integrity may be more critical, for example, when an intervention is first being introduced and students are acquiring skills than after implementation has been sustained and the focus is on establishing fluency (Noell et al., 2002).

This does not mean that we should have severe trepidation that all interventions we attempt need to be implemented with perfect integrity. Even interventions delivered with low integrity may have positive outcomes (Sanetti & Kratochwill, 2009). This surprising finding suggests that making small changes in a classroom may still improve the behavior of students. It should also free us from the fear that only perfectly implemented interventions will improve student outcomes. Rather than allowing the perfect to be the enemy of the good, we need to keep in mind that something is (almost!) always better than nothing. Teachers should therefore be encouraged to put a behavior improvement plan into place for their classrooms even if they know that perfect implementation is unattainable. However, interventions that are implemented as intended will likely give the most effective reinforcement that is delivered at an appropriate dose, at the appropriate time, and with the appropriate nuance.

The concepts of key components of an intervention reflects the expertise that a teacher may have in understanding the unique factors of a group of students. Thus, individualizing the interventions that we recommend in this book may allow a teacher to tailor his or her approach to best suit each classroom. Of course, once an intervention is designed, it should be implemented as intended. Within the next section, we discuss strategies that can be used to help ensure high levels of integrity.

STRATEGIES FOR PROMOTING TREATMENT INTEGRITY

As important as we know that treatment integrity is, difficulties are nonetheless encountered that lead to low levels of implementation. In fact, in a meta-analysis of treatment implementation studies, Noell and colleagues (2014) found that the average level of implementation during baseline was only 36%! For this reason, a burgeoning area of research in recent years has focused on the development and evaluation of strategies for promoting treatment integrity. These strategies can be divided into three phases: those that are used prior to, during, and after implementation (see Coach Card 9.1).

Prior to Implementation

Even before they are ever brought into a classroom, some interventions are simply more likely to be implemented than others. In fact, teachers report that qualities of the intervention itself are the most common barriers to successful implementation (Long et al., 2016). Thus, many interventions are likely to fail before they start because their design does not consider important contextual factors such as feasibility and ease of implementation. It may therefore be possible to increase the probability of successful implementation early on by considering some of the following factors.

Interventions Should Be Acceptable

The first important consideration is that interventions that are deemed acceptable by consumers are more likely to be implemented. Acceptability refers to whether the intervention "is fair, reasonable, and intrusive, and whether the treatment meets with conventional notions about what treatment should be" (Kazdin, 1980, p. 259). A great deal of empirical attention was focused on the concept of treatment acceptability in the 1980s, with researchers documenting consumers' acceptability of a range of school-based treatments (e.g., Martens, Witt, Elliott, & Darveaux, 1985; Witt & Martens, 1983). Interestingly, however, those studies that have directly examined the relationship between treatment acceptability and integrity have suggested that there may be "little overlap between what individuals say they will do and what they actually then do" (Sterling-Turner & Watson, 2002, p. 46). Acceptability should therefore be considered a necessary but not sufficient condition of implementation integrity.

Interventions Should Be Feasible

A second important consideration is that interventions that are feasible are more likely to be implemented. The feasibility of an intervention may be influenced by the amount of time it takes, the level of resources that are needed, or the complexity of the plan. Imagine a plan that requires you to give a token to every student once a minute. Although the students would certainly appreciate the dense reinforcement schedule, it would be unreasonable to expect a teacher to be able to deliver a token to 20 students every minute (for individual students, however, it may be necessary to provide more frequent reinforcement. We discuss this further in Chapter 10). Frequently, when we are developing a classroom management plan, we make it too difficult. If you intend to revamp your classroom, and you attempt to implement everything in this book at once, it will require too much work. As Happe (1982) put it, "the plan that requires the consultee to become a timer-setting, data-taking, token-counting, head-patting octopus has a very low probability of implementation and maintenance" (p. 33).

Interventions Should Be Contextually Appropriate

Interventions also need to work within the specific context of a teacher's classroom setting. If an intervention is fundamentally incompatible with how things are typically done in the classroom (or larger school system), it is much less likely to be implemented with integrity. A teacher who is already using some form of classwide feedback, for example, will have an easier time implementing a classwide token economy or the GBG than one who does not. In a classroom in which independent seatwork is the norm, the teacher may find token independent group contingencies such as token economy systems easy to implement, whereas a teacher who employs more group activities may find dependent group contingencies and routines easier to put into place.

Interventions Should Be Well Understood

When any of us are trying to do something that is new, we first need some level of instruction. Although we can learn about an intervention by reading about it, the research tells us that we are more likely to implement something well if we receive modeling and practice (i.e., direct training; Sterling-Turner, Watson, Wildmon, Watkins, & Little, 2001). Ideally, there would be someone in your building who already has experience with the intervention. In this case, we suggest watching him or her implement the intervention. Many of these interventions seem easy at first glance, but involve more planning than expected. Watching another teacher put it into place can be a great way to understand how the intervention should flow (Joyce & Showers, 2002). After the intervention has been modeled, you can then test it out in the context of a role play. In front of an empty classroom, you can practice the wording and moving around the classroom when implementing a new intervention. Ideally, a colleague or coach would be available who could give you clear feedback on your wording and help you recognize what portions of the intervention you need to practice again. If you need to adapt your intervention after the first test, feel free to do that!

When trying something new, it also works much better to have concrete expectations spelled out. Throughout this book, you will note that we have provided checklists that you can follow along with suggested language for introducing the intervention. We encourage you to use these checklists, but ask you to keep in mind that they should not be treated as perfect documents that must be rigidly followed at all times. Every teacher works in a unique context, and every classroom has unique features. The checklists may be adapted slightly to ensure that they work in your context. After all, the best interventions use research-based practices but make sure that they are appropriately adapted for a local context (Berkel, Mauricio, Schoenfelder, & Sandler, 2011; Rogers, 2003). For example, precision commands often require that teachers get eye contact from the student. There are some students, however, who may find eye contact to be uncomfortable or culturally inappropriate. If an intervention does not work, identify those components that are problematic compared with those that are effective, and systematically tweak those portions that are causing problems. When spelling out the intervention, be sure to consider necessary resources, adjustments needed to make use of daily routines, the best time to implement the intervention, how much time is necessary to implement the intervention, and where the best place is to implement the intervention (e.g., hallway, classroom, playground, lunchroom; Long et al., 2016).

During Implementation

Whereas the suggestions outlined above are designed to help promote treatment integrity before the intervention is actually put into place, there are also strategies that can be used to bolster treatment integrity when you are actually in the thick of things. The use of several of these strategies is dependent upon the availability of a partner or coach. There are four components of effective intervention support: (1) didactic instruction, (2) modeling the intervention, (3) practicing the intervention, and (4) providing ongoing intervention support (Joyce & Showers, 2002). Put another way, simply telling someone what he or she should do does not result in behavior change (Reinke, Lewis-Palmer, & Merrell, 2008). This book is designed to provide you with didactic instruction—informing you of what practices are supported by the research literature. However, putting something into place the first time requires immediate and frequent feedback, and this is as true for educators as it is for students. Many classroom teachers believe that they should be able to run their classrooms and implement changes without support from others. However, most teachers report that they are more likely to put social and behavior supports into place if they have adequate support from others in the school setting (Reinke et al., 2011). Teachers who have support in implementing interventions are more likely to do so with integrity than those who do not (Codding, Feinberg, Dunn, & Pace, 2005). This is because a coach is able to provide an objective assessment of implementation integrity as well as ongoing support to bolster integrity levels.

Include a Cueing Procedure

As much as we may not want to admit our fallacy, as human beings we sometimes forget things. We may have seen a student commit a rule infraction and then fail to follow up on it. Or, we may have intended to remind students about an upcoming deadline but then forgot. Even with the most carefully laid out plan and best of intentions, sometimes we simply forget to do what needs to be done. Incorporating cueing procedures, however, can help to reduce the likelihood of that happening.

One way to remind yourself of what needs to be done is to use an intermittent prompt. In the section on reinforcement schedules, we talked about variable interval and fixed interval schedules. These types of schedules can also be used to remind you to make sure you are doing what you said you would do. A variable interval timer, for example, can be set to provide a prompt every 3–5 minutes to deliver tokens (you can use the self-monitoring interventions described in Chapter 7 on yourself!). This can be done using some type of reminder app on your smartphone or device. Alternatively, visual cues may be used to remind us of what needs to be done. A treatment integrity checklist, for example, can be a great visual reminder of the steps that need to be carried out. It is important, however, that the checklist is kept in a highly visible location that can easily be accessed during the school day. Even the most explicit and easy-to-follow checklist will be of little value if cozily tucked away under a pile of papers or stored in a desk drawer.

Solicit Performance Feedback

One of the strategies for promoting treatment integrity that has received the most attention within the literature is performance feedback. Performance feedback typically involves the teacher meeting with a coach following intervention implementation in order to discuss how well the intervention was carried out as well as what effects the intervention may have had on student behavior (Fallon, Collier-Meek, Maggin, Sanetti, & Johnson, 2015). Within a meta-analysis of studies that examined school-based intervention implementation, Noell and colleagues (2014) found that simply meeting with a coach in the absence of the review of actual data was ineffective in promoting integrity. However, notable improvements in implementer behavior were observed when teachers received explicit performance feedback based on obtained data. In meta-analyzing those studies that specifically examined the use of performance feedback, Fallon and colleagues (2015) found such an approach to be an evidence-based intervention and an effective means for improving classroom behavior.

Research has suggested that the best type of feedback to receive in these situations is visual feedback (Fallon et al., 2015; Reinke et al., 2007). Visual feedback involves graphing both the degree of implementation integrity (e.g., percentage of steps completed) as well as the outcome data (e.g., percentage of time on task) and sharing these data with the implementer. This can be achieved by using the implementation checklist that you created in the first place, and then having your partner or coach take note of those steps that you performed correctly and those you did not. This information can then be graphed and reviewed on a frequent basis to ensure that implementation remains high over time (Joyce & Showers, 2002).

Employ Self-Monitoring

Although ideally everyone would have a partner or coach available to provide ongoing performance feedback, we know that in reality this is not always feasible. In such a case, it is possible to solicit performance feedback from oneself through the use of self-monitoring. As described in Chapter 7, self-monitoring involves the observing and recording of one's own behavior. As one example, in a study by Simonsen, MacSuga, Fallon, and Sugai (2013), teachers' use of praise was found to improve substantially when they tracked the number of praise statements made using either a tally sheet or counter. Each day, these data were then entered into a log and then graphed in order to provide a record of behavior over time. Plavnick, Ferreri, and Maupin (2010) taught early education teachers to complete an implementation checklist at least two times each day when carrying out a token economy system in a special education classroom. Similarly, results suggested notable improvements in implementation behavior when teachers were taught to self-monitor.

After Implementation

Even after we have implemented an intervention for a while and feel like we have mastered it, it is important to remember that we are never immune to drift. Like a car that needs its oil changed periodically, we can also break down from our previous precision performance without a checkup. Think of the diet that worked for a while but then you eventually fell off, or those New Year's resolutions that lasted only until the middle of January. One way to prevent a lapse or drift is to have periodic checkups. These checkups should provide you with several pieces of diagnostic information. First, you want to know if the intervention is being implemented with the appropriate integrity. Are there particular steps of the intervention that you are performing consistently, whereas others seem to have been lost? Second, you want to know if the intervention is still helping to improve student behavior. Has the level of student improvement remained consistent over time or has there been a gradual decline over time as students become more accustomed to the intervention? Finally, the checkup should help to indicate whether the intervention is still necessary. If so, are there small changes that we should make? If not, are there larger changes that we should make?

It is important that these checkup meetings are guided by data rather than gut impressions. Our tendency to use our intuition and emotions for decision making may help us in some situations, but is much less helpful when making decisions regarding implementation effectiveness. The truth is that all of us will implement an intervention imperfectly. This in and of itself is not a problem. The problem occurs if we are unwilling to face that fact and to make improvements. Regular checkup meetings with a colleague or coach are part of a continual improvement process whereby we strive to make improvements knowing that perfection does not exist and will never be reached. Instead, we need to identify good data and use it to improve our practice the best that we can.

CONCLUSIONS

As we've discussed within this chapter, treatment integrity is critical to making decisions regarding intervention effectiveness, particularly within a multi-tiered model of supports. If an evidence-based intervention is in place but is not having the desired effects, the first thing to check is the integrity of implementation. When problems with integrity are identified, it is important to determine why these problems are occurring. Is it, for example, an issue in terms of fundamental understanding of what needs to be done? Or are feasibility constraints interfering with the ability to carry out essential steps? It is only once an intervention has been implemented at appropriately high levels that teachers can then collect data on the effects of their intervention to determine whether or not it is effective. Promotion and maintenance of treatment integrity is best achieved when teachers work with a coach or a partner who is able to provide modeling, troubleshooting, and ongoing performance feedback.

COACH CARD 9.1.
Strategies for Promoting Treatment Integrity

Implementation integrity may be bolstered by considering strategies during three phases.

1. Prior to implementation:

   ☐ Ensure intervention is acceptable to stakeholders.

   ☐ Ensure intervention is sufficiently feasible to be carried out regularly.

   ☐ Make needed modifications to ensure contextual appropriateness.

   ☐ Ensure intervention procedures are well understood.

2. During implementation:

   ☐ Utilize a cueing procedure.

   ☐ Solicit performance feedback from a colleague or coach.

   ☐ Employ self-monitoring.

3. After implementation:

   ☐ Conduct checkups to ensure adequate implementation integrity.

   ☐ Conduct checkups to ensure intervention continues to be effective.

   ☐ Conduct checkups to determine whether intervention is still necessary.

CHAPTER 10

Individualizing Intervention

Throughout this book, we have discussed a range of strategies and interventions for use at the universal level to support *all* students in a classroom. Within the literature, there are many examples of universal supports being used to successfully address the needs of struggling students in particular. In a study by Ling, Hawkins, and Weber (2011), for example, a first-grade student was identified as being frequently off task and not completing many of his assignments. Rather than developing an individualized intervention focused on this one child's behavior, the team instead decided to implement an interdependent group contingency with the entire class. The teacher had three expectations: (1) be seated on the carpet with legs crossed, (2) keep hands and feet to yourself, and (3) talk only when it's your turn. If the students were on task when the teacher was prompted to scan the classroom, they earned a point toward a group prize. Results suggested substantial improvements not only in the behavior of the target student but in the behavior of the larger classroom as well. This is one of many examples of a classwide intervention demonstrating positive effects for both the classroom overall and at-risk students in particular (e.g., Fudge et al., 2008; Hoff & Ervin, 2013; Tanol et al., 2010).

Unfortunately, however, although empirically validated classwide supports are expected to meet the behavioral needs of approximately 80–85% of the students in a classroom, there is no one silver-bullet intervention that will effectively address *all* behavior problems. The techniques discussed in this book will help to make classrooms work more efficiently and safely, but there will inevitably be students who continue to display problem behaviors. In fact, we estimate that one out of every five students will require some level of additional intervention. Within a multi-tiered system, extra support typically consists of a small-group intervention that is provided to students with similar behavioral needs. This targeted intervention is designed to complement—rather than to replace—classroom management practices. In this way, those students believed to be at some level of risk effectively receive a double dose of behavioral support through the (1) universal-level teaching and reinforcement of expected behaviors and (2) receipt of more intensive supports targeted at specific areas of need. For example, a student who has difficulty interacting appropriately with peers might experience the generalized benefits of participation in a classwide token economy system focused on promoting appropriate classroom behavior, but would likely need more explicit social skills instruction outside of the regular classroom in order to effectively address interpersonal deficits. In order to maintain feasibility when working with a sizable percentage of students, it is important for targeted interventions to be easy and efficient to implement across multiple students. For this reason, manualized interventions with explicit protocols (e.g., social skills training, Behavior Education Program) are often used. Although implementation of secondary-level supports is essential to providing all students in a classroom with the appropriate level of support, discussion of these types of interventions is beyond the scope of this book. Interested readers are therefore referred to other Guilford Press resources that provide excellent guidance for supporting the behavioral needs of at-risk students, such as Steege and Watson (2009); Crone, Hawken, and Horner (2010); and Stormont, Reinke, Herman, and Lembke (2012). Within this final chapter, however, we discuss proactive strategies that may be used to intensify existing classwide interventions when particular students are not responding before moving to implement more targeted secondary-level supports.

STRATEGIES FOR INTENSIFYING CLASSWIDE INTERVENTIONS

Within multi-tiered systems of support, it can be easy to fall into the trap of thinking about intervention supports in a linear fashion—consulting the appropriate flowchart to determine what the next steps should be when student behavior has proven unresponsive. If a student continues to struggle after an empirically supported classwide intervention has been implemented with fidelity, for example, we may automatically assume that it is time to move on to a more intensive level of secondary support. Ludlow (2014), however, drew an important analogy between a teacher's use of evidence-based practices and a master chef's use of classic recipes. She argued that just as a celebrity chef may take a standard recipe and "kick it up a notch" by adding new seasonings, teachers may also take an intervention to the next level by simply tweaking some of the ingredients. Within the following section, we discuss three strategies for intensifying classwide interventions to support those students with more defined behavioral needs: increasing intervention dosage, altering intervention delivery, and changing aspects of the environment (IRIS Center, 2015). (See Coach Card 10.1 for an overview of these strategies to intensify classwide interventions.)

Strategy 1: Increase Dosage

The first strategy we can use when particular students are not responding is to increase the dosage or quantity of an intervention. Increasing the amount of time that an intervention is implemented can be incredibly important for struggling students because it provides them with more time to practice appropriate behaviors and receive specific performance feedback. Frequency may be altered by increasing the number of minutes per day or days per week with which an intervention is implemented. If a classwide intervention is being implemented only during a particular time in the day (e.g., morning meeting), for example, implementation could be extended to additional lessons or activities in order to strengthen the dosage. One might consider making this change in schedule for the class as a whole, such that the group contingency or self-management intervention is simply in place for the entire school day. However, if keeping the intervention in place for everyone throughout the day proves logistically complicated, another option is to implement the intervention classwide during the targeted period and then to keep procedures in place only for select students throughout the remainder of the day.

Strategy 2: Alter Intervention Delivery

A second way to intensify intervention is by changing the way in which the intervention is delivered—that is, it may be possible to better support at-risk students if certain changes are made to the classwide intervention to enhance individual fit. Thus, changes to the intervention that make it more developmentally appropriate for a particular student, such as incorporating more explicit instruction, or more frequent and explicit feedback, may help to reduce problem behaviors (National Center on Intensive Intervention, 2014).

Enhance Explicit Instruction

Over the past several chapters, we have presented many different interventions and strategies; however, the common element across all of these different approaches is that implementation begins with the explicit teaching of behavioral expectations. One approach that is often used when teaching new skills is called the "I do, we do, you do" model of instruction. First, the teacher models the task (i.e., desired behavior) for the students, explaining what he or she is doing and why. If, for example, an intervention was in place to improve classroom transitions, the teacher would first demonstrate what appropriate transitioning behavior should look like (e.g., quietly putting away materials, quickly moving to line up by the door, facing forward and waiting quietly to be released) and explain how transitioning quickly and quietly ultimately means that there is more time available for learning. Next, the teacher leads the students through guided practice, having the students perform the task while receiving ongoing feedback to correct any errors. Finally, the students perform the task independently under the supervision of the teacher.

Although most students are able to perform the desired task or behavior after receiving a brief form of this type of instruction, some students require additional scaffolding to be successful. Explicit instruction can be intensified by providing additional modeling, increasing the number of opportunities for practice, or improving the quantity or immediacy of behavioral feedback. In order to avoid drawing unnecessary attention to an individual student, the teacher might have the student stay in for a few minutes at lunch or after school to simulate a classroom transition. Prompts may be used to ensure that the student remembers what to do. The student could then practice the outlined steps for transitioning until they are fully mastered. If any problems were noted, such as the student running to line up instead of walking, the teacher could provide corrective feedback and then ask the student to perform the behavior again. This independent practice could be performed initially under simulated conditions before transitioning into the target setting.

Increase the Frequency and Explicitness of Feedback

For some students, problems may arise if there is too long of a delay between when the student performs the behavior and when he or she receives feedback. After all, many of you learned from the Stanford marshmallow experiments (just to jog your memory, students were offered a second marshmallow if they could avoid eating one marshmallow that was left in front of them for 15 minutes) that some children have difficulty delaying gratification (Mischel, Shoda, & Rodriguez, 1989). This inability to wait for reinforcement is often characteristic of those students who struggle with self-control and impulsive behavior, such as those with ADHD. Whereas the average student in a classroom may be able to wait until the end of the day (or even week!) to receive an earned reward, students with ADHD may need reinforcement to occur much more frequently. If too much time elapses, the student may become distracted by other things and lose sight of the goal and reward. Therefore, providing the student with more frequent, intermittent feedback (whether verbal or in the form of tokens or points) than what is delivered to the rest of the class may be necessary in some cases.

Increase the Power of Reinforcement

Remember from our discussion in Chapter 2 that there is a difference between a reinforcer and a reward—even though we tend to use the terms interchangeably. Rewards are those things that we *believe* someone will like, such as a gold star or a homework pass. Although the majority of students tend to find typical school-based rewards to be desirable, there is no guarantee that every student will respond in the same way. Reinforcers, on the other hand, are those things that have actually been shown to change the frequency or magnitude of a behavior. We know that something is an effective reinforcer if it results in an increase in the desired behavior. Although not all classwide interventions involve a reward component, the effectiveness of those that do may be significantly influenced by the attractiveness of the available rewards. If a student is not sufficiently interested in the selected rewards at the outset, or loses interest in what is available over time, he or she may be less motivated to follow behavioral expectations.

One of the difficulties that can arise when utilizing group-based rewards is that not all of the students will likely find the rewards to be equally appealing. Other students may habituate or grow tired of the reinforcer over time. One approach that addresses these issues, as previously discussed in Chapter 6, is to randomize the reinforcement component of the intervention. Rather than identifying a reward that students will work toward earning at the outset, the reward is instead randomly selected from a pool of possibilities. The idea is that when there exists the possibility that the randomly selected reward will be something that an individual student is very motivated to earn, that student is more likely to remain invested in the intervention (Popkin & Skinner, 2003).

In contrast to interdependent and dependent group contingency interventions, fewer reward-related problems tend to arise within a token economy system. This is because rewards are earned and administered at the individual level. Nevertheless, it is possible that the rewards originally selected may have changed in value over time. A student may suddenly decide that he or she no longer likes playing educational games on the computer or the student may satiate on a particular reward (e.g., stickers) such that it is no longer appealing. For this reason, it is important to periodically readminister a reinforcement preference survey to participating students. As briefly discussed in Chapter 5, a reinforcement preference survey includes a list of possible rewards that are available to the student and have been approved by the classroom teacher (see Table 10.1). Instead of presuming what a student may find to be desirable, asking the student directly what he or she is interested in ultimately avoids lost time and energy (Cooper, Heron, & Heward, 2007). Typically, the student is asked to either (1) check yes or no to indicate whether he or she would be interested in a particular reward or (2) rate how desirable he or she perceives the reward to be using a Likert-type scale (e.g., 0 = not at all interested, 3 = extremely interested). A user-friendly tool for creating your own reinforcement survey is available through the Intervention Central website at *www.interventioncentral.org/teacher-resources/student-rewards-finder*. Another approach to identifying reinforcers is to use a "forced-choice" approach, whereby a student is given pairs of reinforcers, and then chooses the one that is most reinforcing. An example of a "forced-choice" assessment is available at *www.pbis.org/Common/Cms/files/ Forum15_Presentations/B13_Forced-Choice-Reinforcement-Menu.pdf*.

An example of how both the frequency and potency of rewards may be increased in order to achieve stronger effects can be seen in a study by Safer, Heaton, and Parker (1981). When a basic token economy system proved ineffective for a small group of junior high

TABLE 10.1. Ideas for a Reinforcement Preference Survey

Objects	Responsibilities	Activities	Privileges
Allowed to select materials first	Be line leader	Draw on chalk/ whiteboard	Eat special lunch with teacher
Keep a favorite toy on desk	Be teacher's helper for a day	Extra computer time	Receive a no-homework pass
Receive stickers	Design class bulletin board	Free time at the end of the day	Receive positive call home
Select a prize from the prize box	Help in younger classroom	Go to library to get a book	Sit in special chair
Wear a special badge	Take note to main office	Leave to go to lunch/ recess early	

school students who had received multiple office referrals and suspensions for problem behavior, intervention intensity was increased in order to meet their individual needs. Students could earn points every 15 minutes for engaging in appropriate behavior and completing their work, and if at least 90% of the possible points were earned within a day, the student was able to earn an early release from school. In addition, students were also able to earn privileges at home for having a good week at school. Students who participated in this point system performed significantly better on a number of behavioral indicators (e.g., expulsions, disciplinary issues) than peers in a control group.

Change the Role of the Interventionist

Finally, it may be necessary to change the role of the interventionist. Although the primary teacher typically maintains responsibility for implementation of a classwide behavioral intervention, this individual may be spread too thin to provide additional instruction and feedback to select students. In this case, it could be helpful to recruit a classroom aide or paraprofessional to provide supplemental supports.

Strategy 3: Change Aspects of the Environment

A third option for intensifying intervention is to change aspects of the environment. By environment, we mean those factors independent of the intervention itself that may have an effect on student behavior. Context is incredibly important to consider when implementing any intervention. Even if a well-supported plan is implemented precisely as intended, intervention effectiveness may be impeded by a number of environmental factors.

Alter the Difficulty of the Task

If a behavioral intervention is being implemented during academic instruction, one of the first things to consider is whether behavior problems are the result of academic frustration. Several studies have investigated the interaction between assignment difficulty and off-task behavior (Burns & Dean, 2005; Gickling & Armstrong, 1978; Treptow, Burns, & McComas, 2007), and have identified significantly more off-task behavior when assignments were too difficult for students. For example, when Gickling and Armstrong (1978) worked with a group of first graders, they varied the difficulty of the tasks that the students were asked to complete. When the task was too difficult for the students, the rate of off-task behavior increased as did the number of disruptions. When the work was too easy, there was also an increase in off-task behavior. It was only when the work was just at the right level of challenge did the students' off-task levels decrease. Finding this "sweet spot" is not easy for a large group of students; however, particular students may benefit from slight adaptations to their work whereby additional "easy" or "difficult" problems are added. For some students, interspersing easier problems can help to promote a sense of self-efficacy, meaning students may actually do more work with the addition of more problems (Hulac & Benson, 2011).

Identify Competing Sources of Reinforcement

In some cases, a student may not respond to an intervention as hoped despite the availability of preferred rewards. One possible explanation is that the reinforcement that the student is already receiving for engaging in the problem behavior is more powerful than the rewards being provided. The question that we must ask ourselves is whether it is worth it to the student to give up engaging in the problem behavior in order to get what we are offering. For example, consider a student, Omar, whose problem behavior involves turning around in his seat and talking to classmates at inappropriate times. The classroom group contingency intervention rewards students with 10 minutes of free time at the end of the day for meeting the expectations of facing forward, sitting quietly, and taking notes. Although Omar likes having the free time at the end of the day to talk with his friends, at present he is able to talk to his friends throughout the entire day. As such, the free-time reward that will occur later is not powerful enough to convince Omar that sitting quietly during the lecture now is worth the wait.

One way to reduce competing sources of reinforcement may therefore be to change a student's seat. Most often we think about moving a student's seat away from peers who are providing desired attention. This is probably a good time to talk about how David got in trouble in Spanish class during the 12th grade. He was working in a small group while his friend was working in another group across the room. Both David and his friend made several off-task comments loudly enough for the other to hear, which only served to trigger a similar response (though they were speaking Spanish, so it couldn't have been that bad, could it?). The teacher responded by making it impossible for them to shout across the room to each other—and instead having them work by themselves at a table separated from everybody else. In this case, the teacher changed the environment by moving the students closer to each other, so as to avoid disrupting the rest of the classroom.

There are other ways to alter the classroom environment. These may include the use of study carrels for students who need to complete work or increasing the amount of space between students while they are working. Other teachers have used techniques whereby the seating chart and the orientation of the seats have been changed suddenly if there are broader classroom disruptions. Finally, many students benefit from the use of sound amplification whereby the teacher's voice is broadcast via a microphone through speakers in the ceiling. These systems have the benefit of allowing the teacher to be heard without using a strained voice. There is some limited evidence to suggest that they may reduce off-task behaviors for children with attention difficulties (Cornwell & Evans, 2001).

INCORPORATING ADDITIONAL INTERVENTION COMPONENTS TO INTENSIFY CLASSWIDE SUPPORTS

The strategies described above can be used to modify aspects of a classwide intervention to better support the needs of struggling students (see Box 10.1 for a case example). For example, incorporating additional explicit instruction or increasing the amount of time that the intervention is implemented may benefit not only an individual target student, but the larger class as well. However, other strategies require that substantial modifications be made for individual students (see Coach Card 10.2). Making changes to the potency or frequency of rewards, for example, is not a modification that would likely be made for the entire class but rather one that would be applied to select students (see Box 10.2 for a case example). If there is only one student in a classroom for whom individualized intensification of classwide supports is needed, it may be feasible for the classroom teacher to make these modifications without significantly depleting classroom resources. However, as the number of students with more intensive needs increases, the teacher's ability to provide the appropriate level of support for each student can become challenging. For this reason, it may be helpful to consider extending responsibility for implementation to other stakeholders. Specifically, implementation supports may be provided by an external interventionist, parent, or guardian, or even the student him- or herself.

BOX 10.1. Case Example: Making Classwide Modifications to Intensify Intervention Delivery

Mrs. Washington began implementing a tootling intervention last month in an effort to improve the quality of interactions among her students on the playground. Students were encouraged to look for instances in which their classmates were being kind or helpful during recess, and to let Mrs. Washington know by submitting a tootle card. Each tootle card asked the student to identify (1) who was observed doing something good, (2) what that person did, and (3) for whom they did it. When the students returned from lunch, Mrs. Washington would count up all of the tootles, read them aloud, and record the total number submitted on a chart at the front of the room. The class was informed that they would receive an extra recess period once they had reached a total of 100 tootles.

Although Mrs. Washington has generally been impressed by the increased levels of prosocial behavior on the playground after a few weeks of implementation, there continues to be interpersonal concerns in the classroom among a small group of girls. Specifically, she has overheard name-calling and observed one of the students excluding particular classmates during small-group work. She decides to make a couple of modifications in order to intensify intervention delivery. The first modification is to increase the dosage of the intervention. Because interpersonal problems are no longer confined to unstructured periods, Mrs. Washington decides to extend implementation to the classroom as well—that is, students can now submit tootles whenever they observe prosocial behavior throughout the day. The second modification is to increase the frequency of behavioral feedback. Rather than waiting until the end of the day to read and count up all of the tootles, Mrs. Washington chose to review them at two times each day: once before lunch and once before dismissal. She hoped that having a midday review would both reinforce students for their appropriate behavior and prompt those students who hadn't delivered as many tootles to be on the lookout in the afternoon.

BOX 10.2. Case Example: Intensifying Classwide Supports to Meet Individual Needs

Jennifer is a 12-year-old student who frequently disrupts classes by cussing and yelling out things like "This is stupid!" and "When are we ever going to use this?" Although Jennifer is clearly the most disruptive, there are also several other students in the class who routinely talk out of turn and engage their classmates in side conversations. The teacher and behavior specialist therefore decide to implement the Good Behavior Game (GBG) classwide. All teams begin each day with 10 points and point deductions are made if any member of the team disrupts classroom instruction by calling out, engaging in conversations unrelated to instruction, or getting out of his or her seat without permission. At the end of the day, any team that still has at least 7 points will be allowed to have free time on the computer for the last 15 minutes before dismissal.

After 1 week of implementation, the teacher and behavior specialist meet to discuss how the intervention has been going. The teacher is very concerned about the fact that Jennifer has been "ruining the game for everyone" by acting out and causing the rest of her team to lose points. The behavior specialist therefore suggests that they keep the existing teams intact but put Jennifer on her own team so that she does not lose points for the other students. After making this modification, Jennifer's acting-out behavior quickly subsides, and by the second day she has already earned computer time to herself. Although the teacher and behavior specialist are very encouraged by this turnaround in Jennifer's behavior, their ultimate goal is for Jennifer to rejoin a team and participate in the intervention as the rest of the class does. They therefore agree to a modification whereby Jennifer can choose whether she wants to work for 15 minutes of computer time while being on a team or whether she wants to remain on her own and work for only 5 minutes of computer time at the end of the day. Jennifer decides that the 15 minutes sounds like a much better option and rejoins her previous GBG team for the third week of implementation.

Option 1: Add a Self-Monitoring Component

One of the first options that may be considered when individualized supports are needed is to assign the target student increased responsibility for intervention implementation. As described in Chapter 7, shifting responsibility for the assessment of behavior to the student is what is referred to as self-monitoring. Typically, the student is provided with a monitoring card and taught to self-assess his or her behavior. By asking the student to more deliberately reflect on his or her own behavior in this way, self-monitoring is believed to lead to more enduring behavioral change. Although both token economies and group contingencies have been shown to be highly effective in improving student behavior, one potential disadvantage is that the classroom teacher maintains sole responsibility for the assessment of student behavior. Additionally, with interventions such as interdependent group contingencies, the student may not even receive needed feedback with regard to his or her individual performance. Adding a self-monitoring component to an existing classwide intervention may therefore provide the additional individualized support needed to bolster intervention effects.

As highlighted in Chapter 7, there are many ways in which self-management components may be implemented; however, three basic requirements should be met. First, the student should be provided with a personalized monitoring form that lists the classwide expectations and provides space for assessing how well each was met. Individualized expectations may also be added to the form if necessary; however, the total number of behaviors should be kept small (i.e., three to seven) to ensure that proper monitoring can occur. Second, it is necessary to establish a schedule for conducting ratings. When implementing a group contingency, it is most efficient to have the student rate his or her own behavior each time that the teacher assesses the behavior of the larger group or class (e.g., according to a variable interval schedule). The teacher could therefore give the target student a discreet prompt, such as a tap on the shoulder, to signal when it is time to self-assess. When implementing a token economy, however, in which reinforcers are distributed in a more continuous fashion, it may be necessary to establish an independent schedule for self-monitoring. This may entail the student conducting independent ratings at predetermined intervals or at the end of an instructional period (see Chapter 7 for further discussion of options for conducting ratings). Third, the classroom teacher must determine how and when he or she will discuss self-ratings with the student. Debrief meetings with the student can be used to (1) provide the student with feedback regarding the accuracy of ratings or level of performance, (2) administer applicable rewards, and/or (3) discuss how to ensure maintenance of a desired level of performance or what changes may be necessary in order to improve future performance. An example of a self-monitoring card that could be used to supplement classwide supports is provided in Figure 10.1.

One example of how a self-management component may be added to an existing classwide intervention is provided by Wills et al. (2010). The Class-Wide Function-related Intervention Teams (CW-FIT) program is conceptualized as a Tier 2 classwide intervention, which incorporates elements of both a group contingency and self-management intervention. First, explicit teaching is used to ensure that students know how to appropriately gain the attention of the teacher, follow directions, and ignore peers engaging in inappropriate behaviors (Kamps, Conklin, & Wills, 2015). Second, students are divided into small teams. If all team members are observed engaging in the target behaviors when a timer sounds (every 2–3 minutes), the teacher awards a point to the team. Points can then be exchanged for rewards at the end of the class period. For those students who do not demonstrate response to the CW-FIT intervention, a self-management component may also be added—that is, select students may be given more individualized instruction regarding the behavioral expectations and then provided with a recording sheet. Each time that the buzzer sounds, these students could mark a point on their sheet if they were meeting all expectations. Points would then be exchanged in the same manner as they were for the class at large.

Option 2: Introduce an External Interventionist

A second way in which to support individualization is to recruit implementation support from outside of the classroom. If changes are needed in order to increase the intensity of

Name: Asher

Expectations:

- Respect your neighbors' space by keeping your hands and feet to yourself
- Work on assignments without talking to neighbors
- Raise your hand to ask a question or obtain help

Goal for today: Earn 12 of 18 total points

Time of Day	How Well Did I . . . ?	Rating (0 = not at all, 1 = somewhat, 2 = moderately, 3 = very well)			
Morning Meeting	Respect my neighbors' space?	0	1	2	3
	Work quietly?	0	1	2	3
	Raise my hand to ask a question?	0	1	2	3
Literacy	Respect my neighbors' space?	0	1	2	3
	Work quietly?	0	1	2	3
	Raise my hand to ask a question?	0	1	2	3
Comments:					

FIGURE 10.1. Self-monitoring form for classwide token economy.

intervention delivery, introducing an external interventionist can help to facilitate provision of a more targeted level of support. Providing intervention supports outside of the classroom may also help to avoid drawing unnecessary attention to the student. For example, if the classroom teacher needed to provide the student with feedback much more frequently than to his or her typical peers, this not only draws attention to the student but may also interfere with the delivery of instruction.

One popular example of a targeted intervention that incorporates an external interventionist is Check-In, Check-Out (CICO; Crone et al., 2010). CICO was designed for use within schools that have adopted an SWPBIS model and have effective Tier 1 supports in place, including the teaching and systematic reinforcement of schoolwide behavioral expectations. Each participating student begins his or her day by meeting (i.e., check-in) with a central CICO coordinator, who reminds the student of the behavioral expectations and provides him or her with a Daily Progress Report (DPR). Throughout the day, the DPR is completed by the student's teacher(s), who rate the degree to which the student met the expectations. At the end of the day, the student then returns the DPR to the CICO coordinator, who reviews the ratings and provides performance feedback. If the student meets his or her overall goal for the day (e.g., 20/27 points), the coordinator praises the student and may provide him or her with a small reward. Interested readers are referred to Crone et al. (2010), which provides a detailed description of how CICO may be implemented.

If we think about the classwide interventions that were described in Chapters 5–7, there are several ways in which we might think about incorporating an external interventionist. In the case of a token economy, the interventionist could review the classroom expectations with the student at the start of the day and establish a goal for how many tokens he or she will earn. The classroom teacher could then use a monitoring sheet to record the number of tokens the student earned during different blocks of the day (see Figure 10.2). At the end of the day, the interventionist would then meet with the student to review the token data and provide a special reward if the predetermined goal was met. One of the key potential advantages of such a model is that it is possible to flexibly determine how often the student's data will be reviewed and rewards administered. For example, whereas some students may respond to the chance to exchange tokens for a reward once at the end of each week, this may be too long of a wait for other students. Shifting responsibility for rewards to the interventionist therefore allows the schedule of reinforcement to be tailored to the student's needs.

Name: *Benjamin*

Expectations:

- *Keep your eyes on the teacher/lesson*
- *Raise your hand to be called on*
- *Stay seated*

Goal for today: *Earn 10 tokens throughout the day*

Time of Day	Tokens Earned	Teacher Comments
Morning Meeting		
Literacy		
Snack		
Math		
Language Arts		
Lunch		
Science/Social Studies		
Specials		

FIGURE 10.2. Individual monitoring form for classwide token economy.

As we discussed in Chapter 6, perhaps the most commonly used group contingency is the interdependent group contingency. From a feasibility perspective, one of the main advantages is that behavior is both monitored and reinforced at the group—rather than the individual—level. At the same time, however, one potential concern is that at-risk students may not receive the level or frequency of feedback that they require. Additionally, although we hope that group contingencies will invoke a motivating yet gentle level of peer pressure, there is the potential for students to experience a diffusion of responsibility. By this we mean that some students may feel less personal responsibility for behaving appropriately, and exert less effort, knowing that whether or not they receive a reward is contingent on factors outside of their control. To address these concerns, it may be possible to add an additional independent group contingency for select students that is managed by the external interventionist. In order to avoid unnecessary complication, it would be important to align the independent group contingency with the existing classwide expectations. The teacher would therefore keep two separate but parallel records of behavior: one public record for the class or teams and one more discreet record for the target student in particular (see Figure 10.3). The interventionist could then be provided with the individual student data at the end of the day and supplemental, individually administered rewards delivered if the goal or criterion was met.

An interventionist could also be used to support implementation of a self-management intervention. If all students in the classroom are simultaneously assessing their own behavior, it may become challenging for the teacher to provide feedback to individual students. This is why many classwide self-management interventions incorporate group contingency

Name: Eleanor

Expectations:

• Use kind words
• Keep your hands and feet to yourself
• Listen when someone else is talking

Time of Day	Class Rule Violations	Student Rule Violations	Teacher Comments
Morning Meeting	/ / / / /	/ /	Difficulty keeping her hands to herself on the carpet
Literacy	/		
Math	/ /	/	Talking to friends during lesson
Language Arts			
Science/Social Studies	/ / /	/ /	Grabbing science materials from classmates

FIGURE 10.3. Teacher monitoring form for managing multiple contingencies.

components (see Chapter 7). One solution would be for the student to complete a self-monitoring card during the class period and then bring the card to review during a meeting with the interventionist outside of the classroom. The interventionist can then provide the student with more individualized feedback regarding his or her performance and even administer rewards if appropriate.

There are several reasons why incorporating an external interventionist may be beneficial. First, the interventionist can help to intensify intervention efforts by allowing you to change aspects of the environment, increase the intervention dosage, and alter aspects of intervention delivery, all at the same time. By meeting with the student outside of the regular classroom and away from his or her classmates, instruction can be tailored to the student's needs. The student can also receive feedback more frequently, or in greater detail, than is typical within the general classroom. Second, an interventionist can prompt and reinforce the classroom expectations. Although it is important for the classroom teacher to briefly review the behavioral expectations with the entire class on a regular basis, some students may require more in-depth, and therefore time-intensive, review. The student could therefore meet with the interventionist at the start of the day in order to review—and even practice—the expectations, thereby setting the student up for greater success from the start. Additionally, providing the student with performance feedback both within and outside of the classroom can reinforce expectations, thereby promoting generalization of skills. Finally, it can be easier to incorporate rewards that the student finds to be more motivating if reinforcement is provided outside of the general classroom. After all, the rewards that a particular student finds desirable may be more elaborate or intensive than the rewards the rest of the class receives. One can only imagine the resentment that might take place if the classroom teacher gives one student a big reward and the rest of the class a smaller reward!

One of the concerns that may arise when considering use of an external interventionist relates to resources. When thinking about who in the school building would most naturally fall into the role, we often default to someone who already works in a guidance capacity—perhaps a school counselor or social worker. As we have seen in the literature, however, an effective interventionist does not need an advanced degree or specialized credentials. Instead, the individual must be able to connect with students—both effectively and consistently. By effectively, we mean that the individual should be someone who students enjoy interacting with and look forward to seeing each day (Crone et al., 2010). Just as adults are more likely to accept constructive criticism from a respected supervisor, students are much more likely to engage in the intervention process if they like the person responsible for delivery. By consistently, we mean that it is critical that the interventionist's schedule accommodates meeting with the student(s) every day. This consistency ensures that students receive regular feedback and establish a trusting relationship. As long as these basic conditions are met, there are many different individuals who might be asked to serve in this capacity. Paraprofessionals can be useful to serve in this role if their schedules permit sufficient flexibility. Alternatively, the school librarian, main office staff, or a specials teacher may prove to be an effective interventionist. The key is to think openly as to who might have both the personality and the flexibility to take on this task.

Option 3: Incorporate a Home-Based Component

The two options we have discussed thus far involve recruiting help from either within (i.e., self-monitoring) or outside (i.e., using an external interventionist) of the classroom; however, both components are carried out entirely within the regular school day. A third option for intensification extends the scope of the intervention beyond school borders and incorporates the child's home. One successful example of a targeted intervention for which home involvement serves as a key component is the Daily Report Card (DRC; Volpe & Fabiano, 2013). Within a DRC intervention, students are rated throughout the school day on their performance on a small number of individualized target behaviors. Although the classroom teacher meets with the student periodically throughout the day to review DRC ratings and provide performance feedback (e.g., praise when students meet performance goals, constructive feedback when goals are not met), the student's parent or guardian maintains primary responsibility for the delivery of reinforcement—that is, the DRC is sent home at the end of the day for parents or guardians to review with their child, and rewards are administered if performance goals were met during the school day. Interested readers are referred to Volpe and Fabiano (2013), which provides a detailed description of how the DRC may be implemented.

A home-based component may be added to any of the interventions discussed in Chapters 5–7 by establishing a reliable system for sharing information across school and home settings. When implementing a classwide token economy system or other group contingency, individual monitoring forms such as the ones shown in Figures 10.2 and 10.3 could be used to document progress throughout the day and then sent home for the family to review. Similarly, if a classwide self-management system is in place, the teacher could send the student home with a self-monitoring form after reviewing the data at the end of the day. To promote two-way communication, parents could also be provided with space on the data sheet to comment on the student's behavior at home or note any upcoming changes in routine/schedule that may impact the student's behavior.

Incorporating a home-based component may increase the effectiveness of a classwide intervention for several reasons. First, implementing a home-based component increases the degree of communication and collaboration between home and school. All too often, the communication received by the families of those students demonstrating behavioral problems is in one direction and negative in nature—that is, these families tend to hear from school only when things have gone wrong and their input is not always solicited. In contrast, when teachers and families communicate bidirectionally, sharing both successes and challenges, they are able to work together to support student behavior. Many benefits of effective home–school partnerships have been noted within the literature, with regard to both performance in school and beyond (Reschly & Christenson, 2009).

Second, involving families in intervention implementation can serve to support generalization across settings. When parents review behavioral expectations and provide reinforcement for achieved goals, this communicates to their children that the target behaviors are also valued at home. Additionally, families may consider extending the rating of behavior to the home setting as well (see Figure 10.4 for an example of a home–school rating form). In

Name: <u>Gus</u>

Expectations:

- <u>Be respectful of your classmates/siblings</u>
- <u>Be responsible for your belongings</u>
- <u>Start working without reminders</u>

Goal for today: <u>Earn three tokens during each time period</u>

Time of Day	Tokens Earned	Teacher/Parent Comments
School		
Morning		
Afternoon		
Home		
After school		
Comments:		

FIGURE 10.4. Example home–school monitoring form for classwide token economy.

this way, the student receives consistent behavioral feedback throughout all aspects of his or her day.

Third, families may be able to provide more powerful rewards for appropriate behavior than can feasibly be provided in the school setting. If a student is not sufficiently motivated by the available rewards, he or she may be less interested in the intervention. Because a wider variety of rewards can be provided in the home setting than at school, there is a better chance that the student will find available rewards motivating. Home-based rewards can be classified as edible, tangible, activity, or social reinforcers (see Table 10.2). Examples of edible rewards delivered at home include a special after-school snack or getting to have ice cream after dinner. Tangible rewards are objects that the child earns, such as a special toy or game. Activity rewards that are unique to the home setting include being able to go on a hike or bike ride, or being able to stay up late. Finally, home-based social reinforcers would include playing a game with a parent, getting to chat on Skype with a friend, or having a sleepover.

TABLE 10.2. Examples of Home-Based Reinforcers

Edible reinforcers	Tangible reinforcers	Activity reinforcers	Social reinforcers
• After-school snack • After-dinner dessert • Going out for ice cream	• Access to special toys • Board games • Toys	• Extended bedtime • Free time on the computer • Going for a hike/bike ride	• Chatting on Skype • Having a friend sleep over • Playing a game with a parent

MATCHING THE RIGOR OF ASSESSMENT TO THE RIGOR OF INTERVENTION

One of the critical ideas when talking about multi-tiered systems of support is that there is an increase in the intensity of *both* intervention and corresponding assessment as one moves across tiers. As we discussed in Chapter 8, assessment is critically important to understanding whether or not the intervention was actually effective. Even though evidence-based interventions are identified based upon documentation of their effectiveness in the research literature, this does not mean that they will work for every student in every possible situation.

Of the behavioral assessment measures available, we advocate for the use of either systematic direct observation (e.g., frequency count, PLA-Check) or teacher rating-based tools (e.g., DBR, performance-based behavioral recordings) in order to monitor the progress of individual students in response to intervention (see Chapter 8 for a detailed discussion of these methods). These data need to be collected only on a periodic basis (e.g., once a month) when monitoring the effectiveness of a classwide intervention; however, as the intensity of our efforts increase, so, too, should the intensity of our assessment. Therefore, when more targeted, individualized supports are being put into place for one or more students, it may be necessary to increase the frequency of monitoring from once a month to every other week or even weekly.

As we discussed in Chapter 8, it is important to collect outcome data across both baseline and intervention phases. When considering the introduction of individualized modifications, however, the question may arise of what constitutes baseline and intervention. Up until this point, data have typically been collected only at the aggregate (i.e., classwide) level and therefore a true baseline (i.e., in the absence of any intervention) estimate of behavior for an individual student is not available. In this case, the student's performance while the standard classwide intervention is in place should be considered to represent the baseline phase—that is, individual-level data should be collected for the target student prior to implementing any modifications. A phase-change line can then be drawn when any individualized changes are made to the intervention, such as adding a self-monitoring, coaching, or home-based component (see Box 10.3 for a case example).

CONCLUSIONS

Throughout this book, we have presented a number of strategies and interventions that can be used to promote appropriate student behavior. Although the use of these strategies is supported by the research literature, even the best evidence-based interventions are not expected to work for everyone. In other words, these interventions make classrooms better, but not perfect. There will always be students who continue to display behavior struggles—no matter what classwide supports we provide. When our initial efforts to implement classwide supports do prove insufficient for one or more students, we often jump to considering available small-group interventions that can provide the student(s) with more targeted supports. What we have tried to make clear in this chapter, however, is the fact that there is an often-overlooked step that can come between the provision of universal and secondary-level behavioral supports—that is, intensifying an existing classwide intervention may provide struggling students with the necessary level of support while also maintaining a higher level of feasibility. Depending on the student's needs, intensification may be achieved by either changing aspects of the classwide intervention or incorporating additional components to provide individualized supports.

BOX 10.3. Case Example: Evaluating the Effectiveness of Individualized Modifications

Mr. Cohen has been implementing a classwide token economy system for the past month and using daily DBR data to monitor the effectiveness of the intervention in reducing disruptive behavior. Although results have been promising for the large majority of the classroom, Judy continues to disrupt classroom instruction by getting out of her chair to talk to her friends. After talking with the school's behavior specialist, Mr. Cohen decides to introduce a self-monitoring component for Judy. At the end of each instructional block, Judy will be instructed to assess how well she has (1) stayed in her seat, (2) faced the front of the room, (3) listened quietly to instruction, and (4) taken notes. In order to obtain a baseline level of performance, Mr. Cohen continues to complete the classwide DBR each day but then also completes a DBR for Judy more specifically. After collecting these data for a week and finding that Judy's level of disruptive behavior was fairly stable over time, Mr. Cohen meets with Judy to introduce the self-monitoring procedures. A phase line is drawn after the self-monitoring intervention is implemented and Mr. Cohen continues to complete the individualized DBR on a daily basis. The behavior specialist and Mr. Cohen decide to implement the intervention and collect outcome data for 3 weeks before they meet again to evaluate whether and how Judy's behavior has changed.

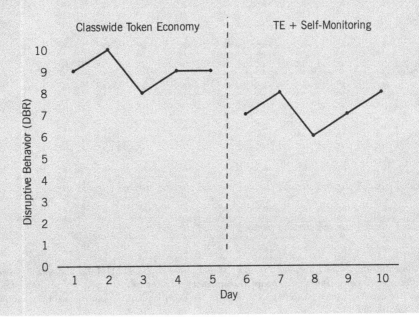

COACH CARD 10.1.
Intensifying Classwide Intervention

When looking to intensify an existing classwide intervention, consider the following options:

1. Increase dosage.

   ☐ Number of minutes in the day

   ☐ Number of days in the week

2. Alter intervention delivery.

   ☐ Provide more explicit instruction.

   ☐ Increase frequency and/or explicitness of performance feedback.

   ☐ Consider whether rewards are adequately motivating.

   ☐ Recruit additional interventionist(s).

3. Change aspects of the environment.

   ☐ Ensure academic work is appropriately challenging.

   ☐ Work to reduce competing sources of reinforcement.

COACH CARD 10.2. Making Individualized Modifications to a Classwide Intervention

Individualized modifications may be made to classwide interventions when a more intensive level of support is needed.

1. Add a self-monitoring component.

   ☐ Determine how the student will monitor how well he or she met classroom expectations.

   ☐ Establish schedule for self-monitoring.

   ☐ Determine how/when ratings will be discussed with the student.

2. Use an external interventionist.

   ☐ Have interventionist review teacher ratings with the student.

   ☐ Have interventionist manage an independent group contingency for the student.

   ☐ Have interventionist review self-ratings with the student.

   ☐ Recruit additional interventionist(s).

3. Incorporate a home-based component.

   ☐ Establish reliable system for sharing information across home and school.

   ☐ Consider whether student behavior will also be rated in the home setting.

   ☐ Identify home-based rewards that are sufficiently motivating.

References

Abramowitz, A. J., O'Leary, S. G., & Futtersak, M. W. (1988). The relative impact of long and short reprimands on children's off-task behavior in the classroom. *Behavior Therapy, 19*(2), 243–247.

Abramowitz, A. J., O'Leary, S. G., & Rosén, L. A. (1987). Reducing off-task behavior in the classroom: A comparison of encouragement and reprimands. *Journal of Abnormal Child Psychology, 15*, 153–163.

Acker, M. M., & O'Leary, S. G. (1987). Effects of reprimands and praise on appropriate behavior in the classroom. *Journal of Abnormal Child Psychology, 15*, 549–557.

Allday, R. A., Hinkson-Lee, K., Hudson, T., Neilsen-Gatti, S., Kleinke, A., & Russel, C. S. (2012). Training general educators to increase behavior-specific praise: Effects on students with EBD. *Behavioral Disorders, 37*, 87–98.

Aloe, A., Amo, L., & Shanahan, M. (2014). Classroom management self-efficacy and burnout: A multivariate meta-analysis. *Educational Psychology Review, 26*(1), 101–126.

Amato-Zech, N. A., Hoff, K. E., & Doepke, K. J. (2006). Increasing on-task behavior in the classroom: Extension of self-monitoring strategies. *Psychology in the Schools, 43*, 211–221.

Ardoin, S. P., Martens, B. K., & Wolfe, L. A. (1999). Using high probability instruction sequences with fading to increase student compliance during transitions. *Journal of Applied Behavior Analysis, 32*, 339–351.

Arlin, M. (1979). Teacher transitions can disrupt time flow in classrooms. *American Educational Research Journal, 16*(1), 42–56.

Armendariz, F., & Umbreit, J. (1999). Using active responding to reduce disruptive behavior in a general education classroom. *Journal of Positive Behavior Interventions, 1*, 152–158.

Axelrod, M. I., & Zank, A. J. (2012). Increasing classroom compliance: Using a high-probability command sequence with noncompliant students. *Journal of Behavioral Education, 21*(2), 119–133.

Axelrod, S. (1973). Comparison of individual and group contingencies in two special classes. *Behavior Therapy, 4*, 83–90.

Axelrod, S., Hall, R. V., & Tams, A. (1979). Comparison of two common classroom seating arrangements. *Academic Therapy, 15*, 29–36.

Baer, R., Ascione, F., & Casto, G. (1977). Relative efficacy of two token economy procedures for decreasing the disruptive classroom behavior of retarded children. *Journal of Abnormal Child Psychology, 5*(2), 135–145.

Ballard, K. D., & Glynn, T. (1975). Behavioral self-management in story writing with elementary school children. *Journal of Applied Behavior Analysis, 8*, 387–398.

Barrish, H. H., Saunders, M., & Wolf, M. M. (1969). Good Behavior Game: Effects of individual contingencies for group consequences on disruptive behavior in a classroom. *Journal of Applied Behavior Analysis, 2*, 119–124.

Barry, L. M., & Messer, J. J. (2003). A practical application of self-management for students diagnosed with attention-deficit/hyperactivity disorder. *Journal of Positive Behavior Interventions, 5*, 238–248.

Baskin, T. W., Slaten, C. D., Sorenson, C., Glover-Russell, J., & Merson, D. N. (2010). Does youth psychotherapy improve academically related outcomes?: A meta-analysis. *Journal of Counseling Psychology, 57*(3), 290.

Beaman, R., & Wheldall, K. (2000). Teachers' use of approval and disapproval in the classroom. *Educational Psychology, 20*, 431–446.

Becker, W. C., Madsen, C. H., Arnold, C. R., & Thomas, D. R. (1967). The contingent use of teacher attention and praise in reducing classroom behavior problems. *Journal of Special Education, 1*, 287–307.

Bennett, N., & Blundell, D. (1983). Quantity and quality of work in rows and classroom groups. *Educational Psychology, 3*, 93–105.

Berkel, C., Mauricio, A. M., Schoenfelder, E., & Sandler, I. N. (2011). Putting the pieces together: An integrated model of program implementation. *Prevention Science, 12*, 23–33.

Birnbrauer, J. S., Wolf, M. M., Kidder, J. D., & Tague, C. E. (1965). Classroom behavior of retarded pupils with token reinforcement. *Journal of Experimental Child Psychology, 2*, 219–235.

Blankenship, T., & Bender, W. N. (2007, Winter). Widely used disciplinary options for aggressive kids: Are the current approaches effective? *Journal of the American Academy of Special Education Professionals*, 5–33.

Blaze, J. T., Olmi, D. J., Mercer, S. H., Dufrene, B. A., & Tingstrom, D. H. (2014). Loud versus quiet praise: A direct behavioral comparison in secondary classrooms. *Journal of School Psychology, 52*, 349–360.

Blondin, C., Skinner, C., Parkhurst, J., Wood, A., & Snyder, J. (2012): Enhancing on-task behavior in fourth-grade students using a modified Color Wheel system. *Journal of Applied School Psychology, 28*, 37–58.

Boegli, R. G., & Wasik, B. H. (1978). Use of the token economy system to intervene on a school-wide level. *Psychology in the Schools, 15*, 72–78.

Bohn, C. M., Roehrig, A. D., & Pressley, M. (2004). The first days of school in the classrooms of two more effective and four less effective primary-grades teachers. *Elementary School Journal, 104*, 269–287.

Bowers, F. E., McGinnis, C., Ervin, R. A., & Friman, P. C. (1999). Merging research and practice: The example of positive peer reporting applied to social rejection. *Education and Treatment of Children, 22*, 218–226.

Bradshaw, C. P., Mitchell, M. M., & Leaf, P. J. (2010). Examining the effects of schoolwide positive behavioral interventions and supports on student outcomes. *Journal of Positive Behavior Interventions, 12*, 133–148.

Brantley, D. C., & Webster, R. E. (1993). Use of an independent group contingency management system in a regular classroom setting. *Psychology in the Schools, 30*, 60–66.

Breyer, N. L., & Allen, G. J. (1975). Effects of implementing a token economy on teacher attending behavior. *Journal of Applied Behavior Analysis, 8*, 373–380.

Briesch, A. M., & Briesch, J. M. (2016). A meta-analysis of behavioral self-management interventions in single-case research. *School Psychology Review, 45*, 3–18.

Briesch, A. M., & Chafouleas, S. M. (2009). Defining behavioral self-management: A review and analysis of the literature 1988–2008. *School Psychology Quarterly, 24*, 106–118.

Briesch, A. M., Hemphill, E. M., & Daniels, B. (2013). Check your SLANT: Adapting self-management for use as a class-wide intervention. *School Psychology Forum, 7*(2), 29–39.

Broden, M., Bruce, C., Mitchell, M. A., Carter, V., & Hall, R. V. (1970). Effects of teacher attention on attending behavior of two boys at adjacent desks. *Journal of Applied Behavior Analysis, 3,* 205–211.

Broden, M., Hall, R. V., Dunlap, A., & Clark, R. (1970). Effects of teacher attention and a token reinforcement system in a junior high school special education class. *Exceptional Children, 36,* 341–349.

Brophy, J. (1981). Teacher praise: A functional analysis. *Review of Education Research, 51,* 5–32.

Brossart, D. F., Parker, R. I., Olson, E. A., & Mahadevan, L. (2006). The relationship between visual analysis and five statistical analyses in a simple A-B single-case research design. *Behavior Modification, 30,* 531–563.

Bruhn, A., McDaniel, S., & Kreigh, C. (2015). Self-monitoring interventions for students with behavior problems: A systematic review of current research. *Behavioral Disorders, 40,* 102–121.

Brulle, A. R., & Repp, A. C. (1984). An investigation of the accuracy of momentary time sampling procedures with time series data. *British Journal of Psychology, 75,* 481–485.

Brunsma, D. L., & Rockquemore, K. A. (1998). Effects of student uniforms on attendance, behavior problems, substance use, and academic achievement. *Journal of Educational Research, 92*(1), 53–62.

Burns, M. K., & Dean, V. J. (2005). Effect of acquisition rates on off-task behavior with children identified as having learning disabilities. *Learning Disability Quarterly, 28*(4), 273–281.

Burns, M. K., & Ysseldyke, J. E. (2008). Reported prevalence of evidence-based instructional practices in special education. *Journal of Special Education, 43,* 3–11.

Busacca, M. L., Anderson, A., & Moore, D. W. (2015). Self-management for primary school students demonstrating problem behavior in regular classrooms: Evidence review of single-case design research. *Journal of Behavioral Education, 24,* 373–401.

Campbell, S., & Skinner, C. H. (2004). Combining explicit timing with an interdependent group contingency program to decrease transition times: An investigation of the Timely Transitions Game. *Journal of Applied School Psychology, 20,* 11–27.

Cancio, E., & Johnson, J. W. (2007). Level systems revisited: An important tool for educating students with emotional and behavioral disorders. *International Journal of Behavioral Consultation and Therapy, 3,* 512–527.

Carnine, D. W. (1976). Effects of two teacher-presentation rates on off-task behavior, answering correctly, and participation. *Journal of Applied Behavior Analysis, 9*(2), 199–206.

Carnine, D. (1997). Bridging the research-to-practice gap. *Exceptional Children, 63*(4), 513–521.

Cavanaugh, R. A., Heward, W. L., & Donelson, F. (1996). Effects of response cards during lesson closure on the academic performance of secondary students in an earth science course. *Journal of Applied Behavior Analysis, 29,* 403–406.

Chafouleas, S. M., Briesch, A. M., Riley-Tillman, T. C., Christ, T. J., Black, A. C., & Kilgus, S. P. (2010). An investigation of the generalizability and dependability of Direct Behavior Rating Single Item Scales (DBR-SIS) to measure academic engagement and disruptive behavior of middle school students. *Journal of School Psychology, 48*(3), 219–246.

Chafouleas, S. M., Hagermoser Sanetti, L. M., Jaffery, R., & Fallon, L. M. (2012). An evaluation of a classwide intervention package involving self-management and a group contingency on classroom behavior of middle school students. *Journal of Behavioral Education, 21*(1), 34–57.

Chafouleas, S. M., Riley-Tillman, T. C., & Sugai, G. (2007). *School-based behavioral assessment: Informing intervention and instruction.* New York: Guilford Press.

Chalk, K., & Bizo, L. A. (2004). Specific praise improves on-task behaviour and numeracy enjoyment: A study of year four pupils engaged in the numeracy hour. *Educational Psychology in Practice, 20*(4), 335–351.

Choate, S. M., Skinner, C. H., Fearrington, J., Kohler, B., & Skolits, G. (2007). Extending the external validity of the Color Wheel procedures: Decreasing out-of-seat behavior in an intact rural first-grade classroom. *Journal of Evidence-Based Practices for Schools, 8,* 120–133.

Cihak, D. F., Kirk, E. R., & Boon, R. T. (2009). Effects of classwide positive peer "tooling" to reduce the disruptive classroom behaviors of elementary students with and without disabilities. *Journal of Behavioral Education, 18,* 267–278.

Codding, R. S., Feinberg, A. B., Dunn, E. K., & Pace, G. M. (2005). Effects of immediate performance feedback on implementation of behavior support plans. *Journal of Applied Behavior Analysis, 38*(2), 205–219.

Cohen, J. (1988). *Statistical power analysis for the behavioral sciences* (2nd ed.). Hillsdale, NJ: Erlbaum.

Colvin, G., Sugai, G., Good, R. H., III, & Lee, Y. (1997). Using active supervision and precorrection to improve transition behaviors in an elementary school. *School Psychology Quarterly, 12,* 344–363.

Connell, M. C., Carta, J. J., & Baer, D. M. (1993). Programming generalization of in-class transition skills: Teaching preschoolers with developmental delays to self-assess and recruit contingent teacher praise. *Journal of Applied Behavior Analysis, 26,* 345–352.

Connell, M. C., Carta, J. J., Lutz, S., Randall, C., Wilson, J., & Lamb, D. R. (1993). Building independence during in-class transitions: Teaching in-class transition skills to preschoolers with developmental delays through choral-response-based self-assessment and contingent praise. *Education and Treatment of Children, 16,* 160–174.

Conyers, C., Miltenberger, R., Maki, A., Barenz, R., Jurgens, M., Sailer, A., et al. (2004). A comparison of response cost and differential reinforcement of other behavior to reduce disruptive behavior in a preschool classroom. *Journal of Applied Behavior Analysis, 37,* 411–415.

Cook, B. G., & Odom, S. L. (2013). Evidence-based practices and implementation science in special education. *Exceptional Children, 79*(2), 135–144.

Cooper, J. O., Heron, T. E., & Heward, W. L. (2007). *Applied behavior analysis.* Upper Saddle River, NJ: Pearson.

Cornwell, S., & Evans, C. J. (2001). The effects of sound-field amplification on attending behaviours. *Journal of Speech Language Pathology and Audiology, 25*(3), 135–144.

Cothran, D. J., Kulinna, P. H., & Garrahy, D. A. (2009). Attributions for and consequences of student misbehavior. *Physical Education and Sport Pedagogy, 14,* 155–167.

Council for Exceptional Children. (2014). *Council for Exceptional Children standards for evidence-based practices in special education.* Arlington, VA: Author.

Crone, D. A., Hawken, L. S., & Horner, R. H. (2010). *Responding to problem behavior in schools: The Behavior Education Program* (2nd ed.). New York: Guilford Press.

Dane, A. V., & Schneider, B. H. (1998). Program integrity in primary and early secondary prevention: Are implementation effects out of control? *Clinical Psychology Review, 18,* 23–45.

Dart, E. H., Radley, K. C., Battaglia, A. A., Dadakhodjaeva, K., Bates, K. E., & Wright, S. J. (2016). The classroom password: A class-wide intervention to increase academic engagement. *Psychology in the Schools, 53*(4), 416–431.

Dart, E. H., Radley, K. C., Briesch, A. M., Furlow, C. M., & Cavell, H. (2016). Assessing the accuracy of classwide direct observation methods: Two analyses utilizing simulated and naturalistic data. *Behavioral Disorders, 41*(3), 148–160.

Davies, S., & Witte, R. (2000). Self-management and peer-monitoring within a group contingency to decrease uncontrolled verbalizations of children with attention-deficit-hyperactivity disorder. *Psychology in the Schools, 37,* 135–147.

De Martini-Scully, D., Bray, M. A., & Kehle, T. J. (2000). A packaged intervention to reduce disruptive behaviors in general education students. *Psychology in the Schools, 37*(2), 149–156.

De Pry, R. L., & Sugai, G. (2002). The effect of active supervision and pre-correction on minor behavioral incidents in a sixth grade general education classroom. *Journal of Behavioral Education, 11*, 255–267.

Delquadri, J., Greenwood, C. R., Whorton, D., Carta, J. J., & Hall, R. V. (1986). Classwide peer tutoring. *Exceptional Children, 52*, 535–542.

Denune, H., Hawkins, R., Donovan, L., McCoy, D., Hall, L., & Moeder, A. (2015). Combining self-monitoring and an interdependent group contingency to improve the behavior of sixth graders with EBD. *Psychology in the Schools, 52*, 562–577.

Dolan, L. J., Kellam, S. G., Brown, C. H., Werthamer-Larsson, L., Rebok, G. W., Mayer, L. S., et al. (1993). The short-term impact of two classroom-based preventive interventions on aggressive and shy behaviors and poor achievement. *Journal of Applied Developmental Psychology, 14*, 317–345.

Donaldson, J. M., Vollmer, T. R., Krous, T., Downs, S., & Berard, K. P. (2011). An evaluation of the Good Behavior Game in kindergarten classrooms. *Journal of Applied Behavior Analysis, 44*(3), 605–609.

Drabman, R., Spitalnik, R., & Spitalnik, K. (1974). Sociometric and disruptive behavior as a function of four types of token reinforcement programs. *Journal of Applied Behavior Analysis, 7*, 93–101.

Drege, P., & Beare, P. L. (1991). The effect of a token reinforcement system with a time-out backup consequence on the classroom behavior of E/BD students. *British Columbia Journal of Special Education, 15*, 39–46.

Dunlap, G., Clarke, S., Jackson, M., Wright, S., Ramos, E., & Brinson, S. (1995). Self-monitoring of classroom behaviors with students exhibiting emotional and behavioral challenges. *School Psychology Quarterly, 10*, 165–177.

DuPaul, G. J., Eckert, T. L., & Vilardo, B. (2012). The effects of school-based interventions for attention deficit hyperactivity disorder: A meta-analysis 1996–2010. *School Psychology Review, 41*(4), 387–412.

Edwards, L., Salant, V., Howard, V. F., Brougher, J., & McLaughlin, T. F. (1995). Effectiveness of self-management on attentional behavior and reading comprehension for children with attention deficit disorder. *Child and Family Behavior Therapy, 17*, 1–17.

Elliott, S. N., Turco, T. L., & Gresham, F. M. (1987). Consumers' and clients' pretreatment acceptability ratings of classroom group contingencies. *Journal of School Psychology, 25*(2), 145–153.

Elwell, W. C., & Tiberio, J. (1994). Teacher praise: What students want. *Journal of Instructional Psychology, 21*, 322–329.

Embry, D. D. (2002). The Good Behavior Game: A best practice candidate as a universal behavioral vaccine. *Clinical Child and Family Psychology Review, 5*, 273–297.

Emmer. E. T. (1984). *Classroom management: Research and implications.* Austin, TX: Research and Development Center for Teacher Education.

Emmer, E. T., Evertson, C. M., & Anderson, L. M. (1980). Effective classroom management at the beginning of the school year. *Elementary School Journal, 80*, 219–231.

Epstein, M., Atkins, M., Cullinan, D., Kutash, K., & Weaver, R. (2008). *Reducing behavior problems in the elementary school classroom: A practice guide* (NCEE #2008-012). Washington, DC: National Center for Education Evaluation and Regional Assistance, Institute of Education Sciences, U.S. Department of Education. Retrieved from *http://ies.ed.gov/ncee/wwc/publications/practiceguides.*

Ervin, R. A., Miller, P. M., & Friman, P. C. (1996). Feed the hungry bee: Using positive peer reports to improve the social interactions and acceptance of a socially rejected girl in a residential placement. *Journal of Applied Behavior Analysis, 29*, 251–253.

Everston, C. M., & Emmer, E. T. (1982). Effective management at the beginning of the school year in junior high classes. *Journal of Educational Psychology, 74*(4), 485.

Every Student Succeeds Act. (2015). Every Student Succeeds Act of 2015, Pub. L. No. 114-95 § 114 Stat. 1177 (2015–2016).

Fabiano, G. A., Pelham, W. E., Jr., Gnagy, E. M., & Burrows-MacLean, L. (2007). The single and combined effects of multiple intensities of behavior modification and methylphenidate for children with attention deficit hyperactivity disorder in a classroom setting. *School Psychology Review, 36*(2), 195.

Fallon, L. M., Collier-Meek, M. A., Maggin, D. M., Sanetti, L. M., & Johnson, A. H. (2015). Is performance feedback for educators an evidence-based practice?: A systematic review and evaluation based on single-case research. *Exceptional Children, 81*(2), 227–246.

Filcheck, H. A., McNeil, C. B., Greco, L. A., & Bernard, R. S. (2004). Using a whole-class token economy and coaching of teacher skills in a preschool classroom to manage disruptive behavior. *Psychology in the Schools, 41*, 351–361.

Finkelhor, D., Turner, H., Ormrod, R., & Hamby, S. L. (2009). Violence, abuse, and crime exposure in a national sample of children and youth. *Pediatrics, 124*(5), 1411–1423.

Fishbein, J. E., & Wasik, B. H. (1981). Effect of the Good Behavior Game on disruptive library behavior. *Journal of Applied Behavior Analysis, 14*, 89–93.

Fixsen, D. L., Naoom, S. F., Blase, K. A., Friedman, R. M., & Wallace, F. (2005). *Implementation research: A synthesis of the literature* (FMHI Publication #231). Tampa: University of South Florida, Louis de la Parte Florida Mental Health Institute, National Implementation Research Network.

Floress, M. T., & Jenkins, L. N. (2015). A preliminary investigation of kindergarten teachers' use of praise in general education classrooms. *Preventing School Failure, 59*, 253–262.

Forehand, R., Gardner, H., & Roberts, M. W. (1978). Maternal response to child compliance and noncompliance: Some normative data. *Journal of Clinical Child Psychology, 7*, 121–124.

Foster, S. L., Laverty-Finch, C., Gizzo, D. P., & Osantowski, J. (1999). Practical issues in self-observation. *Psychological Assessment, 11*, 426–438.

Freedman, D. H. (2012). The perfected self. *The Atlantic, 309*(5), 42–53.

Fry, P. S. (1983). Process measures of problem and non-problem children's classroom behaviour: The influence of teacher behaviour variables. *British Journal of Educational Psychology, 53*, 79–88.

Fudge, D. L., Skinner, C. H., Williams, J. L., Cowden, D., Clark, J., & Bliss, S. L. (2008). Increasing on-task behavior in every student in a second-grade classroom during transitions: Validating the Color Wheel system. *Journal of School Psychology, 46*, 575–592.

Fullerton, E. K., Conroy, M. A., & Correa, V. I. (2009). Early childhood teachers' use of specific praise statements with young children at risk for behavioral disorders. *Behavioral Disorders, 34*, 118–135.

Gable, R. A., Hester, P. H., Rock, M. L., & Hughes, K. G. (2009). Back to basics rules: Praise, ignoring, and reprimands revisited. *Intervention in School and Clinic, 44*(4), 195–205.

Gansle, K. A., & McMahon, C. M. (1997). Component integrity of teacher intervention management behavior using a student self-monitoring treatment: An experimental analysis. *Journal of Behavioral Education, 7*, 405–419.

George, C. L. (2010). Effects of response cards on performance and participation in social studies for middle school students with emotional and behavioral disorders. *Behavioral Disorders, 35*, 200–213.

Gickling, E. E., & Armstrong, D. L. (1978). Levels of instructional difficulty as related to on-task behavior, task completion, and comprehension. *Journal of Learning Disabilities, 11*, 559–566.

Glynn, E. L., & Thomas, J. D. (1974). Effect of cueing on self-control of classroom behavior. *Journal of Applied Behavior Analysis, 7*(2), 299–306.

Glynn, E. L., Thomas, J. D., & Shee, S. M. (1973). Behavioral self-control of on-task behavior in an elementary classroom. *Journal of Applied Behavior Analysis, 6*(1), 105–113.

Godfrey, S. A., Grisham-Brown, J., Schuster, J. W., & Hemmeter, M. L. (2003). The effects of three techniques on student participation with preschool children with attending problems. *Education and Treatment of Children, 26*, 255–272.

Gottman, J. M., & McFall, R. M. (1972). Self-monitoring effects in a program for potential high school dropouts: A time series analysis. *Journal of Consulting and Clinical Psychology, 39,* 273–281.

Greenberg, J., Putnam, H., & Walsh, K. (2014). Training our future teachers: Classroom management. Retrieved from *www.nctq.org/dmsView/Future_Teachers_Classroom_Management_NCTQ_Report.*

Greenwood, C. R., Hops, H., Delquadri, J., & Guild, J. (1974). Group contingencies for group consequences in classroom management: A further analysis. *Journal of Applied Behavior Analysis, 7*(3), 413–425.

Greenwood, C. R., Horton, B. T., & Utley, C. A. (2002). Academic engagement: Current perspectives on research and practice. *School Psychology Review, 31,* 328–349.

Gresham, F. M. (2009). Evolution of the treatment integrity concept: Current status and future directions. *School Psychology Review, 38,* 533–540.

Gresham, F. M., Gansle, K. A., Noell, G. H., Cohen, S., & Rosenblum, S. (1993). Treatment integrity of school-based behavioral intervention studies: 1980–1990. *School Psychology Review, 22*(2), 254–272.

Gresham, F. M., & Gresham, G. N. (1982). Interdependent, dependent, and independent group contingencies for controlling disruptive behavior. *Journal of Special Education, 16,* 101–110.

Grieger, T., Kaufman, J. M., & Grieger, R. (1976). Effects of peer reporting on cooperative play and aggression of kindergarten children. *Journal of School Psychology, 14,* 307–313.

Gross, A. M., & Wojnilower, D. A. (1984). Self-directed behavior change in children: Is it self-directed? *Behavior Therapy, 15*(5), 501–514.

Guttmann, J. (1982). Pupils, teachers' and parents' causal attributions for problem behavior at school. *Journal of Educational Research, 76*(1), 14–21.

Hall, R. V., Lund, D., & Jackson, D. (1968). Effects of teacher attention on study behavior. *Journal of Applied Behavior Analysis, 1,* 1–12.

Hallahan, D. P., & Lloyd, J. W. (1987). Use of self-monitoring of attention with LD students: Research and application. *Learning Disability Quarterly, 10*(2), 139–151.

Hansen, S. D., & Lignugaris/Kraft, B. (2005). Effects of a dependent group contingency on the verbal interactions of middle school students with emotional disturbance. *Behavioral Disorders, 30*(2), 170–184.

Happe, D. (1982). Behavioral intervention: It doesn't do any good in your briefcase. In J. Grimes (Ed.), *Psychological approaches to problems of children and adolescents* (pp. 15–41). Des Moines: Iowa Department of Public Instruction.

Harris, K. R. (1986). Self-monitoring of attentional behavior vs. self-monitoring of productivity: Effects on on-task behavior and academic response rate among learning disabled children. *Journal of Applied Behavior Analysis, 19*(4), 417–423.

Harris, K. R., Friedlander, B. D., Saddler, B., Firzzelle, R., & Graham, S. (2005). Self-monitoring of attention versus self-monitoring of academic performance. *Journal of Special Education, 39,* 145–156.

Harris, K. R., Graham, S., Reid, R., McElroy, K., & Hamby, R. S. (1994). Self-monitoring of attention versus self-monitoring of performance: Replication and cross-task comparison studies. *Learning Disability Quarterly, 17,* 121–139.

Hastings, N., & Schweiso, J. (1995). Tasks and tables: The effects of seating arrangements on task engagement in primary classrooms. *Educational Research, 37,* 279–291.

Hattie, J. (2008). *Visible learning: A synthesis of over 800 meta-analyses relating to achievement.* New York: Routledge.

Hattie, J., & Timperley, H. (2007). The power of feedback. *Review of Educational Research, 77,* 81–112.

Hawkins, R. O., Haydon, T., Denune, H., Larkin, W., & Fite, N. (2015). Improving the transition behavior of high school students with emotional behavioral disorders using a randomized interdependent group contingency. *School Psychology Review, 44*, 208–223.

Hawkins, S. M., & Heflin, L. J. (2011). Increasing secondary teachers' behavior-specific praise using a video self-modeling and visual performance feedback intervention. *Journal of Positive Behavior Interventions, 13*(2), 97–108.

Haydon, T., Conroy, M. A., Scott, T. M., Sindelar, P. T., Barber, B. R., & Orlando, A.-M. (2010). A comparison of three types of opportunities to respond on student academic and social behaviors. *Journal of Emotional and Behavioral Disorders, 18*(1), 27–40.

Heck, A., Collins, J., & Peterson, L. (2001). Decreasing children's risk taking on the playground. *Journal of Applied Behavior Analysis, 34*, 349–352.

Heering, P. W., & Wilder, D. A. (2006). The use of dependent group contingencies to increase on-task behavior in two general education classrooms. *Education and Treatment of Children, 29*, 459–468.

Heller, M., & White, M. (1975). Rates of teacher approval and disapproval to higher and lower ability classes. *Journal of Educational Psychology, 67*, 796–800.

Herrnstein, R. J. (1961). Relative and absolute strength of response as a function of frequency of reinforcement. *Journal of the Experimental Analysis of Behavior, 4*, 267–272.

Hester, P. P., Baltodano, H. M., Hendrickson, J. M., Tonelson, S. W., Conroy, M. A., & Gable, R. A. (2004). Lessons learned from research on early intervention: What teachers can do to prevent children's behavior problems. *Preventing School Failure, 49*(1), 5–10.

Hoff, K. E., & DuPaul, G. J. (1998). Reducing disruptive behavior in general education classrooms: The use of self-management strategies. *School Psychology Review, 27*, 290–303.

Hoff, K. E., & Ervin, R. A. (2013). Extending self-management strategies: The use of a classwide approach. *Psychology in the Schools, 50*(2), 151–164.

Holland, M. L., Malmberg, J., & Gimpel Peacock, G. (2017). *Emotional and behavioral problems of young children: Effective interventions in the preschool and kindergarten years* (2nd ed.). New York: Guilford Press.

Hollo, A., & Hirn, R. G. (2015). Teacher and student behaviors in the contexts of grade-level and instructional grouping. *Preventing School Failure, 59*, 30–39.

Horner, R. H., Sugai, G., Smolkowski, K., Eber, L., Nakasato, J., Todd, A. W., et al. (2009). A randomized, wait-list controlled effectiveness trial assessing school-wide positive behavior support in elementary schools. *Journal of Positive Behavior Interventions, 11*(3), 133–144.

Hosp, J. L., Howell, K. W., & Hosp, M. K. (2003). Characteristics of behavior rating scales: Implications for practice in assessment and behavioral support. *Journal of Positive Behavior Interventions, 5*, 201–208.

Hughes, D. C. (1973). An experimental investigation of the effects of pupil responding and teacher reacting on pupil achievement. *American Educational Research Journal, 10*, 21–37.

Hulac, D. M., & Benson, N. (2010). The use of group contingencies for preventing and managing disruptive behaviors. *Intervention in School and Clinic, 45*(4), 257–262.

Hulac, D. M., & Benson, N. (2011). Getting students to work smarter and harder: Decreasing off-task behavior through interspersal techniques. *School Psychology Forum, 5*(1), 29–36.

Hulac, D., Benson, N., Nesmith, M. C., & Shervey, S. W. (2016). Using variable interval reinforcement schedules to support students in the classroom: An introduction with illustrative examples. *Journal of Educational Research and Practice, 6*(1), 90–96.

IRIS Center. (2015). Intensive intervention (Part 1): Using data-based individualization to intensify instruction. Retrieved from *http://iris.peabody.vanderbilt.edu/module/dbi1*.

Iwata, B. A., & Bailey, J. S. (1974). Reward versus cost token systems: An analysis of the effects on students and teacher. *Journal of Applied Behavior Analysis, 7*, 567–576.

Iwata, B. A., Pace, G. M., Kissel, R. C., Nau, P. A., & Farber, J. M. (1990). Self-Injury Trauma (SIT)

Scale: A method for identifying surface tissue damage caused by self-injurious behavior. *Journal of Applied Behavior Analysis, 23*, 99–110.

Jenkins, L. N., Floress, M. T., & Reinke, W. (2015). Rates and types of teacher praise: A review and future directions. *Psychology in the Schools, 52*(5), 463–476.

Johnson, M. R., Turner, P. F., & Konarski, E. A. (1978). The "Good Behavior Game": A systematic replication in two unruly transitional classrooms. *Education and Treatment of Children, 1*, 25–33.

Johnson-Gros, K. N., Lyons, E. A., & Griffin, J. R. (2008). Active supervision: An intervention to reduce high school tardiness. *Education and Treatment of Children, 31*(1), 39–53.

Jones, K. M., Young, M. M., & Friman, P. C. (2000). Increasing peer praise of socially rejected delinquent youth: Effects on cooperation and acceptance. *School Psychology Quarterly, 15*, 30–39.

Jones, M., Boon, R. T., Fore, C., & Bender, W. N. (2008). Our Mystery Hero!: A group contingency intervention for reducing verbally disrespectful behaviors. *Learning Disabilities, 15*, 61–69.

Jones, R. R., Weinrott, M. R., & Vaught, R. S. (1978). Effects of serial dependency on the agreement between visual and statistical interference. *Journal of Applied Behavior Analysis, 11*, 277–283.

Joyce, B., & Showers, B. (2002). *Student achievement through staff development* (3rd ed.). Alexandria, VA: Association for Supervision and Curriculum Development.

Kalis, T. M., Vannest, K. J., & Parker, R. (2007). Praise counts: Using self-monitoring to increase effective teaching practices. *Preventing School Failure: Alternative Education for Children and Youth, 51*(3), 20–27.

Kamps, D., Conklin, C., & Wills, H. (2015). Use of self-management with the CW-FIT group contingency program. *Education and Treatment of Children, 38*, 1–32.

Kanfer, F. H. (1970). Self-monitoring: Methodological considerations and clinical applications. *Journal of Consulting and Clinical Psychology, 35*, 148–152.

Kartub, D. T., Taylor-Greene, S., March, R. E., & Horner, R. H. (2000). Reducing hallway noise: A systems approach. *Journal of Positive Behavior Interventions, 2*, 179–182.

Kazdin, A. E. (1980). Acceptability of alternative treatments for deviant child behavior. *Journal of Applied Behavior Analysis, 13*, 259–273.

Kellam, S. G., Rebok, G. W., Ialongo, N., & Mayer, L. S. (1994). The course and malleability of aggressive behavior from early first grade into middle school: Results of a developmental epidemiologically-based preventive trial. *Journal of Child Psychology and Psychiatry, 35*(2), 259–281.

Kellam, S. G., Wang, W., Mackenzie, A. C. L., Brown, C. H., Ompad, D. C., Or, F., et al. (2014). The impact of the Good Behavior Game, a universal classroom-based preventive intervention in first and second grades, on high-risk sexual behaviors and srug abuse and dependence disorders into young adulthood. *Prevention Science, 15*(Suppl. 1), 6–18.

Kelshaw-Levering, K., Sterling-Turner, H. E., Henry, J. R., & Skinner, C. H. (2000). Randomized interdependent group contingencies: Group reinforcement with a twist. *Psychology in the Schools, 37*, 523–533.

Kena, G., Musu-Gillette, L., Robinson, J., Wang, X., Rathbun, A., Zhang, J., et al. (2015). The condition of education 2015 (NCES 2015-144). Washington, DC: U.S. Department of Education, National Center for Education Statistics. Retrieved from *http://nces.ed.gov/pubsearch*.

Killu, K., Sainato, D. M., Davis, C. A., Ospelt, H., & Paul, J. N. (1998). Effects of high-probability request sequences on preschoolers' compliance and disruptive behavior. *Journal of Behavioral Education, 8*, 347–368.

Kirk, E. R., Becker, J. A., Skinner, C. H., Fearrington, J. Y., McCane-Bowling, S. J., Amburn, C., et al. (2010). Decreasing inappropriate vocalizations using classwide group contingencies and Color Wheel procedures: A component analysis. *Psychology in the Schools, 47*, 931–943.

Kleinman, K. E., & Saigh, P. A. (2011). The effects of the Good Behavior Game on the conduct of regular education New York City high school students. *Behavior Modification, 35*, 95–105.

Klimas, A., & McLaughlin, T. F. (2007). The effects of a token economy system to improve social and academic behavior with a rural primary aged child with disabilities. *International Journal of Special Education, 22,* 72–77.

Kounin, J. S. (1970). *Discipline and group management in classrooms.* New York: Holt, Rinehart & Winston.

Kowalewicz, E. A., & Coffee, G. (2014). Mystery Motivator: A Tier 1 classroom behavioral intervention. *School Psychology Quarterly, 29,* 138–156.

Krasch, D., & Carter, D. R. (2009). Monitoring classroom behavior in early childhood: Using group observation data to make decisions. *Early Childhood Education Journal, 36,* 475–482.

Kratochwill, T. R., Hitchcock, J., Horner, R. H., Levin, J. R., Odom, S. L., Rindskopf, D. M., et al. (2010). What Works Clearinghouse: Single-case design technical documentation (Version 1.0). Retrieved from *http://ies.ed.gov/ncee/wwc/pdf/wwc_scd.pdf.*

Kratochwill, T. R., & Levin, J. R. (2014). *Single-case intervention research: Methodological and statistical advances.* Washington, DC: American Psychological Association.

Kritchevsky, S., & Prescott, E. (1969). *Planning environments for young children: Physical space.* Washington DC: National Association for the Education of Young Children.

Lambert, A. M., Tingstrom, D. H., Sterling, H. E., Dufrene, B. A., & Lynne, S. (2015). Effects of tootling on classwide disruptive and appropriate behavior of upper-elementary students. *Behavior Modification, 39*(3), 413–430.

Lambert, M. C., Cartledge, G., Heward, W. L., & Lo, Y. (2006). Effects of response cards on disruptive behavior and academic responding during math lessons by fourth-grade urban students. *Journal of Positive Behavior Interventions, 8,* 88–99.

Lane, K. L., Menzies, H. M., Ennis, R. P., & Bezdek, J. (2013). School-wide systems to promote positive behaviors and facilitate instruction. *Journal of Curriculum and Instruction, 7,* 6–31.

Lane, K. L., Wehby, J. H., Robertson, E. J., & Rogers, L. A. (2007). How do different types of high school students respond to schoolwide positive behavior support programs?: Characteristics and responsiveness of teacher-identified students. *Journal of Emotional and Behavioral Disorders, 15*(1), 3–20.

Lannie, A. L., & McCurdy, B. L. (2007). Preventing disruptive behavior in the urban classroom: Effects of the Good Behavior Game on student and teacher behavior. *Education and Treatment of Children, 30,* 85–98.

Lee, D. L. (2005). Increasing compliance: A quantitative synthesis of applied research on high-probability requests. *Exceptionality, 13,* 141–154.

Lee, S., Simpson, R. L., & Shogren, K. A. (2007). Effects and implications of self-management for students with autism: A meta-analysis. *Focus on Autism and Other Developmental Disabilities, 22,* 2–13.

Levendoski, L. S., & Cartledge, G. (2000). Self-monitoring for elementary school children with serious emotional disturbances: Classroom applications for increased academic responding. *Behavioral Disorders, 25,* 211–224.

Lewis, T. J., Colvin, G., & Sugai, G. (2000). The effects of precorrection and active supervision on the recess behavior of elementary students. *Education and Treatment of Children, 23,* 109–121.

Ling, S., Hawkins, R. O., & Weber, D. (2011). Effects of a classwide interdependent group contingency designed to improve the behavior of an at-risk student. *Journal of Behavioral Education, 20,* 103–116.

Litow, L., & Pumroy, D. K. (1975). A brief review of classroom group-oriented contingencies. *Journal of Applied Behavior Analysis, 8,* 341–347.

Little, S. G., Akin-Little, A., & O'Neill, K. (2015). Group contingency interventions with children—1980–2010: A meta-analysis. *Behavior Modification, 39*(2), 322–341.

Lloyd, J. W., Bateman, D. F., Landrum, T. J., & Hallahan, D. P. (1989). Self-recording of attention versus productivity. *Journal of Applied Behavior Analysis, 22,* 315–323.

Lloyd, M. E., & Hilliard, A. M. (1989). Accuracy of self-recording as a function of repeated experience with different self-control contingencies. *Child and Family Behavior Therapy, 11*, 1–14.

Long, A. C. J., Sanetti, L. M. H., Collier-Meek, M. A., Gallucci, J., Altschaefl, M., & Kratochwill, T. R. (2016). An exploratory investigation of teachers' intervention planning and perceived implementation barriers. *Journal of School Psychology, 55*, 1–26.

Ludlow, B. (2014). Intensifying intervention: Kicking it up a notch. *Teaching Exceptional Children, 4*, 4.

Lutzker, J. R., & White-Blackburn, G. (1979). The Good Behavior Game: Increasing work performance in a rehabilitation setting. *Journal of Applied Behavior Analysis, 12*, 488.

Maag, J. W. (2001). Rewarded by punishment: Reflections on the disuse of positive reinforcement in schools. *Exceptional Children, 67*(2), 173–186.

Maag, J. W., Reid, R., & DiGangi, S. A. (1993). Differential effects of self-monitoring attention, accuracy, and productivity. *Journal of Applied Behavior Analysis, 26*, 329–344.

Maag, J. W., Rutherford, R. B., & DiGangi, S. A. (1992). Effects of self-monitoring and contingent reinforcement on on-task behavior and academic productivity of learning-disabled students: A social validation study. *Psychology in the Schools, 29*, 157–172.

Mackay, S., McLaughlin, T. F., Weber, K., & Derby, K. M. (2001). The use of precision requests to decrease noncompliance in the home and neighborhood: A case study. *Child and Family Behavior Therapy, 23*, 41–50.

Madaus, M. R., Kehle, T. J., Madaus, J., & Bray, M. A. (2003). Mystery Motivator as an intervention to promote homework completion and accuracy. *School Psychology International, 24*, 369–377.

Madsen, C. H., Becker, W. C., & Thomas, D. R. (1968). Rules, praise, and ignoring: Elements of elementary classroom control. *Journal of Applied Behavior Analysis, 1*(2), 139–150.

Maggin, D. M., Johnson, A. H., Chafouleas, S. M., Ruberto, L. M., & Berggren, M. (2012). A systematic evidence review of school-based group contingency interventions for students with challenging behavior. *Journal of School Psychology, 50*, 625–654.

Mahar, M. T., Murphy, S. K., Rowe, D. A., Golden, J., Shields, A. T., & Raedeke, T. D. (2006). Effects of a classroom-based program on physical activity and on-task behavior. *Medicine and Science in Sports and Exercise, 38*, 2086–2094.

Maheady, L., Michielli-Pendl, J., Mallette, B., & Harper, G. F. (2002). A collaborative research project to improve the academic performance of a diverse sixth grade science class. *Teacher Education and Special Education, 25*(1), 55–70.

Main, G. C., & Munro, B. C. (1977). A token reinforcement program in a public junior high school. *Journal of Applied Behavior Analysis, 10*, 93–94.

Martens, B. K., Witt, J. C., Elliott, S. N., & Darveaux, D. X. (1985). Teacher judgments concerning the acceptability of school-based interventions. *Professional Psychology: Research and Practice, 16*, 191–198.

Mastropieri, M. A., Jenne, T., & Scruggs, T. E. (1988). A level system for managing problem behaviors in a high school resource program. *Behavioral Disorders, 13*, 202–208.

Mavropoulou, S., & Padeliadu, S. (2002). Teachers' causal attributions for behavior problems in relation to perception of control. *Educational Psychology, 22*, 191–202.

Mayer, M. J., & Leone, P. E. (1999). A structural analysis of school violence and disruption: Implications for creating safer schools. *Education and Treatment of Children, 22*, 333–356.

McCurdy, B. L., Lannie, A. L., & Barnabas, E. (2009). Reducing disruptive behavior in an urban school cafeteria: An extension of the Good Behavior Game. *Journal of School Psychology, 47*(1), 39–54.

McFall, R. M. (1970). Effects of self-monitoring on normal smoking behavior. *Journal of Consulting and Clinical Psychology, 35*, 135–142.

McGoey, K. E., & DuPaul, G. J. (2000). Token reinforcement and response cost procedures: Reducing the disruptive behavior of preschool children with attention-deficit/hyperactivity disorder. *School Psychology Quarterly, 15*, 330–343.

McHugh, M. B., Tingstrom, D. H., Radley, K. C., Barry, C. T., & Walker, K. M. (2016). Effects of tootling on classwide and individual disruptive and academically engaged behavior of lower-elementary students. *Behavioral Interventions, 31*(4), 332–354.

McKissick, C., Hawkins, R. O., Lentz, F. E., Hailley, J., & McGuire, S. (2010). Randomizing multiple contingency components to decrease disruptive behaviors and increase student engagement in an urban second-grade classroom. *Psychology in the Schools, 47*, 944–959.

McLaughlin, T., & Malaby, J. (1972). Reducing and measuring inappropriate verbalizations in a token classroom. *Journal of Applied Behavior Analysis, 5*(3), 329–333.

McNeely, C. A., Nonnemaker, J. M., & Blum, R. W. (2002). Promoting school connectedness: Evidence from the National Longitudinal Study of Adolescent Health. *Journal of School Health, 72*, 138–146.

Medland, M. B., & Stachnik, T. J. (1972). Good Behavior Game: A replication and systematic analysis. *Journal of Applied Behavior Analysis, 5*, 45–51.

Melnick, S. A., & Meister, D. G. (2008). A comparison of beginning and experienced teachers' concerns. *Educational Research Quarterly 31*(3), 40–56.

Mendham, R. P., & Thorne, M. T. (1984). A description and evaluation of a "levelled token economy" operating within the school day in a residential school for junior maladjusted boys. *Behavioural Psychotherapy, 12*, 151–162.

Merrett, F., & Blundell, D. (1982). Self-recording as a means of improving classroom behavior in the secondary school. *Educational Psychology, 2*, 147–157.

Merrett, F., & Wheldall, K. (1987). Natural rates of teacher approval and disapproval in British primary and middle school classrooms. *British Journal of Educational Psychology, 57*(1), 95–103.

Merriam-Webster. (2017). Retrieved March 15, 2017, from *www.merriam-webster.com.*

Metcalf, T. (n.d.). What's your plan?: Accurate decision making within a multi-tier system of supports: Critical areas in Tier 2. Retrieved from *www.rtinetwork.org/essential/tieredinstruction/ tier2/whats-your-plan-accurate-decision-making-within-a-multi-tier-system-of-supports-critical-areas-in-tier-2.*

Miller, L. J., Strain, P. S., Boyd, K., Jarzynka, J., & McFetridge, M. (1993). The effects of classwide self-assessment on preschool children's engagement in transition, free play, and small group instruction. *Early Education and Development, 4*, 162–181.

Mischel, W., Shoda, Y., & Rodriguez, M. L. (1989). Delay of gratification in children. *Science, 244*, 933–938.

Mitchem, K. J., & Young, K. R. (2001). Adapting self-management programs for classwide use: Acceptability, feasibility, and effectiveness. *Remedial and Special Education, 22*, 75–88.

Mitchem, K. J., Young, K. R., West, R. P., & Benyo, J. (2001). CWPASM: A classwide peer assisted self-management program for general education classrooms. *Education and Treatment of Children, 24*(2), 111–140.

Morrison, J. Q., & Jones, K. M. (2007). The effects of positive peer reporting as a class-wide positive behavior support. *Journal of Behavioral Education, 16*(2), 111–124.

Murphy, G., & Goodall, E. (1980). Measurement error in direct observation: A comparison of common recording methods. *Behaviour Research and Therapy, 18*, 147–150.

Murphy, K. A., Theodore, L. A., Aloiso, D., Alric-Edwards, J. M., & Hughes, T. L. (2007). Interdependent group contingency and mystery motivators to reduce preschool disruptive behavior. *Psychology in the Schools, 44*, 53–63.

Musser, E. H., Bray, M. A., Kehle, T. J., & Jenson, W. R. (2001). Reducing disruptive behaviors in students with serious emotional disturbance. *School Psychology Review, 30*, 294–304.

Myers, D., Simonsen, B., & Sugai, G. (2011). Increasing teachers' use of praise with a response-to-intervention approach. *Education and Treatment of Children, 34*, 35–59.

Nafpaktitis, M., Mayer, G. R., & Butterworth, T. (1985). Natural rates of teacher approval and disapproval and their relation to student behaviour in intermediate school classrooms. *Journal of Educational Psychology, 77,* 363–367.

Narayan, J. S., Heward, W. L., Gardner, R., III, Courson, F. H., & Omness, C. K. (1990). Using response cards to increase student participation in an elementary school classroom. *Journal of Applied Behavior Analysis, 23,* 483–490.

National Center on Intensive Intervention. (2014). *So what do I do now?: Strategies for intensifying intervention when standard approaches don't work.* Washington, DC: U.S. Department of Education, Office of Special Education Programs, National Center on Intensive Intervention.

Neff, N. A., Shafer, M. S., Egel, A. L., Cataldo, M. F., & Parrish, J. M. (1983). The class specific effects of compliance training with "do" and "don't" requests: Analogue analysis and classroom application. *Journal of Applied Behavioral Analysis, 16*(1), 81–99.

Nelson, R. O., & Hayes, S. C. (1981). Theoretical explanations for reactivity in self-monitoring. *Behavior Modification, 5,* 3–14.

New Teacher Project. (2013). Perspectives of irreplaceable teachers. Retrieved May 28, 2014, from *http://tntp.org/assets/documents/TNTP_Perspectives_2013.pdf.*

Noell, G. H. (2007). Research examining the relationships among consultation process, treatment integrity, and outcomes. In W. P. Erchul & S. M. Sheridan (Eds.), *Handbook of research in school consultation: Empirical foundations for the field* (pp. 315–334). Mahwah, NJ: Erlbaum.

Noell, G. H., Gansle, K. A., Mevers, J. L., Knox, R. M., Mintz, J. C., & Dahir, A. (2014). Improving treatment plan implementation in schools: A meta-analysis of single subject design studies. *Journal of Behavioral Education, 23,* 168–191.

Noell, G. H., Gresham, F. M., & Gansle, K. A. (2002). Does treatment integrity matter?: A preliminary investigation of instructional implementation and mathematics performance. *Journal of Behavioral Education, 11,* 51–67.

Noell, G. H., Witt, J. C., Slider, N. J., Connell, J. E., Gatti, S. L., Williams, K. L., et al. (2005). Treatment implementation following behavioral consultation in schools: A comparison of three follow-up strategies. *School Psychology Review, 34,* 87–106.

O'Leary, K. D., & Becker, W. C. (1967). Behavior modification of an adjustment class: A token reinforcement program. *Exceptional Children, 33,* 637–642.

O'Leary, K. D., Becker, W. C., Evans, M. B., & Saudargas, R. A. (1969). A token reinforcement program in a public school: A replication and systematic analysis. *Journal of Applied Behavior Analysis, 2,* 3–13.

O'Leary, K. D., & Drabman, R. (1971). Token reinforcement programs in the classroom: A review. *Psychological Bulletin, 75,* 379–398.

O'Leary, K. D., Drabman, R., & Kass, R. E. (1973). Maintenance of appropriate behavior in a token program. *Journal of Abnormal Child Psychology, 1,* 127–138.

O'Leary, K. D., Kaufman, K. F., Kass, R. E., & Drabman, R. S. (1970). The effects of loud and soft reprimands on behavior of disruptive students. *Exceptional Children, 37*(2), 145–155.

Oliver, R., & Skinner, C. H. (2002). Applying behavioral momentum theory to increase compliance: Why Mrs. H. RRRevved up the elementary students with the hokey-pokey. *Journal of Applied School Psychology, 19*(1), 75–94.

Oliver, R. M., Wehby, J. H., & Reschly, D. J. (2011). Teacher classroom management practices: Effects on disruptive or aggressive student behavior. *Campbell Systematic Reviews, 2011*(4), 1–55.

O'Neill, S. C., & Stephenson, J. (2011). The measurement of classroom management self-efficacy: A review of measurement instrument development and influences. *Educational Psychology, 31*(3), 261–299.

Ottenbacher, K. J. (1990). Visual inspection of single-subject data: An empirical analysis. *Mental Retardation, 28,* 283–290.

PACER Center. (2011). Evidence-based practices at school: A guide for parents. Retrieved January 11, 2017, from *www.pacer.org/publications/all-68.pdf*.

Parker, R. I., Brossart, D. F., Vannest, K. J., Long, J. R., Garcia De-Alba, R., Baugh, F. G., et al. (2005). Effect sizes in single case research: How large is large? *School Psychology Review, 34,* 116–132.

Parker, R. I., Hagan-Burke, S., & Vannest, K. (2007). Percentage of all non-overlapping data (PAND): An alternative to PND. *Journal of Special Education, 40,* 194–204.

Partin, T. C. M., Robertson, R. E., Maggin, D. M., Oliver, R. M., & Wehby, J. H. (2009). Using teacher praise and opportunities to respond to promote appropriate behavior. *Preventing School Failure, 54,* 172–178.

Patrick, C. A., Ward, P., & Crouch, D. W. (1998). Effects of holding students accountable for social behaviors during volleyball games in elementary physical education. *Journal of Teaching in Physical Education, 17,* 143–156.

Peterson, L. D., Young, K. R., Salzberg, C. L., West, R. P., & Hill, M. (2006). Using self-management procedures to improve classroom social skills in multiple general education settings. *Education and Treatment of Children, 29,* 1–21.

Pipkin, C., Vollmer, T. R., & Sloman, K. N. (2010). Effects of treatment integrity failures during differential reinforcement of alternative behaviors: A translational model. *Journal of Applied Behavior Analysis, 43,* 47–70.

Planty, M., Hussar, W., Snyder, T., Kena, G., KewalRamani, A., Kemp, J., et al. (2009). The condition of education 2009 (NCES 2009-081). Washington, DC: National Center for Education Statistics, Institute of Education Sciences, U.S. Department of Education.

Plavnick, J. B., Ferreri, S. J., & Maupin, A. N. (2010). The effects of self-monitoring on the procedural integrity of a behavioral intervention for young children with developmental disabilities. *Journal of Applied Behavior Analysis, 43,* 315–320.

Pokorski, E. A., Barton, E. E., & Ledford, J. R. (2017). A review of the use of group contingencies in preschool settings. *Topics in Early Childhood Special Education, 36*(4), 230–241.

Popkin, J., & Skinner, C. H. (2003). Enhancing academic performance in a classroom serving students with serious emotional disturbance: Interdependent group contingencies with randomly selected components. *School Psychology Review, 32,* 282–295.

Powell, J., Martindale, A., & Kulp, S. (1975). An evaluation of time-sample measures of behavior. *Journal of Applied Behavior Analysis, 8*(4), 463–469.

Powell, J., Martindale, B., Kulp, S., Martindale, A., & Bauman, R. (1977). Taking a close look: Time sampling and measurement error. *Journal of Applied Behavior Analysis, 10*(2), 325–332.

Prater, M. A, Hogan, S., & Miller, S. R. (1992). Using self-monitoring to improve on-task behavior and academic skills of an adolescent with mild handicaps across special and regular education settings. *Education and Treatment of Children, 15*(1), 43–55.

Prater, M. A., Joy, R., Chilman, B., Temple, J., & Miller, S. R. (1991). Self-monitoring of on-task behavior by adolescents with learning disabilities. *Learning Disability Quarterly, 14,* 164–177.

Prout, S. M., & Prout, H. T. (1998). A meta-analysis of school-based studies of counseling and psychotherapy: An update. *Journal of School Psychology, 36*(2), 121–136.

Rafferty, L. A., & Raimondi, S. L. (2009). Self-monitoring of attention versus self-monitoring of performance: Examining the differential effects among students with emotional disturbance engaged in independent math practice. *Journal of Behavioral Education, 18,* 279–299.

Raspa, M. J., McWilliam, R. A., & Maher Ridley, S. (2001). Child care quality and children's engagement. *Early Education and Development, 12*(2), 209–224.

Redd, W. H., Morris, E. K., & Martin, J. A. (1975). Effects of positive and negative adult–child interactions on children's social preference. *Journal of Experimental Child Psychology, 19,* 153–164.

Reed, D. D., & Martens, B. K. (2011). Temporal discounting predicts student responsiveness to exchange delays in a classroom token system. *Journal of Applied Behavior Analysis, 44,* 1–18.

Reid, R. (1996). Research in self-monitoring with students with learning disabilities: The present, the prospects, the pitfalls. *Journal of Learning Disabilities, 29,* 317–331.

Reid, R., & Harris, K. H. (1993). Self-monitoring of attention versus self-monitoring of performance: Effects on attention and academic performance. *Exceptional Children, 60,* 29–40.

Reid, R., Trout, A. L, & Schartz, M. (2005). Self-regulation interventions for children with attention deficit/hyperactivity disorder. *Exceptional Children, 71,* 361–377.

Reilly, E., Buskist, C., & Gross, M. K. (2012). Movement in the classroom: Boosting brain power, fighting obesity. *Kappa Delta Pi Record, 48*(2), 62–66.

Reinke, W. M., Herman, K. C., & Stormont, M. (2013). Classroom-level positive behavior supports in schools implementing SW-PBIS: Identifying areas for enhancement. *Journal of Positive Behavior Interventions, 15*(1), 39–50.

Reinke, W. M., Lewis-Palmer, T., & Martin, E. (2007). The effect of visual performance feedback on teacher use of behavior-specific praise. *Behavior Modification, 31*(3), 247–263.

Reinke, W. M., Lewis-Palmer, T., & Merrell, K. (2008). The classroom check-up: A classwide teacher consultation model for increasing praise and decreasing disruptive behavior. *School Psychology Review, 37*(3), 315.

Reinke, W. M., Stormont, M., Herman, K. C., Puri, R., & Goel, N. (2011). Supporting children's mental health in schools: Teacher perceptions of needs, roles, and barriers. *School Psychology Quarterly, 26,* 1–13.

Reschly, A. L., & Christenson, S. L. (2009). Parents as essential partners for fostering students' learning outcomes. In M. J. Furlong, R. Gilman, & E. S. Huebner (Eds.), *Handbook of positive psychology in schools* (pp. 257–272). New York: Routledge.

Reynolds, C. R., & Kamphaus, R. W. (2015). *Behavior Assessment System for Children* (3rd ed.). Bloomington, MN: Pearson.

Rhode, G., Jenson, W. R., & Reavis, H. K. (1992). *The tough kid book: Practical classroom management strategies.* Longmont, CO: Sopris West.

Rhode, G., Morgan, D. P., & Young, K. R. (1983). Generalization and maintenance of treatment gains of behaviorally handicapped students from resource rooms to regular classrooms using self-evaluation procedures. *Journal of Applied Behavior Analysis, 16,* 171–188.

Riley-Tillman, T. C., & Burns, M. K. (2009). *Evaluating educational interventions: Single-case design for measuring response to intervention.* New York: Guilford Press.

Riley-Tillman, T. C., Methe, S. A., & Weegar, K. (2009). Examining the use of Direct Behavior Rating on formative assessment of class-wide engagement: A case study. *Assessment for Effective Intervention, 34,* 224–230.

Ringer, V. M. J. (1973). The use of a "token helper" in the management of classroom behavior problems and in teacher training. *Journal of Applied Behavior Analysis, 6*(4), 671–677.

Risley, T., & Cataldo, M. (1973). *Evaluation of planned activities: The PLA-Check measure of classroom participation.* Lawrence, KS: Center for Applied Behavior Analysis.

Robichaux, N. M., & Gresham, F. M. (2014). Differential effects of the Mystery Motivator intervention using student-selected and mystery rewards. *School Psychology Review, 43,* 286–298.

Rock, M. L., & Thead, B. K. (2007). The effects of fading a strategic self-monitoring intervention on students' academic engagement, accuracy, and productivity. *Journal of Behavioral Education, 16,* 389–412.

Rogers, E. M. (2003). *Diffusion of innovations* (5th ed.). New York: Free Press.

Rooney, K. J., Hallahan, D. P., & Lloyd, J. W. (1984). Self-recording of attention by learning disabled students in the regular classroom. *Journal of Learning Disabilities, 17,* 360–364.

Rosén, L. A., O'Leary, S. G., Joyce, S. A, Conway, G., & Pfiffner, L. J. (1984). The importance of prudent negative consequences for maintaining the appropriate behavior of hyperactive children. *Journal of Abnormal Child Psychology, 12*(4), 581–604.

Rubie-Davies, C. M. (2007). Classroom interactions: Exploring the practices of high‐ and low‐expectation teachers. *British Journal of Educational Psychology, 77*(2), 289–306.

Russell, A., & Lin, L. G. (1977). Teacher attention and classroom behavior. *The Exceptional Child, 24*, 148–155.

Safer, D. J., Heaton, R. C., & Parker, F. C. (1981). A behavioral program for disruptive junior high school students: Results and follow-up. *Journal of Abnormal Child Psychology, 9*, 483–494.

Saigh, P. A., & Umar, A. M. (1983). The effects of a Good Behavior Game on the disruptive behavior of Sudanese elementary school students. *Journal of Applied Behavior Analysis, 16*, 339–344.

Sainato, D. M., Goldstein, H., & Strain, P. S. (1992). Effects of self-evaluation on preschool children's use of social interaction strategies with their classmates with autism. *Journal of Applied Behavior Analysis, 25*, 127–141.

Sainato, D. M., Strain, P. S., Lefebvre, D., & Rapp, N. (1990). Effects of self-evaluation on the independent work skills of preschool children with disabilities. *Exceptional Children, 56*, 540–549.

Salend, S. J., Reynolds, C. J., & Coyle, E. M. (1989). Individualizing the Good Behavior Game across type and frequency of behavior with emotionally disturbed adolescents. *Behavior Modification, 13*, 108–126.

Salzberg, R. S., & Greenwald, M. A. (1977). Effects of a token system on attentiveness and punctuality in two string instrument classes. *Journal of Music Therapy, 14*, 27–38.

Sanetti, L. M. H., & Kratochwill, T. R. (2009). Toward developing a science of treatment integrity: Introduction to the special series. *School Psychology Review, 38*, 445–459.

Sanford, J. P., & Evertson, C. M. (1981). Classroom management in a low SES junior high: Three case studies. *Journal of Teacher Education, 32*, 34–38.

Santogrossi, D. A., O'Leary, K. D., Romanczyk, R. G., & Kaufman, K. F. (1973). Self-evaluation by adolescents in a psychiatric hospital school token program. *Journal of Applied Behavior Analysis, 6*(2), 277–287.

Sargeant, J. (2012). Prioritising student voice: "Tween" children's perspectives on school success. *Education 3–13, 42*(2), 190–200.

Saudargas, R. A., & Zanolli, K. (1990). Momentary time sampling as an estimate of percentage time: A field validation. *Journal of Applied Behavior Analysis, 23*, 533–537.

Schanding, G. T., Jr., & Sterling-Turner, H. E. (2010). Use of the Mystery Motivator for a high school class. *Journal of Applied School Psychology, 26*(1), 38–53.

Schuldheisz, J. M., & Mars, H. (2001). Active supervision and students' physical activity in middle school physical education. *Journal of Teaching in Physical Education, 21*(1), 75–90.

Scruggs, T. E., & Mastropieri, M. A. (1998). Summarizing single-subject research: Issues and applications. *Behavior Modification, 22*(3), 221–242.

Scruggs, T. E., & Mastropieri, M. A. (2013). PND at 25: Past, present, and future trends in summarizing single-subject research. *Remedial and Special Education, 34*, 9–19.

Sharp, S. R., & Skinner, C. H. (2004). Using interdependent group contingencies with randomly selected criteria and paired reading to enhance class-wide reading performance. *Journal of Applied School Psychology, 20*, 29–45.

Shearer, D. D., Kohler, F. W., Buchan, K. A., & McCullough, K. M. (1996). Promoting independent interactions between preschoolers with autism and their nondisabled peers: An analysis of self-monitoring. *Early Education and Development, 7*, 205–220.

Simonsen, B., Fairbanks, S., Briesch, A. M., Myers, D., & Sugai, G. (2008). Evidence-based practices in classroom management: Considerations for research to practice. *Education and Treatment of Children, 31*, 351–380.

Simonsen, B., MacSuga, A. S., Fallon, L. M., & Sugai, G. (2013). The effects of self-monitoring on teachers' use of specific praise. *Journal of Positive Behavior Interventions, 15*(1), 5–15.

Sindelar, P. T., Bursuck, W. D., & Halle, J. W. (1986). The effects of two variations of teacher questioning on student performance. *Education and Treatment of Children, 9*, 56–66.

Skiba, R. J., & Knesting, K. (2001). Zero tolerance, zero evidence: An analysis of school disciplinary practice. *New Directions for Youth Development, 2001*(92), 17–43.

Skinner, B. F. (1966). Contingencies of reinforcement in the design of a culture. *Behavioral Science, 11*, 159–166.

Skinner, C. H., Cashwell, T. H., & Skinner, A. L. (2000). Increasing tootling: The effects of a peer-monitored group contingency program on students' reports of peers' prosocial behaviors. *Psychology in the Schools, 37*, 263–270.

Skinner, C. H., Neddenriep, C. E., Robinson, S. L., Ervin, R., & Jones, K. (2002). Altering educational environments through positive peer reporting: Prevention and remediation of social problems associated with behavior disorders. *Psychology in the Schools, 39*, 191–202.

Skinner, C. H., Scala, G., Dendas, D., & Lentz, F. E. (2007). The Color Wheel: Implementation guidelines. *Journal of Evidence-Based Practices for Schools, 8*, 134–140.

Skinner, C. H., & Skinner, A. L. (2007). Establishing an evidence base for a classroom management procedure with a series of studies: Evaluating the Color Wheel. *Journal of Evidence-Based Practices for Schools, 8*, 88–101.

Skinner, C. H., Skinner, C. F., Skinner, A. L., & Cashwell, T. H. (1999). Using interdependent contingencies with groups of students: Why the principal kissed the pig. *Educational Administration Quarterly, 35*, 806–820.

Skinner, C. H., Williams, R. L., & Neddenriep, C. E. (2004). Using interdependent group-oriented reinforcement to enhance academic performance in general education classrooms. *School Psychology Review, 33*, 384–397.

Soodak, L. C., & Podell, D. M. (1994). Teachers' thinking about difficult-to-teach students. *Journal of Educational Research, 88*, 44–51.

Stage, S. A., Jackson, H. G., Jensen, M. J., Moscovitz, K. K., Bush, J. W., Violette, H. D., et al. (2008). A validity study of functionally-based behavioral consultation with students with emotional/behavioral disabilities. *School Psychology Quarterly, 23*(3), 327.

Stage, S. A., & Quiroz, D. R. (1997). A meta-analysis of interventions to decrease disruptive classroom behavior in public education settings. *School Psychology Review, 26*, 333–368.

Stahmer, A. C., & Schreibman, L. (1992). Teaching children with autism appropriate play in unsupervised environments using a self-management treatment package. *Journal of Applied Behavior Analysis, 25*, 447–459.

Stanley, P., & Simmons, G. (1975). Rock and roll all nite. On *Dressed to kill* [Record]. New York: Casablanca Records.

Steege, M. W., Davin, T., & Hathaway, M. (2001). Reliability and accuracy of a performance-based behavioral recording procedure. *School Psychology Review, 30*, 252–261.

Steege, M. W., & Watson, T. S. (2009). *Conducting school-based functional behavioral assessments: A practitioner's guide* (2nd ed.). New York: Guilford Press.

Sterling-Turner, H. E., & Watson, T. S. (2002). An analog investigation of the relationship between treatment acceptability and treatment integrity. *Journal of Behavioral Education, 11*, 39–50.

Sterling-Turner, H. E., Watson, T. S., & Moore, J. W. (2002). The effects of direct training and treatment integrity on treatment outcomes in school consultation. *School Psychology Quarterly, 17*, 47–77.

Sterling-Turner, H. E., Watson, T. S., Wildmon, M., Watkins, C., & Little, E. (2001). Investigating the relationship between training type and treatment integrity. *School Psychology Quarterly, 16*, 56–67.

Stormont, M., & Reinke, W. (2008). The importance of precorrective statements and behavior-specific praise and strategies to increase their use. *Beyond Behavior, 18*(3), 26–32.

Stormont, M., Reinke, W. M., Herman, K. C., & Lembke, E. S. (2012). *Academic and behavioral supports for at-risk students*. New York: Guilford Press.

Strain, P. S., Kohler, F. K., Storey, K., & Danko, C. D. (1994). Teaching preschoolers with autism to self-monitor their social interactions: An analysis of results in home and school settings. *Journal of Emotional and Behavioral Disorders, 2*, 78–88.

Suitts, S., Barba, P., & Dunn, K. (2015). *A new majority: Low income students now a majority in the nation's public schools*. Atlanta, GA: Southern Education Foundation.

Sutcliffe, K., Thomas, J., Stokes, G., & Bangpan, M. (2015, October 29). Intervention Component Analysis (ICA): A pragmatic approach for identifying the critical features of complex interventions. *Systematic Reviews, 4*, 140.

Sutherland, K. S., Alder, N., & Gunter, P. L. (2003). The effect of varying rates of opportunities to respond to academic requests on the classroom behavior of students with EBD. *Journal of Emotional and Behavioral Disorders, 11*, 239–248.

Sutherland, K. S., Wehby, J. H., & Copeland, S. R. (2000). Effect of varying rates of behavior-specific praise on the on-task behavior of students with EBD. *Journal of Emotional and Behavioral Disorders, 8*(1), 2–8.

Swain, J. J., Allard, G. B., & Holborn, S. W. (1982). The Good Toothbrushing Game: A school-based dental hygiene program for increasing the toothbrushing effectiveness of children. *Journal of Applied Behavior Analysis, 15*, 171–176.

Tanol, G., Johnson, L., McComas, J., & Cote, E. (2010). Responding to rule violations or rule following: A comparison of two versions of the Good Behavior Game with kindergarten students. *Journal of School Psychology, 48*, 337–355.

Theodore, L. A., DioGuardi, R. J., Hughes, T. L., Aloiso, D., Carlo, M., & Eccles, D. (2009). A class-wide intervention for improving homework performance. *Journal of Educational and Psychological Consultation, 19*(4), 275–299.

Thomas, J. D., Presland, I. E., Grant, M. D., & Glynn, T. (1978). Natural rates of teacher approval and disapproval in grade 7 classrooms. *Journal of Applied Behavior Analysis, 11*, 91–94.

Thompson, M. T., Marchant, M., Anderson, D., Prater, M. A., & Gibb, G. (2012). Effects of tiered training on general educators' use of specific praise. *Education and Treatment of Children, 35*, 521–546.

Thorndike, E. L. (1898). Animal intelligence: An experimental study of the associative processes in animals. *Psychological Review:Monograph Supplements, 2*(4), i–109.

Tingstrom, D. H., Sterling-Turner, H. E., & Wilczynski, S. M. (2006). The Good Behavior Game: 1969–2002. *Behavior Modification, 30*, 225–253.

Turkewitz, H., O'Leary, K. D., & Ironsmith, M. (1975). Generalization and maintenance of appropriate behavior through self-control. *Journal of Consulting and Clinical Psychology, 43*(4), 577.

Treiber, F. A., & Lahey, B. B. (1983). Toward a behavioral model of academic remediation with learning disabled children. *Journal of Learning Disabilities, 16*(2), 111–116.

Treptow, M. A., Burns, M. K., & McComas, J. J. (2007). Reading at the frustration, instructional, and independent levels: The effects on students' reading comprehension and time on task. *School Psychology Review, 36*(1), 159.

Trevino-Maack, S. I., Kamps, D., & Wills, H. (2015). A group contingency plus self-management intervention targeting at-risk secondary students' class-work and active engagement. *Remedial and Special Education, 36*, 347–360.

Trice, A. D., & Parker, F. C. (1983). Decreasing adolescent swearing in an instructional setting. *Education and Treatment of Children, 6*, 29–35.

Ttofi, M. M., & Farrington, D. P. (2012). Risk and protective factors, longitudinal research, and bullying prevention. *New Directions for Youth Development, 2012*(133), 85–98.

U.S. Department of Education, Institute of Education Sciences. (2003). *Identifying and implement-*

ing educational practices supported by rigorous evidence: A user friendly guide. Washington, DC: U.S. Government Printing Office.

U.S. Department of Education, National Center for Education Statistics. (2000–2001). *Teacher follow-up survey ("Questionnaire for current teachers" and "Questionnaire for former teachers").* Washington, DC: U.S. Government Printing Office.

U.S. Department of Health and Human Services, Administration on Children, Youth, and Families. (2007). *Child maltreatment 2005.* Washington, DC: U.S. Government Printing Office.

Van Acker, R., Grant, S. H., & Henry, D. (1996). Teacher and student behavior as a function of risk for aggression. *Education and Treatment of Children, 19*(3), 316–334.

Van Houten, R., Nau, P. A., MacKenzie-Keating, S. E., Sameoto, D., & Colavecchia, B. (1982). An analysis of some variables influencing the effectiveness of reprimands. *Journal of Applied Behavior Analysis, 15*(1), 65–83.

Vollmer, T. R., Iwata, B. A., Zarcone, J. R., Smith, R. G., & Mazaleski, J. L. (1993). The role of attention in the treatment of attention-maintained self-injurious behavior: Noncontingent reinforcement and differential reinforcement of other behavior. *Journal of Applied Behavior Analysis, 26*(1), 9–21.

Volpe, R. J., & Briesch, A. M. (2012). Generalizability and dependability of single-item and multiple-item Direct Behavior Rating scales for engagement and disruptive behavior. *School Psychology Review, 41*, 246–261.

Volpe, R. J., & Fabiano, G. A. (2013). *Daily behavior report cards: An evidence-based system of assessment and intervention.* New York: Guilford Press.

Wannarka, R., & Ruhl, K. (2008). Seating arrangements that promote positive academic and behavioural outcomes: A review of empirical research. *Support for Learning, 23*, 89–93.

Wehby, J. H., & Hollahan, M. S. (2000). Effects of high-probability requests on the latency to initiate academic tasks. *Journal of Applied Behavior Analysis, 33*, 259–262.

Weiner, B. (1993). On sin versus sickness: A theory of perceived responsibility and social motivation. *American Psychologist, 48*, 957–965.

West, R. P., & Sloane, H. N. (1986). Teacher presentation rate and point delivery rate effects on classroom disruption, performance accuracy, and response rate. *Behavior Modification, 10*(3), 267–286.

Wheldall, K., Houghton, S., & Merrett, F. (1989). Natural rates of teacher approval and disapproval in British secondary school classrooms. *British Journal of Educational Psychology, 59*, 38–48.

Wheldall, K., & Lam, Y. Y. (1987). Rows versus tables II: The effects of two classroom seating arrangements on classroom disruption rate, on-task behaviour and teacher behaviour in three special school classes. *Educational Psychology, 7*, 303–312.

Wheldall, K., Morris, M., Vaughan, P., & Ng, Y. Y. (1981). Rows versus tables: An example of the use of behavioural ecology in two classes of eleven-year-old children. *Educational Psychology, 1*, 171–184.

White, M. A. (1975). Natural rates of teacher approval and disapproval in the classroom. *Journal of Applied Behavior Analysis, 8*, 367–372.

Wickstrom, K. F., Jones, K. M., LaFleur, L. H., & Witt, J. C. (1998). An analysis of treatment integrity in school-based behavioral consultation. *School Psychology Quarterly, 13*, 141–154.

Wiley, A. L., Tankersley, M., & Simms, A. (2012). Teachers' causal attributions for student problem behavior: Implications for school-based behavioral interventions and research. In B. G. Cook, M. Tankersley, & T. J. Landrum (Eds.), *Advances in learning and behavioral disabilities* (Vol. 25, pp. 279–300). Bingley, UK: Emerald Group.

Williamson, B. D., Campbell-Whatley, G. D., & Lo, Y. (2009). Using a random dependent group contingency to increase on-task behaviors of high school students with high incidence disabilities. *Psychology in the Schools, 46*, 1074–1083.

Wills, H. P., Kamps, D., Hansen, B., Conklin, C., Bellinger, S., Neaderhiser, J., et al. (2010). The classwide function-based intervention team program. *Preventing School Failure, 54,* 164–171.

Winter, S. (1990). Teacher approval and disapproval in Hong Kong secondary school classrooms. *British Journal of Educational Psychology, 60,* 88–92.

Witmer, J. M., Bornstein, A. V., & Dunham, R. M. (1971). The effects of verbal approval and disapproval upon the performance of third and fourth grade children on four subtests of the Wechsler Intelligence Scale for Children. *Journal of School Psychology, 9*(3), 347–356.

Witt, J. C., & Martens, B. K. (1983). Assessing the acceptability of behavioral interventions used in classrooms. *Psychology in the Schools, 20,* 510–517.

Witt, J. C., VanDerHeyden, A. M., & Gilbertson, D. (2004). Troubleshooting behavioral interventions: A systematic process for finding and eliminating problems. *School Psychology Review, 33,* 363–383.

Wood, C. L., Mabry, L. E., Kretlow, A. G., Lo, Y., & Galloway, T. W. (2009). Effects of preprinted response cards on students' participation and off-task behavior in a rural kindergarten classroom. *Rural Special Education Quarterly, 28,* 39–47.

Wood, S. J., Murdock, J. Y., & Cronin, M. E. (2002). Self-monitoring and at-risk middle school students. *Behavior Modification, 26,* 605–626.

Wright, R. A., & McCurdy, B. L. (2011). Class-wide positive behavior support and group contingencies: Examining a positive variation of the Good Behavior Game. *Journal of Positive Behavior Interventions, 14*(3), 173–180.

Yarborough, J. L., Skinner, C. H., Lee, Y. J., & Lemmons, C. (2004). Decreasing transition times in a second grade classroom: Scientific support for the Timely Transitions Game. *Journal of Applied School Psychology, 20,* 85–107.

Yawkey, T. D. (1971). Conditioning independent work behavior in reading with seven-year-old children in a regular early childhood classroom. *Child Study Journal, 2,* 23–34.

Zaghlawan, H. Y., Ostrosky, M. M., & Al-Khateeb, J. M. (2007). Decreasing the inattentive behavior of Jordanian children: A group experiment. *Education and Treatment of Children, 30*(3), 49–64.

Zifferblatt, S. M. (1972). Architecture and human behavior: Toward increased understanding of a functional relationship. *Educational Technology, 12*(8), 54–57.

Index

Note. "f" or "t" following a page number indicates a figure or a table.

Class-Wide Function-related Intervention Teams (CW-FIT) program, 209
Classwide interventions. *See also* Group contingencies; Self-management of behavior; Token economies
  coach cards for, 218–219
  incorporating additional intervention components, 206–215, 210*f*, 211*f*, 212*f*, 215*f*
  intensifying, 201–206, 204*t*
  overview, 216–217
Classwide peer tutoring management (CWPASM) program, 141–142
Classwide system of reinforcement, 83. *See also* Group contingencies
Coach cards
  feedback and, 73, 76–78
  group contingencies and, 121–125
  individualized intervention and, 207, 218–219
  overview, 11
  prevention strategies and, 44, 53–56
  self-management techniques and, 146–148
  token economy and, 89, 99–101
  treatment integrity and, 199
Color Wheel intervention, 38–39, 39*t*
Communication techniques, 45–51, 47*t*, 49*t*
Consequences, 17*t*, 18–19
Context, 195, 205
Contingency. *See also* Group contingencies
  feedback as a part of, 58–61
  forms for, 212, 212*f*
  response cost and, 90–93, 91*f*, 92*t*
  types of, 103–111, 103*t*, 105*t*, 108*t*–109*t*
Continuous reinforcement schedules, 21, 21*t*. *See also* Reinforcement; Schedules of reinforcement
Control, 12–13, 14, 14*t*
Cueing
  intensifying classwide interventions and, 202–203
  self-monitor performance (SMP) techniques and, 135
  treatment integrity and, 196–197

D

Daily Progress Report (DPR), 210
Daily Report Card (DRC), 214
Data collection. *See also* Classwide data collection
  evaluating data, 175–179, 176*f*, 179*f*
  methods of, 173–174, 174*f*
"Dead-man test," 157–158
Dependent group contingencies. *See also* Group contingencies
  coach cards for, 121
  intensifying classwide interventions and, 204
  Mystery Motivator intervention and, 113
  overview, 103*t*, 105*t*, 106–109, 108*t*–109*t*
  self-management techniques and, 141
Depression, 70
Deprivation, 17*t*, 25–26, 26*f*
Developmental delays, 143
Didactic instruction, 196

Differential reinforcement of an alternative behavior (DRA), 74. *See also* Planned ignoring
Direct Behavior Rating (DBR) scale, 140, 168, 169*f*, 170
Direct observation. *See* Observation
Discriminative stimulus, 17*t*, 26–27
Disruption, 62
Drift, 198

E

Edible reinforcers. *See also* Rewards
  group contingencies and, 110–111
  home-based intervention components and, 215*t*
  overview, 88, 88*t*
Education programs, teacher. *See* Teacher education programs
Embarrassment, 64–65
Emotional/behavioral disorders (EBDs)
  praise and, 68, 70
  self-management techniques and, 141
  token economy and, 90
Engagement, 8. *See also* Active engagement; Instruction
Environment. *See also* Classroom environment
  behavioral techniques and, 30
  home environment, 15, 34
  intensifying classwide interventions and, 205–206
  overview, 33–34
Evaluation. *See also* Classwide data collection; Observation; Self-monitoring
  feedback and, 60–61
  matching assessment to intervention, 216
  overview, 11
  self-management techniques and, 136–137, 140–142
Event behaviors
  overview, 158–159, 159*t*
  rating-based tools for assessing, 166–168, 166*f*, 169*f*
  recording, 159–163, 160*f*, 162*f*
Every Student Succeeds Act (2015), 7
Evidence-based classroom management
  overview, 7–9
  prevention strategies and, 35
  treatment integrity and, 195–196
Expectations. *See also* Rules
  "Big Five" classroom management strategies and, 8
  coach cards for, 53
  feedback and, 59–60
  overview, 10
  teaching to students, 36–44, 39*t*, 43*t*
  token economy and, 84–86, 86*t*
Explicit instruction. *See* Instruction
Extant data, 169–172, 171*f*
External interventionists, 209–213, 211*f*, 212*f*, 218
External reinforcement, 81–82. *See also* Reinforcement; Rewards; Token economies
Extinction
  overview, 23–24
  planned ignoring and, 73, 74
  principles of behavior and, 17*t*